영문법 판매 1위, 중학영문법 3800제의 초등시리즈

# 초등영문법 3800제

LEVEL 8

실력 2단계

**발행** 초판 13쇄(2024년 2월 12일)
**책임편집** 서은숙 **편집** 성은혜 **원고집필** 정다혜, 권은정, 김주현, 정은주, 김유미, 홍주희 **연습문제집필** 조윤경, 권은정, 김송이, 김주희
**워크북집필** 윤정한, 정다혜, 김주희, 김송이 **원고검토** 유예슬, 최희찬, 박문정, 백경빈, 김미경, 김규은, 양원석, 고민정 **영문감수** Kathryn O'Handley
**감수** 최주영(대치 위자듀학원 강사) **교정** 황희진, 정다혜, 김주희, 이은영, 하은옥, 홍성경, 오정훈, 심가원, 이은혜, 신영은, 김송이, 하새롬
**베타테스트** 신재진, 이옥현, 유윤정, 정요한, 신소미, 장신혜, 변선영, 정은주
**녹음** 와이알 미디어 **녹음대본정리** 신소미, 김소정, 김건탁, 김윤아, 최안나 **녹음검수** 이상미, 신소미, 김소정, 김주희, 윤수경, 이옥현, 이유진, 최안나
**사진검색** 신의진, 김윤아, 이은혜, 손주연 **삽화** 박현주 **표지디자인** 김연실 **인디자인편집** 정은영, 박정민, 박경아, 김미라, 고연화
**제작** 이주영 **발행처** ㈜마더텅 **발행인** 문숙영 **주소** 서울시 금천구 가마산로 96, 708호



마더텅 교재를 풀면서 궁금한 점이 생기셨나요?
교재 관련 내용 문의나 오류신고 사항이 있으면 아래 문의처로 보내주세요! 문의하신 내용에 대해 성심성의껏 답변해 드리겠습니다. 또한 교재의 내용 오류 또는 오·탈자, 그 외 수정이 필요한 사항에 대해 가장 먼저 신고해 주신 분께는 감사의 마음을 담아 CU 모바일 편의점 상품권 1천 원권을 보내드립니다!

*기한: 2024년 12월 31일 *오류신고 이벤트는 당사 사정에 따라 조기 종료될 수 있습니다. *홈페이지에 게시된 정오표 기준으로 최초 신고된 오류에 한하여 상품권을 보내드립니다.

카카오톡 mothertongue 이메일 mothert1004@toptutor.co.kr 문자 010-6640-1064(문자수신전용)
홈페이지 www.toptutor.co.kr 교재Q&A게시판 고객센터 전화 1661-1064(07:00~22:00)

# 초등 영문법3800제 실력 2단계

이 렇 게   공 부 하 세 요 .

LEVEL 8

STEP 1

문법 개념을 익힌 후 확인테스트를 풀어보면서 제대로 이해했는지 확인해요.

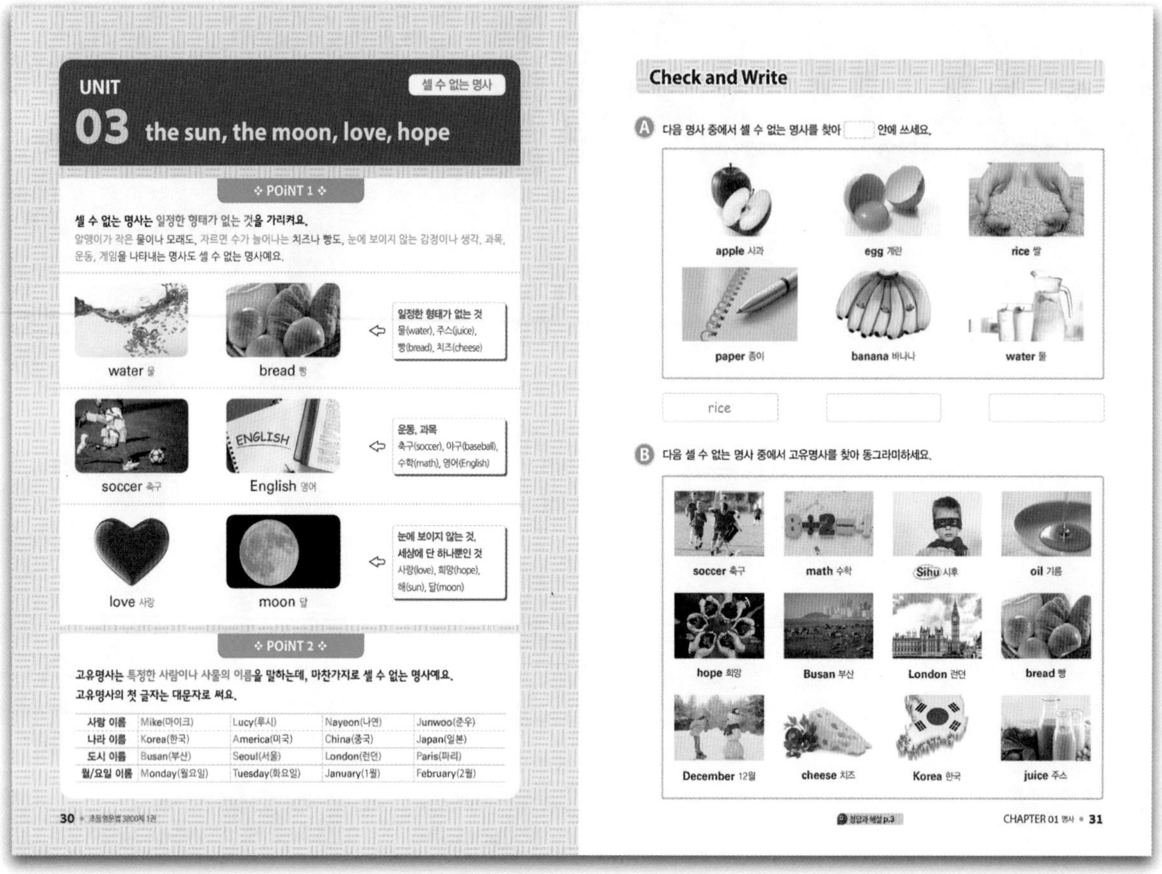
UNIT 셀 수 없는 명사

03 the sun, the moon, love, hope

POiNT 1

**셀 수 없는 명사는 일정한 형태가 없는 것을 가리켜요.**
알갱이가 작은 물이나 모래도, 자르면 수가 늘어나는 치즈나 빵도, 눈에 보이지 않는 감정이나 생각, 과목, 운동, 게임을 나타내는 명사도 셀 수 없는 명사예요.

water 물 / bread 빵 — 일정한 형태가 없는 것: 물(water), 주스(juice), 빵(bread), 치즈(cheese)

soccer 축구 / English 영어 — 운동, 과목: 축구(soccer), 야구(baseball), 수학(math), 영어(English)

love 사랑 / moon 달 — 눈에 보이지 않는 것, 세상에 단 하나뿐인 것: 사랑(love), 희망(hope), 해(sun), 달(moon)

POiNT 2

**고유명사는 특정한 사람이나 사물의 이름을 말하는데, 마찬가지로 셀 수 없는 명사예요. 고유명사의 첫 글자는 대문자로 써요.**

| | | | | |
|---|---|---|---|---|
| 사람 이름 | Mike(마이크) | Lucy(루시) | Nayeon(나연) | Junwoo(준우) |
| 나라 이름 | Korea(한국) | America(미국) | China(중국) | Japan(일본) |
| 도시 이름 | Busan(부산) | Seoul(서울) | London(런던) | Paris(파리) |
| 월/요일 이름 | Monday(월요일) | Tuesday(화요일) | January(1월) | February(2월) |

30 초등영문법 3800제 1권

Check and Write

A 다음 명사 중에서 셀 수 없는 명사를 찾아 [ ] 안에 쓰세요.

apple 사과 / egg 계란 / rice 쌀 / paper 종이 / banana 바나나 / water 물

rice

B 다음 셀 수 없는 명사 중에서 고유명사를 찾아 동그라미하세요.

soccer 축구 / math 수학 / Sihu 시후 / oil 기름 / hope 희망 / Busan 부산 / London 런던 / bread 빵 / December 12월 / cheese 치즈 / Korea 한국 / juice 주스

정답과 해설 p.3

CHAPTER 01 명사 31

STEP 2

**Practice 1, 2, 3**

Practice 1, 2, 3로 구성된 연습문제를 풀면서 앞에서 배운 문법이 적용된 풍부한 예문을 접할 수 있어요. 연습 문제들을 풀다보면, 서술형 문제도 더 이상 어렵지 않아요!

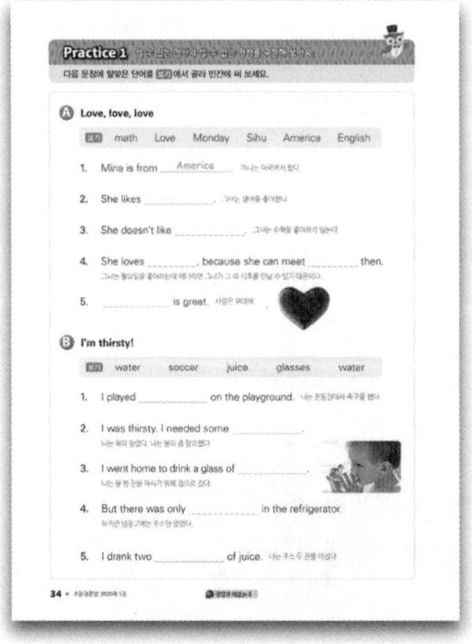
Practice 1

A Love, love, love

math Love Monday Sihu America English

1. Mina is from America.
2. She likes ________.
3. She doesn't like ________.
4. She loves ________, because she can meet ________ then.
5. ________ is great.

B I'm thirsty!

water soccer juice glasses water

1. I played ________ on the playground.
2. I was thirsty. I needed some ________.
3. I went home to drink a glass of ________.
4. But there was only ________ in the refrigerator.
5. I drank two ________ of juice.

34

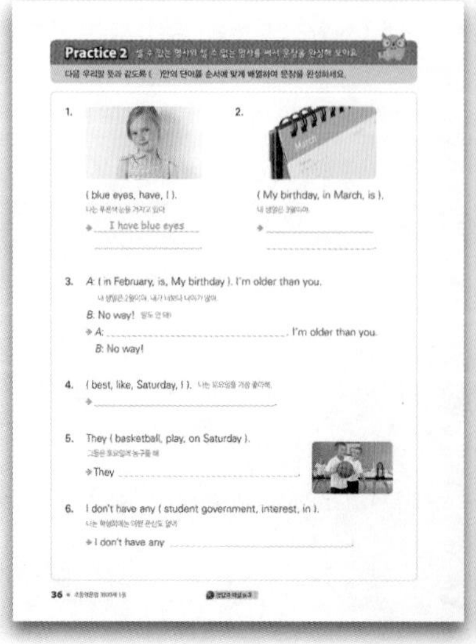
Practice 2

1. ( blue eyes, have, I ).
→ I have blue eyes
2. ( My birthday, in March, is ).
3. A: ( in February, is, My birthday ). I'm older than you.
B: No way!
→ A: ________ I'm older than you.
B: No way!
4. ( best, like, Saturday, I ).
5. They ( basketball, play, on Saturday ).
→ They ________
6. I don't have any ( student government, interest, in ).
→ I don't have any ________

36

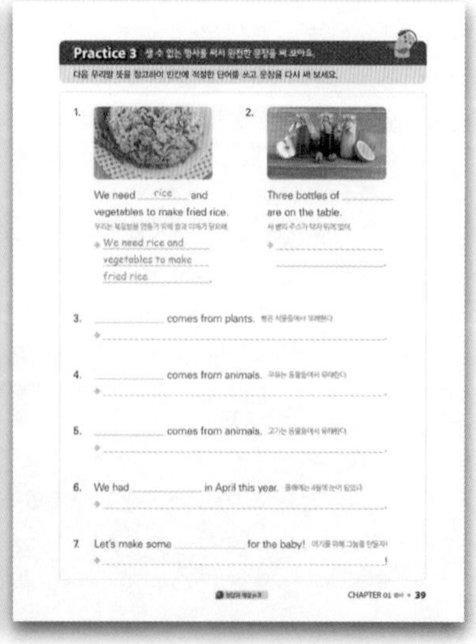
Practice 3

1. We need rice and vegetables to make fried rice.
→ We need rice and vegetables to make fried rice.
2. Three bottles of ________ are on the table.
3. ________ comes from plants.
4. ________ comes from animals.
5. ________ comes from animals.
6. We had ________ in April this year.
7. Let's make some ________ for the baby!

CHAPTER 01 명사 39

STEP 3

## Let's Practice More!

문법 내용을 제대로 이해했는지 확인할 수 있도록 SET 01~08까지 다양한 유형의 연습문제를 실었어요. 문제를 하나하나 풀다보면 해당 UNIT의 핵심 개념을 제대로 익히게 될 거에요.

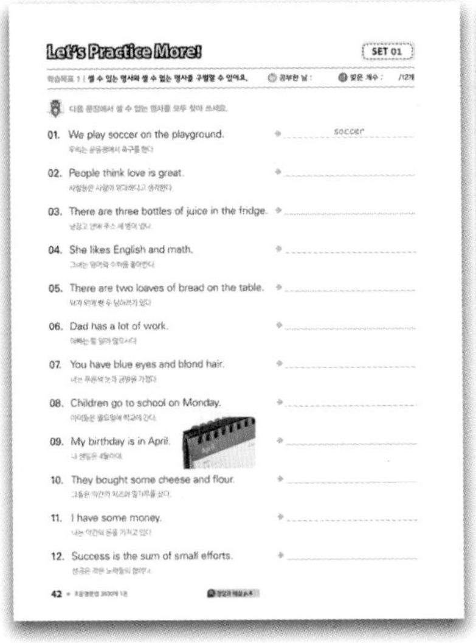

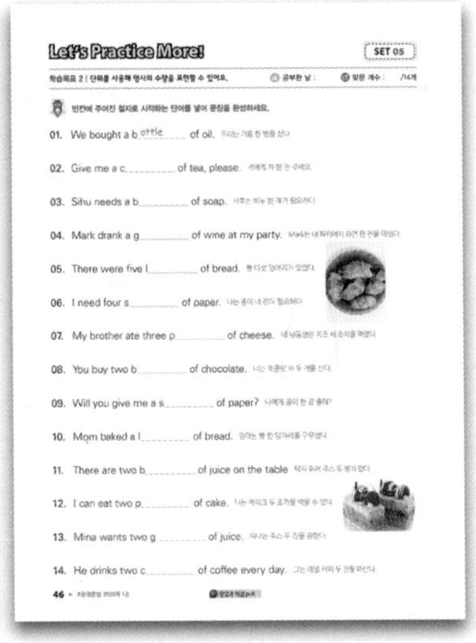

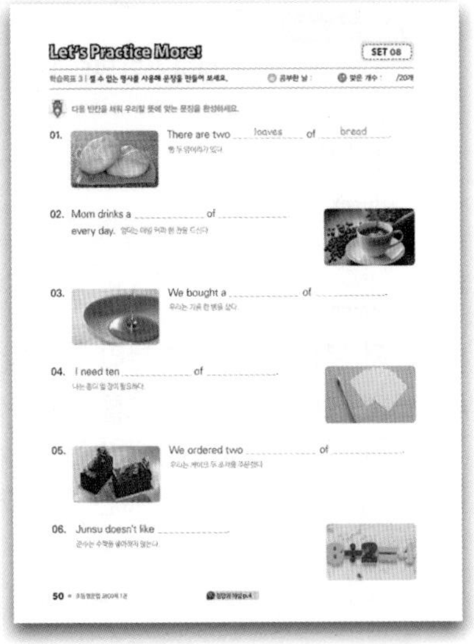

STEP 4

## 마무리 실전테스트

최종 마무리 테스트로서 권당 2회분의 실전테스트를 실었어요. 총 30문제의 진단평가 및 교내평가 유형의 실전문제로 앞에서 배운 내용을 복습하고 취약한 부분을 파악해 봐요.

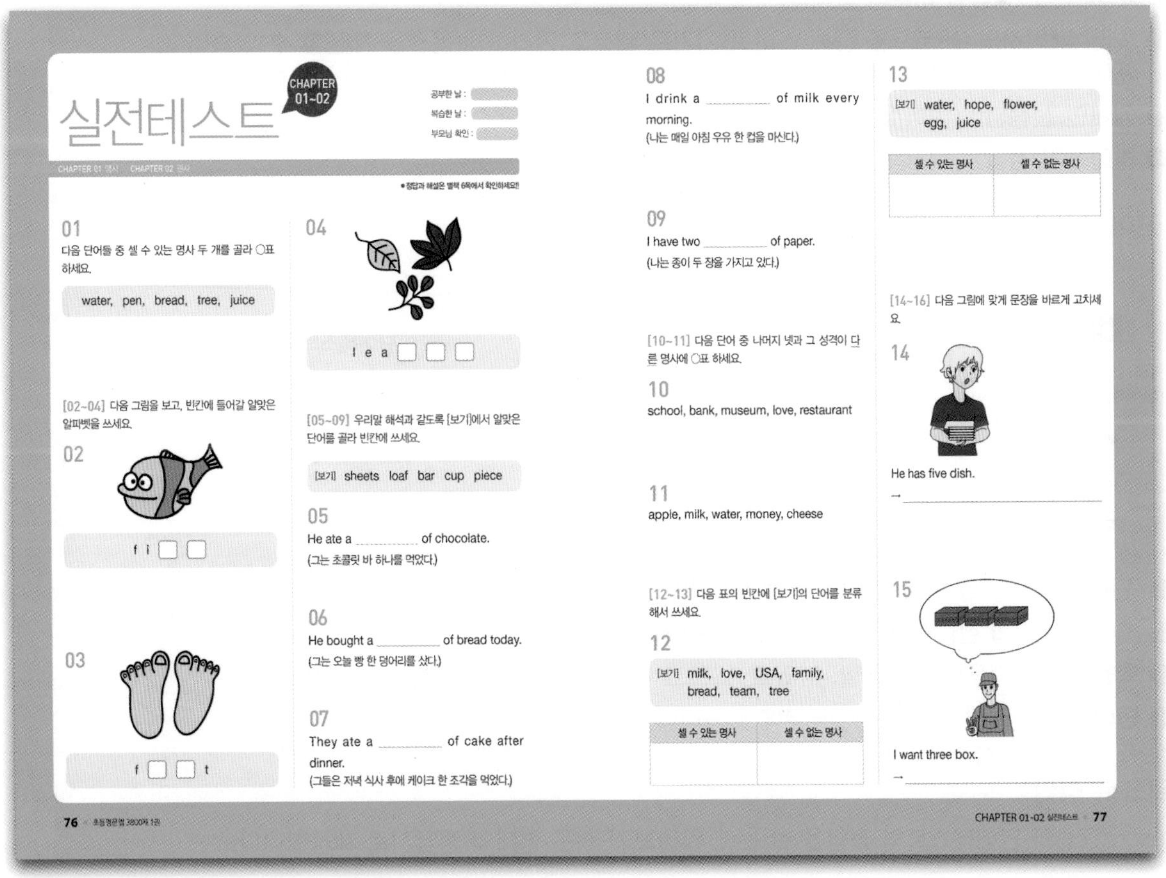

# 실전테스트

CHAPTER 01~02

공부한 날 :
복습한 날 :
부모님 확인 :

CHAPTER 01 명사 CHAPTER 02 명사

* 정답과 해설은 별책 6쪽에서 확인하세요!

01
다음 단어들 중 셀 수 있는 명사 두 개를 골라 ○표 하세요.

water, pen, bread, tree, juice

[02~04] 다음 그림을 보고, 빈칸에 들어갈 알맞은 알파벳을 쓰세요.

02
f i ☐ ☐

03
f ☐ ☐ t

04
l e a ☐ ☐ ☐

[05~09] 우리말 해석과 같도록 [보기]에서 알맞은 단어를 골라 빈칸에 쓰세요.

[보기] sheets loaf bar cup piece

05
He ate a ________ of chocolate.
(그는 초콜릿 바 하나를 먹었다.)

06
He bought a ________ of bread today.
(그는 오늘 빵 한 덩어리를 샀다.)

07
They ate a ________ of cake after dinner.
(그들은 저녁 식사 후에 케이크 한 조각을 먹었다.)

08
I drink a ________ of milk every morning.
(나는 매일 아침 우유 한 컵을 마신다.)

09
I have two ________ of paper.
(나는 종이 두 장을 가지고 있다.)

[10~11] 다음 단어 중 나머지 넷과 그 성격이 다른 명사에 ○표 하세요.

10
school, bank, museum, love, restaurant

11
apple, milk, water, money, cheese

[12~13] 다음 표의 빈칸에 [보기]의 단어를 분류해서 쓰세요.

12
[보기] milk, love, USA, family, bread, team, tree

| 셀 수 있는 명사 | 셀 수 없는 명사 |
|---|---|
| | |

13
[보기] water, hope, flower, egg, juice

| 셀 수 있는 명사 | 셀 수 없는 명사 |
|---|---|
| | |

[14~16] 다음 그림에 맞게 문장을 바르게 고치세요.

14
He has five dish.
→ ________

15
I want three box.
→ ________

76 초등영문법 3800제 1권

CHAPTER 01-02 실전테스트 77

## 워크북 구성 및 활용법 워크북은 아래와 같은 방법으로 활용하세요.

### 1. 단어쓰기 연습

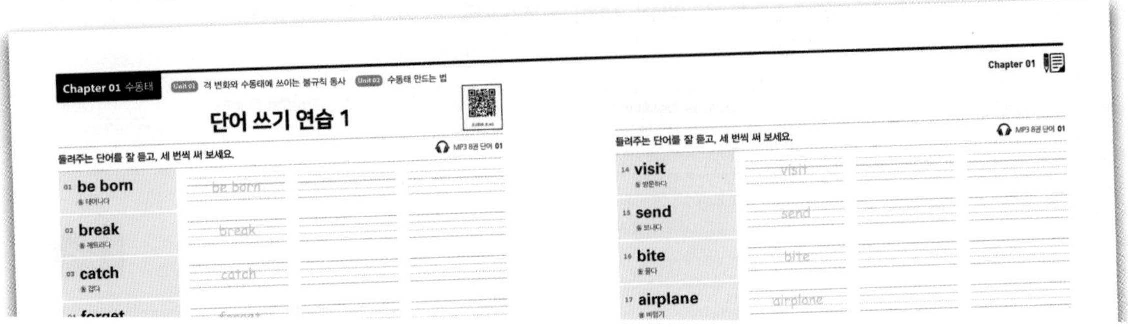
Chapter 01 수동태 Unit 01 격 변화와 수동태에 쓰이는 불규칙 동사 Unit 02 수동태 만드는 법

단어 쓰기 연습 1

들려주는 단어를 잘 듣고, 세 번씩 써 보세요.

01 be born 태어나다 be born
02 break 깨뜨리다 break
03 catch 잡다 catch

Chapter 01

들려주는 단어를 잘 듣고, 세 번씩 써 보세요.

14 visit 방문하다 visit
15 send 보내다 send
16 bite 물다 bite
17 airplane 비행기 airplane

❶ 먼저 본문 학습을 마무리 합니다.
❷ 해당 페이지의 QR코드를 통해 스마트 기기로 빠르고 편리하게 음원을 재생할 수 있습니다.
전체 음원 파일은 마더텅 홈페이지(www.toptutor.co.kr)에서 다운로드 가능합니다.
❸ 원어민 선생님이 읽어주는 영단어를 잘 듣고 안내선 안에 영어 단어 철자를 세 번씩 쓰세요.

### 2. 받아쓰기 시험 (Dictation Test)

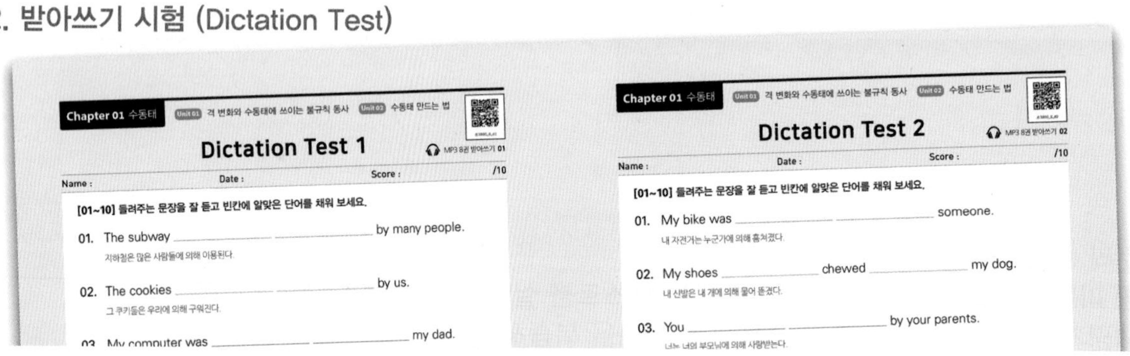
Chapter 01 수동태 Unit 01 격 변화와 수동태에 쓰이는 불규칙 동사 Unit 02 수동태 만드는 법

Dictation Test 1

Name : Date : Score : /10

[01~10] 들려주는 문장을 잘 듣고 빈칸에 알맞은 단어를 채워 보세요.

01. The subway ______ ______ by many people.
지하철은 많은 사람들에 의해 이용된다.

02. The cookies ______ ______ by us.
그 쿠키들은 우리에 의해 구워진다.

Chapter 01 수동태 Unit 01 격 변화와 수동태에 쓰이는 불규칙 동사 Unit 02 수동태 만드는 법

Dictation Test 2

Name : Date : Score : /10

[01~10] 들려주는 문장을 잘 듣고 빈칸에 알맞은 단어를 채워 보세요.

01. My bike was ______ ______ someone.
내 자전거는 누군가에 의해 훔쳐졌다.

02. My shoes ______ chewed ______ my dog.
내 신발은 내 개에 의해 물어 뜯겼다.

03. You ______ ______ by your parents.

❶ 먼저 본문 학습을 마무리 합니다.
❷ 해당 페이지의 QR코드를 통해 스마트 기기로 빠르고 편리하게 음원을 재생할 수 있습니다.
전체 음원 파일은 마더텅 홈페이지(www.toptutor.co.kr)에서 다운로드 가능합니다.
❸ 원어민 선생님이 읽어주는 문장을 잘 듣고, 빈칸을 채우세요.
❹ 받아쓰기 정답은 워크북 뒷부분에 있습니다.

### 3. 단어테스트

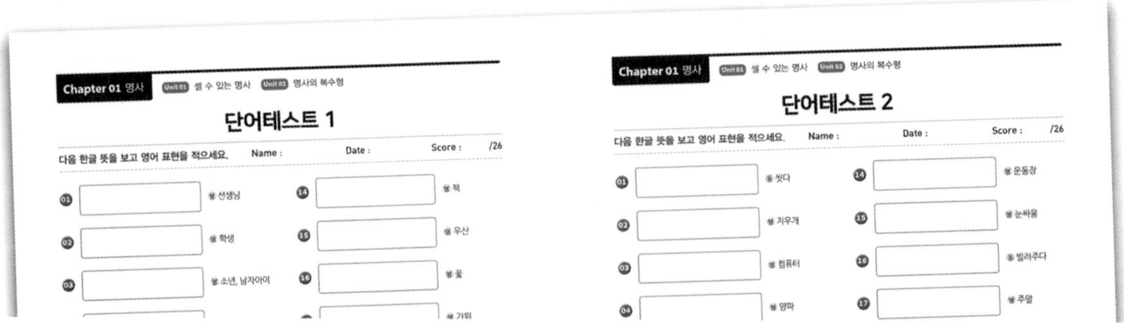
Chapter 01 명사 Unit 01 셀 수 있는 명사 Unit 02 명사의 복수형

단어테스트 1

다음 한글 뜻을 보고 영어 표현을 적으세요. Name : Date : Score : /26

01 명 선생님
02 명 학생
03 명 소년, 남자아이
14 명 책
15 명 우산
16 명 꽃

Chapter 01 명사 Unit 01 셀 수 있는 명사 Unit 02 명사의 복수형

단어테스트 2

다음 한글 뜻을 보고 영어 표현을 적으세요. Name : Date : Score : /26

01 동 씻다
02 명 지우개
03 명 컴퓨터
04 명 양파
14 명 운동장
15 명 눈싸움
16 동 빌려주다
17 명 주말

❶ 단어쓰기 연습을 하며, 단어들을 암기합니다.
❷ 단어테스트의 한글 뜻을 보고 암기한 영단어를 써 보세요.
❸ 학원에서 평가용으로 활용할 수 있고, 스스로 확인하는 용도로 활용할 수도 있습니다.
❹ 단어테스트 정답은 워크북 뒷부분에 있습니다.

### 4. 워크북 정답

Dictation Test와 단어테스트의 정답을 한 눈에 알아보기 쉬운 형태의 정답지로 제공합니다.

영문법 판매 1위, 중학영문법 3800제의 초등시리즈

# 초등영문법 3800제

LEVEL 8

실력2단계 CONTENTS

# Chapter 01 수동태

이 챕터에서는 '~가 ~되어지다'로 해석되는
'수동태'를 배워 보아요.

☆ 학습 방향 및 배울 내용 미리보기 ☆

## ☐ Unit 01 : I love you.

**격 변화와 수동태에 쓰이는 불규칙 동사**

수동태 문장을 쓰려면 인칭대명사의 격 변화와 동사의 과거분사 형태에 대해 알아야 해요. 주격이냐 목적격이냐에 따라 형태가 달라지는 인칭대명사의 격 변화에 대해 알아보고, 동사원형-과거-과거분사형이 불규칙하게 변화하는 동사에 대해 배워 보아요.

▼

## ☐ Unit 02 : This cookie was made by me.

**수동태 만드는 법**

능동태 문장을 수동태 문장으로 바꾸는 법에 대해 알아보아요.

▼

## ☐ Unit 03 : This house is not used anymore.

**수동태의 부정문**

수동태의 부정문을 만드는 방법과 줄여 쓰는 방법에 대해 배워 보아요.

▼

## ☐ Unit 04 : Are these cell phones made in Korea?

**수동태의 의문문**

수동태의 의문문을 만드는 방법과 의문사가 포함된 수동태 의문문을 만드는 방법에 대해 배워 보아요.

## 단어 미리보기

이 챕터에 나올 단어들 중 이미 알고 있는 단어가 있나요?
맞는 뜻을 골라 체크해 봐요.

날짜 : 이름 : 알고 있는 단어의 수 : /24개

| No. | 아는 단어 | 단어 | 품사 | 알맞은 뜻에 체크 표시해 봐요. | | | |
|---|---|---|---|---|---|---|---|
| 1 | ☑ | bear | 동사 | 낳다 | ☑ | 죽다 | ☐ |
| 2 | ☐ | hit | 동사 | 격려하다 | ☐ | 치다 | ☐ |
| 3 | ☐ | think | 동사 | 미워하다 | ☐ | 생각하다 | ☐ |
| 4 | ☐ | gift | 명사 | 선물 | ☐ | 가방 | ☐ |
| 5 | ☐ | prince | 명사 | 공주 | ☐ | 왕자 | ☐ |
| 6 | ☐ | darkness | 명사 | 빛 | ☐ | 어둠 | ☐ |
| 7 | ☐ | use | 동사 | 사용하다 | ☐ | 버리다 | ☐ |
| 8 | ☐ | bike | 명사 | 자동차 | ☐ | 자전거 | ☐ |
| 9 | ☐ | wall | 명사 | 벽 | ☐ | 시계 | ☐ |
| 10 | ☐ | stamp | 명사 | 편지 | ☐ | 우표 | ☐ |
| 11 | ☐ | police | 명사 | 경찰 | ☐ | 소방관 | ☐ |
| 12 | ☐ | understand | 동사 | 이해하다 | ☐ | 숨다 | ☐ |
| 13 | ☐ | why | 부사 | 무엇 | ☐ | 왜 | ☐ |
| 14 | ☐ | seat | 명사 | 좌석 | ☐ | 안전벨트 | ☐ |
| 15 | ☐ | leg | 명사 | 팔 | ☐ | 다리 | ☐ |
| 16 | ☐ | bite | 동사 | 물다 | ☐ | 묻다 | ☐ |
| 17 | ☐ | wood | 명사 | 나무 | ☐ | 인형 | ☐ |
| 18 | ☐ | plan | 동사 | 심다 | ☐ | 계획하다 | ☐ |
| 19 | ☐ | ship | 명사 | 비행기 | ☐ | 배 | ☐ |
| 20 | ☐ | mobile | 형용사 | 정지한 | ☐ | 움직이는 | ☐ |
| 21 | ☐ | attack | 동사 | 공격하다 | ☐ | 막다 | ☐ |
| 22 | ☐ | yet | 부사 | 예전에 | ☐ | 아직 | ☐ |
| 23 | ☐ | heavy | 형용사 | 무거운 | ☐ | 가벼운 | ☐ |
| 24 | ☐ | snack | 명사 | 군것질거리 | ☐ | 뱀 | ☐ |

UNIT

# 01 I love you.

격 변화와 수동태에 쓰이는 불규칙 동사

**수동태 문장 만드는 법을 배우려면 인칭대명사의 격 변화와 동사의 과거분사 형태를 알아야 해요.**

## ❖ POiNT 1 ❖

격 변화 – 주격과 목적격

**인칭대명사만이 격 변화가 있고, 명사는 주격과 목적격의 형태가 같아요.**

| | | | | | | | |
|---|---|---|---|---|---|---|---|
| 주격(~은, 는) | I | you | he | she | it | we | they |
| 목적격(~을, 를) | me | you | him | her | it | us | them |

## ❖ POiNT 2 ❖

수동태에 많이 쓰이는 불규칙 동사

| 동사원형 | 과거 | 과거분사 | 동사원형 | 과거 | 과거분사 |
|---|---|---|---|---|---|
| be | was/were | been | know | knew | known |
| bear | bore | born | lose | lost | lost |
| break | broke | broken | make | made | made |
| buy | bought | bought | meet | met | met |
| catch | caught | caught | read | read | read |
| do | did | done | say | said | said |
| drink | drank | drunk(en) | see | saw | seen |
| eat | ate | eaten | sell | sold | sold |
| feel | felt | felt | send | sent | sent |
| find | found | found | set | set | set |
| forget | forgot | forgotten | speak | spoke | spoken |
| get | got | got(ten) | steal | stole | stolen |
| give | gave | given | take | took | taken |
| hear | heard | heard | teach | taught | taught |
| hide | hid(ed) | hid(den) | tell | told | told |
| hit | hit | hit | think | thought | thought |
| keep | kept | kept | win | won | won |

# Check and Write

## A 우리말 해석에 맞게 주어진 단어를 알맞은 형태로 바꾸어 빈칸에 쓰세요.

1. she

[ She ] can understand them.
그녀는 그들을 이해할 수 있어.
They can understand [ her ].
그들은 그녀를 이해할 수 있어.

2. the cat

[ ] is looking at me.
그 고양이는 나를 바라보고 있어.
I'm looking at [ ].
나는 그 고양이를 바라보고 있어.

3. they

[ ] visited their grandparents.
그들은 그들의 조부모님을 방문했어.
Their grandparents visited [ ].
그들의 조부모님은 그들을 방문하셨어.

## B 다음 동사의 과거형과 과거분사를 쓰세요.

1. give – [ gave ] – [ given ]
2. tell – [ ] – [ ]
3. write – [ ] – [ ]
4. take – [ ] – [ ]
5. send – [ ] – [ ]
6. catch – [ ] – [ ]
7. eat – [ ] – [ ]
8. do – [ ] – [ ]
9. hide – [ ] – [ ]
10. win – [ ] – [ ]
11. feel – [ ] – [ ]
12. hit – [ ] – [ ]

정답과 해설 p.2

UNIT 수동태 만드는 법

# 02 This cookie was made by me.

**능동태는 주어가 능동적으로 행동할 때 쓰고, 수동태는 주어가 행동을 받을 때(당할 때) 써요.**
**능동태 문장은 '~가 ~을 하다'로 해석하고, 수동태 문장은 '~가 ~되어지다'로 해석해요.**

❖ POiNT ❖

## 수동태 만드는 법

| 능동태 | I | made | this cookie. |
|---|---|---|---|
| | 나는 | 만들었다 | 이 쿠키를 |
| | ① | ② | ③ |
| 수동태 | This cookie | was made | by me. |
| | 이 쿠키는 | 만들어졌다 | 나에 의해서 |

① 능동태의 목적어를 수동태의 주어로 한다.
this cookie → This cookie
② 능동태의 동사를 「be+과거분사」의 형태로 바꾼다.
이때, be동사는 바뀐 주어의 인칭과 수, 동사의 시제에 일치시킨다.
made → was made
③ 능동태의 주어를 「by+목적격」의 형태로 바꾼다.
I → by me

| 능동태 | My brother | reads | the book. |
|---|---|---|---|
| | 나의 오빠는 | 읽는다 | 그 책을 |
| | ① | ② | ③ |
| 수동태 | The book | is read | by my brother. |
| | 그 책은 | 읽혀진다 | 나의 오빠에 의해서 |

# Check and Write

**다음 문장을 보고 능동태 문장은 수동태로, 수동태 문장은 능동태로 바꿔보세요.**

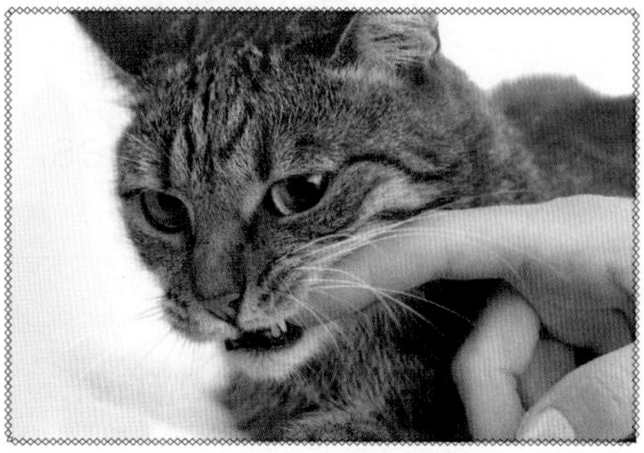

1. A cat bites my sister.

→ My sister is bitten by a cat.

내 여동생이 고양이에게 물렸어.

2. This airplane was made by me.

→ ______________________.

나는 이 비행기를 만들었어.

3. The subway is used by many people.

→ ______________________.

많은 사람들이 지하철을 이용해.

4. My dad fixed my computer.

→ ______________________.

내 컴퓨터는 우리 아빠에 의해서 고쳐졌어.

정답과 해설 p.2

## Practice 1 인칭대명사의 주격, 목적격 형태와 동사의 과거분사 형태를 익혀 보아요.

[1 – 10] 다음 수동태 문장의 빈칸을 채워 보세요.

1. We bake cookies.
   ➜ ___Cookies___ are baked by ___us___. 쿠키들은 우리에 의해 구워져.

2. Sihu invited me.
   ➜ __________ was invited by __________. 나는 시후에게 초대받았어.

3. He cancelled the meeting.
   ➜ __________ was cancelled by __________. 회의는 그에 의해 취소되었다.

4. The news surprised me.
   ➜ __________ was surprised by __________.
   나는 그 소식에 놀랐다.

5. He sends a present.
   ➜ __________ is sent by __________. 선물은 그에 의해서 보내진다.

6. The news pleased her.
   ➜ __________ was pleased by __________. 그녀는 그 소식에 기뻤다.

7. He writes it.
   ➜ __________ is written by __________. 그것은 그에 의해서 쓰여.

8. Many people love them.
   ➜ __________ are loved by __________. 그들은 많은 사람들에게 사랑 받는다.

9. You read a book.
   ➜ __________ is read by __________.
   책 한 권이 너에게 읽혀져.

10. I forgot him.
    ➜ __________ was forgotten by __________. 그는 나에게서 잊혀졌다.



정답과 해설 p.2

[11 – 20] (   ) 안에 주어진 동사의 과거분사 형태를 빈칸에 써 보세요.

11.

I am interested in music. ( interest )

나는 음악에 흥미가 있다.

12.

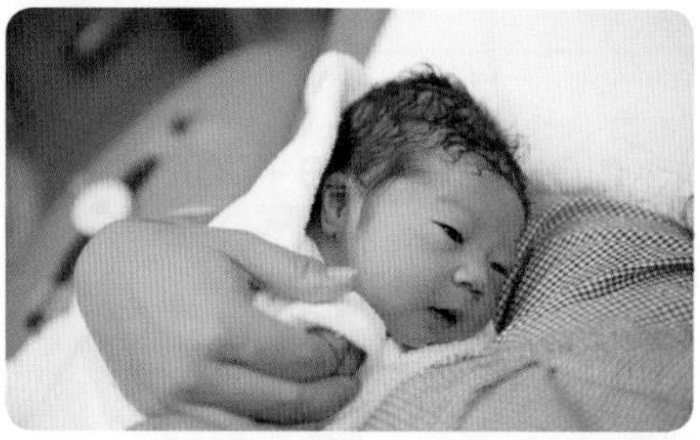

Sion was ________________ in 2005. ( bear )

시온이는 2005년에 태어났어.

13. We are ________________ by him. ( teach ) 우리는 그에게 가르침을 받는다.

14. He is ________________ as the writer of a best seller. ( know )

그는 베스트셀러의 작가로 알려져 있다.

15. Many famous books are ________________ here. ( find )

많은 유명한 책들이 여기서 발견된다.

16. Classical music is ________________ in this book store. ( hear )

고전음악이 이 서점에서 들린다.

17. Andersen's books are ________________ by many children. ( read )

안데르센의 책들은 많은 아이들에게 읽힌다.

18. Eggs are ________________ out today. ( sell ) 달걀은 오늘 다 팔렸어요.

19.

Trees are ________________ by Tom. ( plant )

나무들은 Tom에 의해 심어져.

20.

The cupcake was ________________ by me. ( eat )

그 컵케이크는 나에 의해 먹어졌어.

정답과 해설 p.2

## Practice 2 수동태 문장을 완성해 보아요.

다음 우리말 뜻과 같도록 주어진 표현을 순서에 맞게 배열하여 문장을 완성하세요.

1. ( is cleaned, The room, by me ).
그 방은 나에 의해서 청소되어져.

→ The room is cleaned by me.

2. ( was, scolded, He ) by his mom.
그는 그의 엄마에게 꾸지람을 들었어.

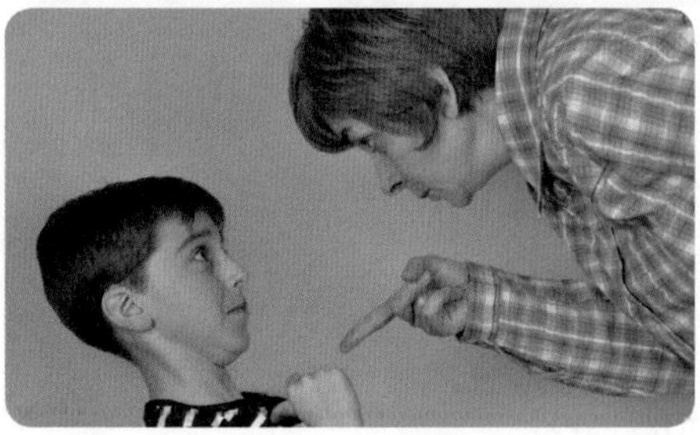

→ ______________________ by his mom.

3. ( to her room, is sent, She ). 그녀는 그녀의 방으로 보내져.
→ ______________________.

4. ( from school, sent home, She was ), because she is sick.
그녀는 학교에서 집으로 보내졌는데, 왜냐하면 그녀는 아프기 때문이야.

→ ______________________, because she is sick.

5. ( a trouble maker, is called, Junwoo ). 준우는 사고뭉치로 불려.
→ ______________________.

6. The window ( was, by Junwoo, broken ). 그 창문은 준우에 의해서 깨졌어.
→ The window ______________________.



정답과 해설 p.2

7. ( are, You, grounded ) for a week! (*ground: 외출을 금지하다, 나가 놀지 못하게 하다)
너는 일주일 동안 외출금지야!
➔ ________________________ for a week!

8. ( at that, was surprised, Justin ).
Justin은 그것에 깜짝 놀랐어.

➔ ________________________
________________________.

9. ( loved, by your parents, You are ).
너는 너의 부모님에게 사랑받아.

➔ ________________________
________________________.

10. ( was sent, by the prince, I ) to save you.
나는 당신을 구하기 위해 왕자로부터 보내졌습니다.
➔ ________________________ to save you.

11. Yesterday is history, tomorrow is a mystery, and today is a gift. So ( is called, the present, today )
어제는 역사, 내일은 미스터리, 그리고 오늘은 선물이다. 그래서 오늘은 선물이라고 불린다.
➔ Yesterday is history, tomorrow is a mystery, and today is a gift. So ________________________.

12. Maria ( introduced, is, by her ). Maria는 그녀에 의해 소개되어져.
➔ Maria ________________________.

13. ( is found, Happiness, in the darkness ). 행복은 어둠 속에서 발견된다.
➔ ________________________.

정답과 해설 p.2

14. ( by us, are remembered, They ). 그들은 우리에 의해 기억된다.

➔ ______________________________.

15. We are twins.
( were, raised, We ) together.
우린 쌍둥이야. 우린 함께 길러졌어.

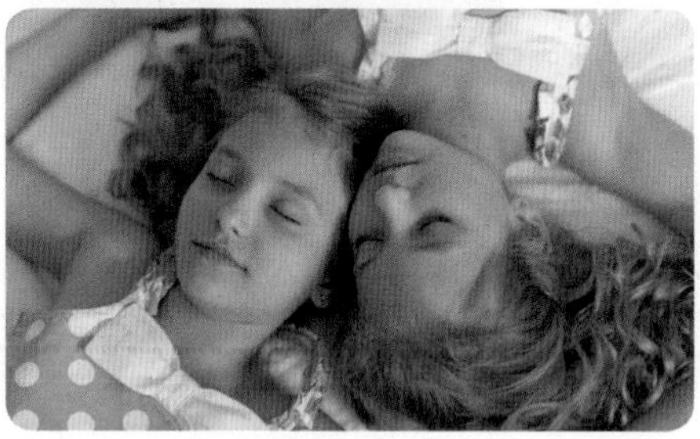

➔ We are twins.
______________
together.

16. ( Clara, by grandma, is invited ) to her birthday party.
Clara는 할머니에 의해 생일파티에 초대된다.

➔ ______________
______________
to her birthday party.

17. ( is written, The letter, by Sihu ). 그 편지는 시후에 의해 쓰여진다.

➔ ______________________________.

18. ( by my mother, was cooked, The fish ).
그 생선은 나의 어머니에 의해 요리되었어.

➔ ______________________________.

19. ( was painted, by her, This picture ). 이 그림은 그녀에 의해 그려졌어.

➔ ______________________________.

20. ( This box, by me, was opened ). 이 상자는 나에 의해 열렸다.

➔ ______________________________.



정답과 해설 p.2

## Practice 3 완전한 수동태 문장을 써 보아요.

**다음 능동태 문장을 수동태로 바꿔보세요.**

1. I collect stamps.

→ Stamps are collected by me.

우표는 나에 의해서 수집된다.

2. The vet treated the dog.

(*vet : 수의사)

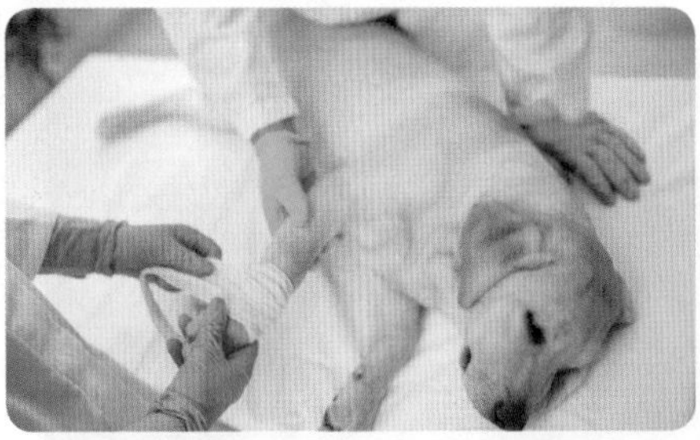

→ ______________________.

그 개는 수의사에게 치료받았어.

3. A car hit a dog.

→ ______________________.

개 한 마리가 차에 치였어.

4. Mori hid(ed) his toys.

→ ______________________.

그의 장난감들은 모리에 의해서 숨겨졌어.

5. My mother made the skirt.

→ ______________________.

그 치마는 우리 엄마에 의해 만들어졌어.

6. They opened a new restaurant.

→ ______________________.

새로운 식당이 그들에 의해 열렸다.

정답과 해설 p.2

7. Some people saw the thief.

➔ ______________________________________________.

도둑은 몇몇 사람들에게 목격되었어.

8. The police caught the thief.

➔ ____________________

____________________.

도둑은 경찰에게 잡혔어.

9. She paints the wall.

➔ ____________________

____________________.

그 벽은 그녀에 의해서 페인트칠 되어져.

10. They kept a secret.

➔ ______________________________________________.

비밀은 그들에 의해 지켜졌어.

11. I told the story.

➔ ______________________________________________.

그 이야기는 나에 의해서 말해졌어.

12. Junwoo broke the window.

➔ ______________________________________________.

그 창문은 준우에 의해서 깨졌어.

13. His mom scolds him.

➔ ______________________________________.

그는 그의 엄마에게 야단맞아.



정답과 해설 p.2

14. I finished the work.

➔ ______________________________________________.

그 일은 나에 의해 마무리되었어.

15. Someone stole my bike.

➔ ______________________________________________.

내 자전거는 누군가에게 도둑맞았다.

16. My dog chews my shoes.

➔ ______________________

______________________.

내 신발은 내 강아지에 의해서 물어뜯어져.

17. Kevin broke the flowerpot.

➔ ______________________

______________________.

화분은 Kevin에 의해서 깨졌다. (*flowerpot: 화분)

18. My grandfather built this house.

➔ ______________________________________________.

이 집은 나의 할아버지에 의해 지어졌어.

19. The teacher answers the question.

➔ ______________________________________________.

질문은 선생님에 의해 답변되어져.

20. Mom baked a chocolate cake.

➔ ______________________________________.

초콜릿 케이크는 엄마에 의해서 구워졌어.

정답과 해설 p.2

# Let's Practice More!

SET 01

학습목표 1 | 인칭대명사의 주격, 목적격 형태를 익혀 보아요. 공부한 날 : 맞은 개수 : /12개

우리말 뜻과 같아지도록 다음 문장의 빈칸을 채우세요.

01. Many people love ___them___.
많은 사람들이 그들을 사랑해.

02. ________ was scolded by his mom.
그는 그의 엄마에게 꾸지람을 들었어.

03. ________ are loved by your parents.
너는 너의 부모님에게 사랑받아.

04. Sihu invited ________.
시후는 나를 초대했어.

05. The cupcake was eaten by ________.
그 컵케이크는 나에 의해 먹어졌어.

06. Maria is introduced by ________.
Maria는 그녀에 의해 소개되어져.

07. The news pleased ________.
그 소식은 그녀를 기쁘게 했어.

08. The room is cleaned by ________.
그 방은 나에 의해서 청소되어져.

09. ________ bake cookies.
우리는 쿠키들을 구워.

10. ________ was sent home from school.
그녀는 학교에서 집으로 보내졌어.

11. ________ read a book.
너는 책 한 권을 읽어.

12. The news surprised ________.
그 소식은 나를 놀라게 했어.



정답과 해설 p.2

# Let's Practice More!

SET 02



학습목표 2 | 동사의 과거분사 형태를 익혀 보아요. 공부한 날 : 맞은 개수 : /14개

다음 동사의 과거분사 형태를 빈칸에 써 보세요.

01. write (글을) 쓰다 → written

02. introduce 소개하다 → ______

03. find 찾다 → ______

04. remember 기억하다 → ______

05. raise 기르다 → ______

06. invite 초대하다 → ______

07. hit 치다 → ______

08. call 전화하다, ~라고 불리다 → ______

09. cook 요리하다 → ______

10. paint 페인트를 칠하다, (그림을) 그리다 → ______

11. open 열다 → ______

12. surprise 놀라게 하다 → ______

13. break 깨뜨리다 → ______

14. send 보내다 → ______

정답과 해설 p.3

# Let's Practice More!

SET 03

학습목표 3 | 능동태와 수동태를 구분해 보아요.　　공부한 날 :　　맞은 개수 :　　/14개

다음 문장이 능동태면 '능', 수동태면 '수'를 쓰세요.

01. A dog was hit by a car. → 수
개 한 마리가 차에 치였어.

02. Many people love them. → ______
많은 사람들이 그들을 사랑해.

03. Sihu invited me. → ______
시후는 나를 초대했어.

04. The dog was treated by the vet. → ______
그 개는 수의사에게 치료받았어.

05. He cancelled the meeting. → ______
그는 회의를 취소했어.

06. Coins are collected by me. → ______
동전들은 나에 의해서 수집되어져.

07. The wall is painted by her. → ______
그 벽은 그녀에 의해서 페인트칠 되어져.

08. He sends a present. → ______
그는 선물을 보낸다.

09. The cake was made by my mother. → ______
그 케이크는 우리 엄마에 의해 만들어졌어.

10. The news pleased her. → ______
그 소식은 그녀를 기쁘게 했어.

11. The thief was seen by some people. → ______
도둑은 몇몇 사람들에게 목격되었어.

12. He writes it. → ______
그는 그것을 써.

13. I forgot him. → ______
나는 그를 잊었어.

14. His toys were hidden by Mori. → ______
그의 장난감들은 모리에 의해서 숨겨졌어.



정답과 해설 p.3

# Let's Practice More!

SET 04

학습목표 3 | 능동태와 수동태를 구분해 보아요.  공부한 날 :  맞은 개수 : /12개

다음 밑줄 친 부분에 대한 우리말 해석으로 가장 적절한 것을 고르세요.

01. I am interested in music. (흥미롭게 하다 / 관심이 있다)

02. He is known as the writer of a best seller. (알려져 있다 / 알리다)

03. Many famous books are found here. (발견되다 / 발견하다)

04. Trees are planted by Jaejun. (심다 / 심어지다)

05. Andersen's books are read by many children. (읽히다 / 읽다)

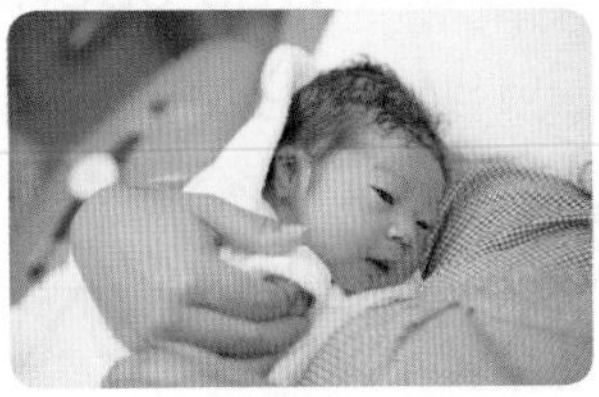

06. Sion was born in 2005. (태어났다 / 낳았다)

07. She is sent to her room. (보내다 / 보내지다)

08. Junwoo is called a trouble maker. (불리다 / 부르다)

09. The window was broken by Junwoo. (깨졌다 / 깨뜨렸다)

10. Justin was surprised at that. (놀라게 했다 / 놀랐다)

11. We were raised together. (길렀다 / 길러졌다)

12. Clara is invited by grandma. (초대되다 / 초대하다)

정답과 해설 p.3

# Let's Practice More!

SET 05

학습목표 4 | 수동태의 형태를 확실히 다져 보아요. 공부한 날 : 맞은 개수 : /14개

다음 ( ) 안의 말을 'by + 행위자'로 고쳐 빈칸에 알맞게 써 보세요.

01. They are remembered ______by us______. (we) 그들은 우리에 의해 기억되어져.

02. The letter is written ____________________. (Sihu)
그 편지는 시후에 의해 쓰여져.

03. The fish was cooked ____________________. (my mother)
그 생선은 나의 어머니에 의해 요리되었어.

04. This picture was painted ____________________. (she) 이 그림은 그녀에 의해 그려졌어.

05. This box was opened ____________________. (I)
이 상자는 나에 의해 열렸어.

06. A new restaurant was opened ____________________. (they)
새로운 식당이 그들에 의해 열렸다.

07. The thief was caught ____________________. (the police)
도둑은 경찰에게 잡혔어.

08. My bike was stolen ____________________. (someone)
내 자전거는 누군가에게 도둑맞았어.

09. Clara is invited ____________________. (grandma) Clara는 할머니에 의해 초대되어져.

10. The wall is painted ____________________. (she)
그 벽은 그녀에 의해서 페인트칠 되어져.

11. The meeting was cancelled ____________________. (he) 회의는 그에 의해서 취소되었어.

12. Cookies are baked ____________________. (we) 쿠키들은 우리에 의해 구워져.

13. A book is read ____________________. (you) 책 한 권이 너에게 읽혀져.

14. He was forgotten ____________________. (I) 그는 나에게 잊혀졌어.



정답과 해설 p.3

# Let's Practice More!

SET 06



학습목표 4 | **수동태의 형태를 확실히 다져 보아요.** 공부한 날 : 맞은 개수 : /14개

다음 문장을 읽고 ( ) 안에서 가장 적절한 것을 고르세요.

01. Many famous books are ( finded / found ) here.
많은 유명한 책들이 여기서 발견된다.

02. They are ( remembered / remembering ) by us.
그들은 우리에 의해 기억된다.

03. Classical music is ( hearded / heard ) in this book store.
고전음악이 이 서점에서 들린다.

04. We were ( raised / raising ) together. 우린 함께 길러졌다.

05. The letter is ( written / wrote ) by Sihu.
그 편지는 시후에 의해 쓰여진다.

06. Trees are ( planting / planted ) by Jane.
나무들은 Jane에 의해서 심어져.

07. Andersen's books are ( reading / read ) by many children.
안데르센의 책들은 많은 어린이들에게 읽혀.

08. You are ( grounding / grounded ) for a week! 너는 일주일 동안 외출금지야!

09. A secret was ( kept / keeped ) by them. 비밀은 그들에 의해 지켜졌어.

10. The story was ( told / telling ) by me. 그 이야기는 나에 의해서 말해졌어.

11. I was ( sended / sent ) by the prince to save you.
나는 당신을 구하기 위해 왕자로부터 보내졌습니다.

12. The window was ( broken / breaking ) by Junwoo. 그 창문은 준우에 의해서 깨졌어.

13. Today is ( calling / called ) the present. 오늘은 선물이라고 불린다.

14. My shoes are ( chewed / chewing ) by my dog.
내 신발은 내 강아지에 의해서 물어뜯어져.

정답과 해설 p.3

# Let's Practice More!

SET 07

학습목표 4 | 수동태의 형태를 확실히 다져 보아요. 공부한 날 : 맞은 개수 : /20개

다음 문장을 읽고 밑줄 친 부분이 맞으면 ○, 틀리면 고쳐 써 보세요.

01.

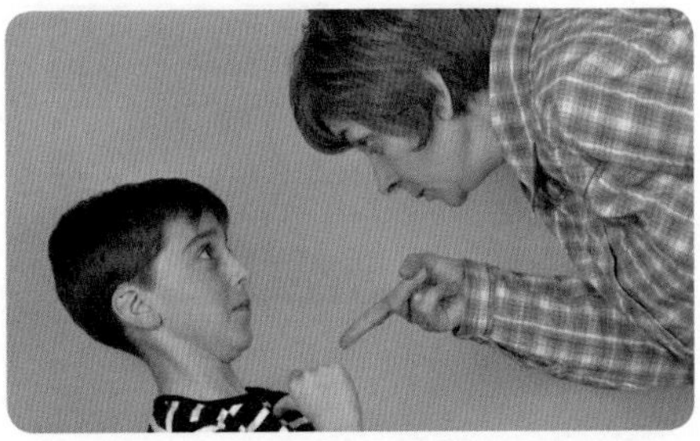

Jade is scolded by his mom.
Jade는 그의 엄마에게 꾸지람을 들어.
→ ○

02.

I was surprising by the news.
나는 그 소식에 깜짝 놀랐어.
→ ______

03. The work was finished by me. → ______
그 일은 나에 의해 마무리되었어.

04. The flowerpot was broken by Kevin. → ______
화분은 Kevin에 의해서 깨졌다.

05. The question is answered by the teacher. → ______
질문은 선생님에 의해 답변되어져.

06. A present is send by him. → ______
선물은 그에 의해서 보내진다.

07. This house was built by my grandfather. → ______
이 집은 나의 할아버지에 의해 지어졌어.

08. It is writing by him. → ______
그것은 그에 의해서 쓰여져.

09. Sion was bearing in 2005. → ______
시온이는 2005년에 태어났어.


정답과 해설 p.3

10. A chocolate cake was baked by mom. ➔ ____________
초콜릿 케이크는 엄마에 의해서 구워졌어.

11. 

The cupcake was eat by me.
그 컵케이크는 나에 의해 먹어졌어.

➔ ____________

12. 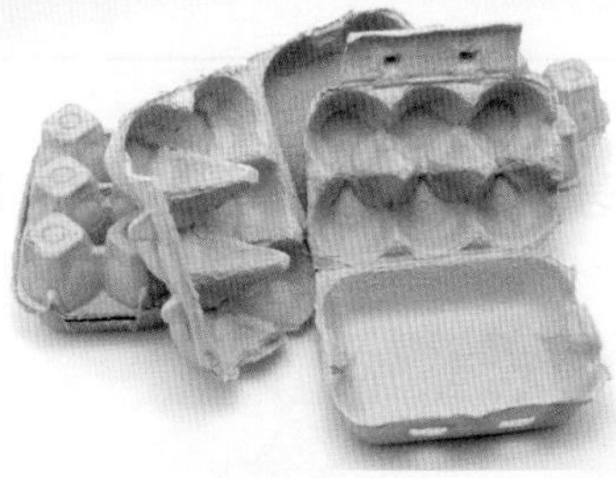

Eggs are selling out today.
달걀은 오늘 다 팔렸어요.

➔ ____________

13. Maria is introduced by her. ➔ ____________
Maria는 그녀에 의해 소개되어져.

14. Junwoo is call a trouble maker. ➔ ____________
준우는 사고뭉치로 불려.

15. The window was breaking by Junwoo. ➔ ____________
그 창문은 준우에 의해서 깨졌어.

16. Happiness is found in the darkness. ➔ ____________
행복은 어둠 속에서 발견된다.

17. You are ground for a week! ➔ ____________
너는 일주일 동안 외출금지야!

18. This picture was painted by her. ➔ ____________
이 그림은 그녀에 의해 그려졌어.

19. A dog was hitting by a car. ➔ ____________
개 한 마리가 차에 치였어.

20. This box was opened by me. ➔ ____________
이 상자는 나에 의해 열렸다.

정답과 해설 p.3

# Let's Practice More!

SET 08

학습목표 5 | 능동태와 수동태 문장을 비교하며 다양한 표현을 만들어 보아요.  공부한 날 :  맞은 개수 : /20개

다음 문장에서 능동태는 수동태로, 수동태는 능동태로 고쳐 보세요.

01. 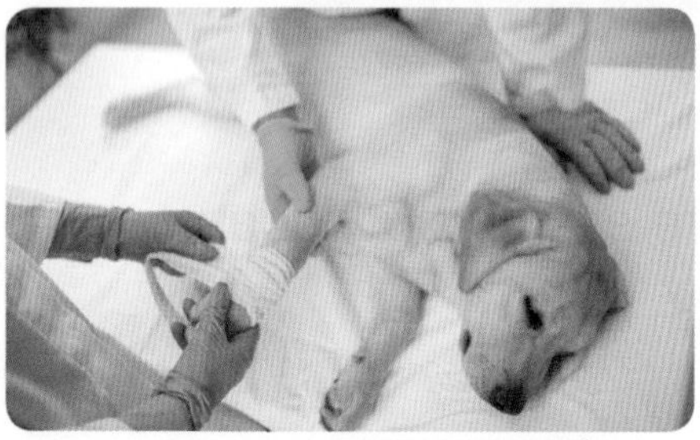

The vet treated the dog.

➔ The dog was treated by the vet.

그 개는 수의사에게 치료받았어.

02. 

I collect stamps.

➔ ______________________.

우표는 나에 의해서 수집된다.

03. The room is cleaned by me.

➔ ______________________. 나는 그 방을 청소한다.

04. Mori hided his toys.

➔ ______________________. 그의 장난감들은 모리에 의해서 숨겨졌어.

05. We are taught by him.

➔ ______________________. 그는 우리들을 가르치셔.

06. My mother made the skirt.

➔ ______________________.

그 치마는 우리 엄마에 의해 만들어졌어.

07. They opened a new restaurant.

➔ ______________________. 새로운 식당이 그들에 의해 열렸다.

08. You are loved by your parents.

➔ ______________________. 너의 부모님은 너를 사랑하셔.

09. I was sent by the prince to save you.

➔ ______________________. 왕자님은 너를 구하기 위해 나를 보내셨어.



정답과 해설 p.3

10. The fish was cooked by my mother.

➔ ______________________________. 나의 어머니는 그 생선을 요리하셨어.

11. 

The flowerpot was broken by Kevin.

➔ ______________________.

Kevin은 꽃병을 깨뜨렸어.

12. 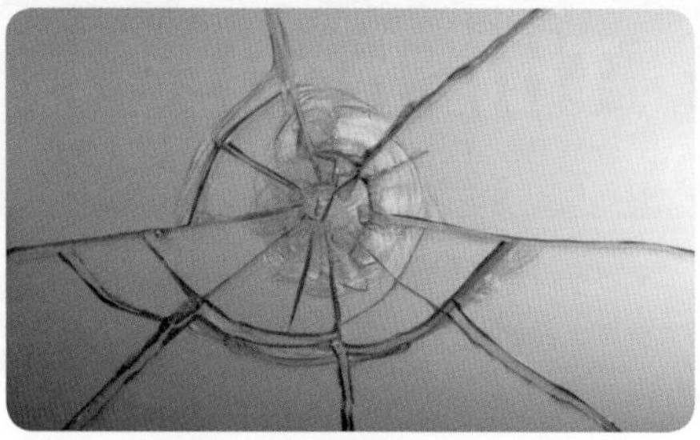

The window was broken by Junwoo.

➔ ______________________.

준우가 그 창문을 깼어.

13. My bike was stolen by someone.

➔ ______________________________. 누군가가 내 자전거를 훔쳤어.

14. The police caught the thief.

➔ ______________________________. 도둑은 경찰에게 잡혔어.

15. Some people saw the thief.

➔ ______________________________. 도둑은 몇몇 사람들에게 목격되었어.

16. They kept a secret.

➔ ______________________________. 비밀은 그들에 의해 지켜졌어.

17. I told the story.

➔ ______________________________. 그 이야기는 나에 의해서 말해졌어.

18. This house was built by my grandfather.

➔ ______________________________. 나의 할아버지가 이 집을 지으셨어.

19. The question is answered by the teacher.

➔ ______________________________.

선생님은 질문에 대답하셔.

20. My dog chews my shoes.

➔ ______________________________. 내 신발은 내 강아지에 의해서 물어뜯어져.

정답과 해설 p.3

# UNIT 03 This house is not used anymore.

수동태의 부정문

## ❖ POiNT 1 ❖

**수동태의 부정문**
**be동사 뒤에 not을 붙여요!**

| 주어 | + | be동사 | + | not | + | 과거분사 |
|---|---|---|---|---|---|---|

This house is not used anymore.
이 집은 더 이상 사용되지 않아.

This house was not used anymore.
이 집은 더 이상 사용되지 않았어.

These pictures are not painted by John.
이 그림들은 John에 의해서 그려지지 않아.

These pictures were not painted by John.
이 그림들은 John에 의해서 그려지지 않았어.

## ❖ POiNT 2 ❖

**be동사 뒤에 not이 오면 축약이 가능해요!**

This house isn't used anymore.
이 집은 더 이상 사용되지 않아.

This house wasn't used anymore.
이 집은 더 이상 사용되지 않았어.

These pictures aren't painted by John.
이 그림들은 John에 의해서 그려지지 않아.

These pictures weren't painted by John.
이 그림들은 John에 의해서 그려지지 않았어.

## Check and Write

**다음 수동태 문장을 부정문, 부정문의 축약형으로 바꿔보세요.**

1. I was caught by Mina.

➔ I was not caught by Mina.

➔ I wasn't caught by Mina.

나는 미나에게 잡히지 않았어.

2. These cookies were made by me.

➔ ______________________.

➔ ______________________.

이 쿠키들은 나에 의해서 만들어지지 않았어.

3. The candy was eaten by Cathy.

➔ ______________________.

➔ ______________________.

그 사탕은 Cathy에 의해 먹어지지 않았어.

4. These shoes were made for me.

➔ ______________________.

➔ ______________________.

이 신발은 나를 위해 만들어진 게 아니었어.

정답과 해설 p.3

수동태의 의문문

UNIT
# 04 Are these cell phones made in Korea?

❖ POiNT 1 ❖

수동태의 의문문

**be동사와 주어의 순서를 바꾸고 뒤에 물음표를 붙이면 돼요.**

be동사 + 주어 + 과거분사 + ?

These cell phones **are** **made** in Korea.

**Are** these cell phones **made** in Korea?

이 핸드폰들은 한국에서 만들어지니?

These trees **were** **planted** by you.

**Were** these trees **planted** by you?

이 나무들은 너희들에 의해 심어졌니?

❖ POiNT 2 ❖

의문사가 있을 경우

**의문사를 가장 앞에 두고 be동사와 주어의 순서를 바꾼 후 물음표를 붙이면 돼요.**

의문사 + be동사 + 주어 + 과거분사 + ?

**Why was** the window **broken**?

왜 그 창문이 깨졌니?

**What was invented** by him?

그에 의해서 무엇이 발명되었니?

## Check and Write

**다음 수동태 문장을 의문문으로 바꿔보세요.**

1. This room was cleaned by him.
➔ Was this room cleaned by him
______________________________?
이 방은 그에 의해서 청소되었니?

2. Tomatoes are grown by your grandmother.
➔ ______________________________
______________________________?
토마토는 너의 할머니에 의해서 키워지니?

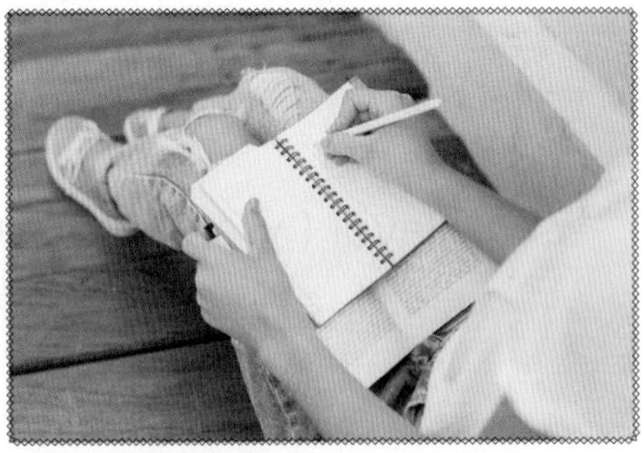

3. The diary was written by Nayeon.
➔ ______________________________
______________________________?
그 일기는 나연이에 의해서 쓰였니?

4. These pictures were taken by you.
➔ ______________________________
______________________________?
이 사진들은 너에 의해서 찍힌 거니?

정답과 해설 p.3

# Practice 1 문제를 풀면서 수동태의 부정문과 의문문을 익혀 보아요.

[1-10] 다음 ( ) 안에서 알맞은 것을 골라 수동태의 부정문을 완성해 보세요.

1. They ( are not / not are ) lost in the forest.
   그들은 숲에서 길을 잃어버리지 않아.

2. I ( am not / not am ) worried about her.
   나는 그녀가 걱정되지 않아.

3. That seat ( was not / not was ) taken.
   저 자리는 주인이 없었어.

4. The music ( is not / not is ) played by Jackson.
   그 음악은 Jackson에 의해서 연주되는 게 아니야.

5. His name ( was not / not was ) called by the teacher.
   그의 이름은 선생님에 의해서 불리지 않았어.

6. My name ( is not / am not ) written on the paper.
   종이에 내 이름이 적혀있지 않아.

7. Hayul ( was not / were not ) invited by Yura.
   하율이는 유라에게 초대받지 않았어.

8. We ( was not / were not ) pleased by the news.
   우리는 그 소식에 기쁘지 않았어.

9. Dinner ( was not / are not ) prepared by dad. (*prepare: 준비하다)
   저녁은 아빠에 의해서 준비되지 않았어.

10. The bag ( was not / were not ) made by Dana.
    그 가방은 다나에 의해서 만들어지지 않았어.


정답과 해설 p.3

[11 – 20] 다음 (   ) 안에서 알맞은 것을 골라 수동태의 의문문을 완성해 보세요.

11. ( Is this seat / Does this seat ) taken?
이 자리는 주인이 있니?

12. ( Were those books / Did those books ) borrowed by Jane? (*borrow: 빌리다)
그 책들은 Jane에 의해 빌려졌니?

13. ( Could this bread / Was this bread ) baked by Paul?
이 빵은 Paul에 의해서 구워졌니?

14. ( Is it / Does it ) filled with butter cream?
그것은 버터크림으로 채워져 있니? (*fill: 채우다, 메우다)

15. ( Would this picture / Was this picture ) painted by him?
이 그림은 그에 의해서 그려졌니?

16. ( Was the meeting / Did the meeting ) cancelled by her? (*cancel: 취소하다)
그 회의는 그녀에 의해서 취소되었니?

17. ( Was the building / Would the building ) built by them?
그 건물은 그들에 의해서 지어졌니?

18. ( Did the memo / Was the memo ) written by Dana?
그 메모는 다나에 의해서 쓰여졌니?

19. ( Will the dishes / Were the dishes ) washed by dad?
그릇들은 아빠에 의해서 씻어졌니? (아빠는 설거지를 하셨니?)

20. ( Was the bathroom / Did the bathroom ) cleaned by Hayul?
화장실은 하율이에 의해서 청소되었니?

정답과 해설 p.3

## Practice 2 문법에 맞게 수동태 문장을 완성해 보아요.

**[1 – 10] 다음 우리말 뜻과 같도록 (    ) 안에서 알맞은 것을 골라 동그라미 하세요.**

1. 

My file was not ( saving / saved )!

내 파일이 저장되지 않았어!

2. 

The letter was ( writing / written ) by David.

그 편지는 David에 의해서 쓰여졌어.

3. Was the soccer game ( cancel / cancelled ) because of heavy rain?

축구 경기가 폭우 때문에 취소됐어?

4. No, it was ( delaying / delayed ). (*delay: 미루다, 연기하다)

아니야, 그건 미뤄졌어.

5. Is your leg ( breaking / broken )? 너의 다리가 부러진 거니?

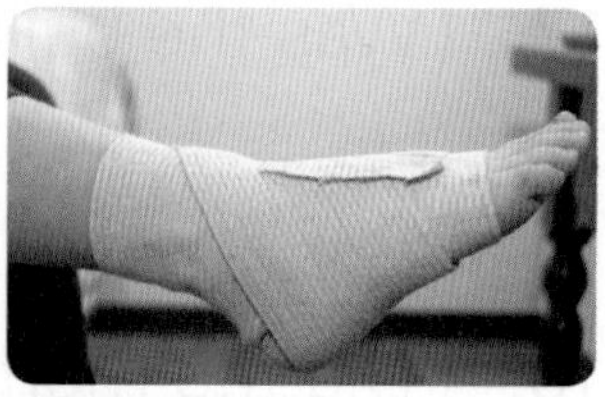

6. No, I was ( bitting / bitten ) by a dog. (*bite: 물다)

아니, 나는 개에게 물렸어.

7. Were you ( attacked / attacking ) by Mina's dog?

너는 미나의 개에 의해서 공격당했니?



정답과 해설 p.4

8. The dress ( was / were ) designed by a young designer.
그 드레스는 젊은 디자이너에 의해서 디자인되었어.

9. The piano is ( playing / played ) by my father.
그 피아노는 나의 아버지에 의해서 연주돼.

10. The airplane ( invent / was invented ) by the Wright brothers.
비행기는 라이트형제에 의해서 발명되었어. (*invent: 발명하다)

**[11 – 20] 다음 우리말 뜻과 같도록 주어진 표현을 순서에 맞게 배열하여 문장을 완성하세요.**

11. ( is cleaned, The park, by us).
그 공원은 우리에 의해 청소된다.

➔ The park is cleaned by us.

12. ( you, excited, Are )?
너 신나니?

➔ ____________________?

13. ( is visited, by many people, The museum ).
그 박물관은 많은 사람들에 의해서 방문된다.

➔ ____________________.

14. ( you, grounded, Are )? (*ground: 외출을 금지시키다)
너 외출금지 된 거야?

➔ ____________________?

정답과 해설 p.4

**15.** ( not, I, grounded, am ). I stay at home because I am sick.

나는 외출금지 된 게 아니야. 나는 아프기 때문에 집에 있는 거야.

➔ ______________________________. I stay at home because I am sick.

**16.** ( was, His room, cleaned )!

그의 방이 청소되었어!

➔ ______________________

______________________!

**17.** ( by many fans, are loved, They ).

그들은 많은 팬들로부터 사랑받아.

➔ ______________________

______________________.

**18.** ( Was, fixed, the computer, by him )? 컴퓨터가 그에 의해서 고쳐졌나요?

➔ ______________________________________________?

**19.** ( is, fixed, It, not ) yet. 그건 아직 고쳐지지 않았어.

➔ ______________________________ yet.

**20.** ( The school picnic, not, was, cancelled ).

학교 소풍은 취소되지 않았어.

➔ ______________________________________.

정답과 해설 p.4

# Practice 3 수동태의 부정문과 의문문을 확실히 다져 보아요.

[1 – 10] 다음 주어진 수동태 문장을 부정문으로 바꿔 써 보세요.

1. These cookies were baked yesterday.

➔ These cookies were not[weren't] baked yesterday.

이 쿠키들은 어제 구워지지 않았어.

2. This building was built in 1989.

➔ ______________________________.

이 건물은 1989년에 지어지지 않았어.

3. My cell phone was lost.

➔ ______________________________.

나의 핸드폰은 분실되지 않았어.

4. This seat is taken.

➔ ______________________________.

이 자리는 주인이 없어.

5. Her grades were raised.

➔ ______________________________.

그녀의 성적은 오르지 않았어.

6. I am bored.

➔ ______________________________.

나는 심심하지 않아요.

정답과 해설 p.4

7. I am interested in mobile games.

→ ______________________________________________.

나는 모바일 게임에 관심이 없어요.

8. This bench was made of wood.

→ ______________________________________.

이 벤치는 나무로 만들어지지 않았어.

9. I was fired. (*fire: 해고하다)

→ ______________________________________________.

나는 해고되지 않았어.

10. My allowance was spent on buying snacks. (*allowance: 용돈)

→ ______________________________________________.

내 용돈은 군것질거리를 사는 데 쓰이지 않았어.

[11 – 20] 다음 주어진 수동태 문장을 의문문으로 바꿔 써 보세요.

11. Your allowance was raised.

→ Was your allowance raised?

너의 용돈은 올랐니?

12. He is disappointed.

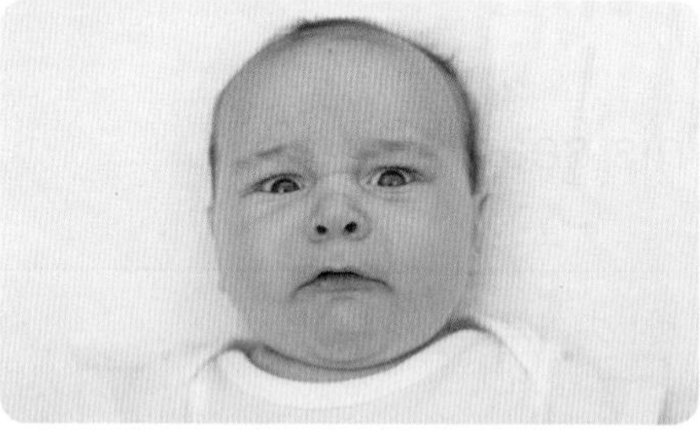

→ ______________________________________?

그는 실망했니? (*disappoint: 실망시키다)

13. We are sent to the haunted house. (*haunted: 유령이 나오는)

→ ______________________________________?

우리는 유령의 집으로 보내지니?



정답과 해설 p.4

14. Your smart phone was stolen.

➔ ____________________________________________?

너의 스마트폰은 도난당했니?

15. This soup was cooked by mom.

➔ ____________________

____________________?

이 스프는 엄마가 요리하셨니?

16. This party was planned by Jane.

➔ ____________________

____________________?

이 파티는 Jane에 의해 계획되었니?

17. Spanish is spoken in many countries.

➔ ____________________________________?

스페인어는 많은 나라에서 말해지니(쓰이니)?

18. The ship was made in Greece.

➔ ____________________________________?

그 배는 그리스에서 만들어졌니?

19. This seat is taken.

➔ ____________________________________________?

이 자리는 주인이 있니?

20. She was born in Korea.

➔ ____________________________________________?

그녀는 한국에서 태어났니?

정답과 해설 p.4

# Let's Practice More!

SET 01

학습목표 1 | 수동태의 부정문을 연습해 보아요.　　공부한 날 :　　맞은 개수 :　　/12개

다음 (　) 안에서 알맞은 것을 고르세요.

01. The letter was ( not written / written not ) by David.
그 편지는 David에 의해서 쓰여지지 않았어.

02. I ( not am / am not ) worried about her.
나는 그녀가 걱정되지 않아.

03. That seat was ( not taken / taken not ).
저 자리는 주인이 없었어.

04. The music is ( not played / played not ) by Jackson.
그 음악은 Jackson에 의해서 연주되는 게 아니야.

05. His name ( not was / was not ) called by the teacher.
그의 이름은 선생님에 의해서 불리지 않았어.

06. My name ( not is / is not ) written on the paper.
내 이름이 종이에 적혀있지 않아.

07. Hayul was ( not invited / invited not ) by Yura.
하율이는 유라에게 초대받지 않았어.

08. We ( not were / were not ) pleased by the news.
우리는 그 소식에 기쁘지 않았어.

09. Dinner was ( not prepared / prepared not ) by Dad.
저녁은 아빠에 의해서 준비되지 않았어.

10. The bag ( not was / was not ) made by Dana.
그 가방은 다나에 의해서 만들어지지 않았어.

11. My file was ( not saved / saved not )!
내 파일이 저장되지 않았어!

12. They ( were not / not were ) lost in the forest.
그들은 숲에서 길을 잃어버리지 않았어.



정답과 해설 p.4

# Let's Practice More!

SET 02



학습목표 1 | 수동태의 부정문을 연습해 보아요. 　공부한 날 : 　맞은 개수 : /14개

다음 수동태 문장을 부정문으로 고쳐 보세요.

01. It was delayed.
➔ It was not[wasn't] delayed. 그건 미뤄지지 않았어.

02. I was bitten by a dog.
➔ ______________________. 나는 개에게 물리지 않았어.

03. The dress was designed by a young designer.
➔ ______________________.
그 드레스는 젊은 디자이너에 의해서 디자인되지 않았어.

04. The piano is played by my father.
➔ ______________________. 그 피아노는 나의 아버지에 의해서 연주되지 않아.

05. The airplane was invented by him.
➔ ______________________. 그 비행기는 그에 의해 발명되지 않았어.

06. The park is cleaned by us.
➔ ______________________. 그 공원은 우리에 의해 청소되지 않아.

07. The museum is visited by many people.
➔ ______________________. 그 박물관은 많은 사람들에 의해서 방문되지 않아.

08. I am grounded.
➔ ______________________. 나는 외출금지 된 게 아니야.

09. His room was cleaned!
➔ ______________________! 그의 방이 청소되지 않았어!

10. They are loved by many fans.
➔ ______________________. 그들은 많은 팬들로부터 사랑받지 않아.

11. It is fixed.
➔ ______________________. 그건 고쳐지지 않았어.

12. The school picnic was cancelled.
➔ ______________________. 학교 소풍은 취소되지 않았어.

13. These cookies were baked yesterday.
➔ ______________________. 이 쿠키들은 어제 구워지지 않았어.

14. This building was built in 1989.
➔ ______________________. 이 건물은 1989년에 지어지지 않았어.

정답과 해설 p.4

# Let's Practice More!

SET 03

**학습목표 2 | 수동태의 의문문을 연습해 보아요.** 공부한 날 : 맞은 개수 : /14개

**다음 수동태 문장을 의문문으로 고쳐 보세요.**

01. The dishes were washed by Dad.
➜ Were the dishes washed by Dad ?
그릇들은 아빠에 의해서 씻어졌니?(아빠가 설거지를 하셨니?)

02. The soccer game was cancelled because of heavy rain.
➜ ______________________________ ?
축구 경기가 폭우 때문에 취소됐어?

03. It was delayed.
➜ ______________________________ ? 그건 미뤄졌어?

04. Your leg is broken.
➜ ______________________________ ? 너의 다리가 부러진 거니?

05. You were attacked by Mina's dog.
➜ ______________________________ ? 너는 미나의 개에 의해서 공격당했니?

06. This seat is taken.
➜ ______________________________ ? 이 자리는 주인이 있니?

07. Those books were borrowed by Jane.
➜ ______________________________ ? 저 책들은 Jane에 의해 빌려졌니?

08. This bread was baked by Paul.
➜ ______________________________ ? 이 빵은 Paul에 의해서 구워졌니?

09. It is filled with butter cream.
➜ ______________________________ ? 그것은 버터크림으로 채워져 있니?

10. This picture was painted by him.
➜ ______________________________ ? 이 그림은 그에 의해서 그려졌니?

11. The meeting was cancelled by her.
➜ ______________________________ ? 그 회의는 그녀에 의해서 취소되었니?

12. The building was built by them.
➜ ______________________________ ? 그 건물은 그들에 의해서 지어졌니?

13. The memo was written by Dana.
➜ ______________________________ ? 그 메모는 다나에 의해서 쓰여졌니?

14. You are excited.
➜ ______________________________ ? 너 신나니?



정답과 해설 p.4

# Let's Practice More!

SET 04



**학습목표 2 | 수동태의 의문문을 연습해 보아요.** 공부한 날 : 맞은 개수 : /12개

**다음 ( ) 안에서 적절한 것을 고르세요.**

01. ( Was / Were ) your allowance raised? 너의 용돈은 올랐니?

02. ( Are / Is ) he disappointed? 그는 실망했니?

03. Are we ( sent / send ) to the haunted house?
우리는 유령의 집으로 보내지니?

04. ( Was / Were ) your smart phone stolen? 너의 스마트폰은 도난당했니?

05. Was this cake ( make / made ) by you?
이 케이크는 너에 의해 만들어졌니?

06. Was this party ( plan / planned ) by Jane? 이 파티는 Jane에 의해 계획되었니?

07. Is Spanish ( speak / spoken ) in many countries? 스페인어는 많은 나라에서 말해지니(쓰이니)?

08. ( Was / Were ) the ship made in Greece? 그 배는 그리스에서 만들어졌니?

09. ( Are / Is ) this seat taken? 이 자리는 주인이 있니?

10. ( Was / Were ) she born in Korea? 그녀는 한국에서 태어났니?

11. Was the bathroom ( clean / cleaned ) by Hayul?
화장실은 하율이에 의해서 청소되었니?

12. ( Are / Is ) you grounded? 너 외출금지 된 거야?

정답과 해설 p.5

# Let's Practice More!

SET 05

학습목표 3 | 다양한 수동태 문제를 풀어 보아요.  공부한 날 :  맞은 개수 : /14개

다음 밑줄 친 부분을 축약형으로 알맞게 써 보세요.

01. My cell phone was not lost. → wasn't
나의 핸드폰은 분실되지 않았어.

02. This seat is not taken. → ______
이 자리는 주인이 없어.

03. Her grades were not raised. → ______
그녀의 성적은 오르지 않았어.

04. They are not lost in the forest. → ______
그들은 숲에서 길을 잃어버리지 않았어.

05. I was not worried about her. → ______
나는 그녀가 걱정되지 않았어.

06. That seat was not taken. → ______
저 자리는 주인이 없었어.

07. The music is not played by Jackson. → ______
그 음악은 Jackson에 의해서 연주되는 게 아니야.

08. His name was not called by the teacher. → ______
그의 이름은 선생님에 의해서 불리지 않았어.

09. My name is not written on the paper. → ______
내 이름이 종이에 적혀있지 않아.

10. I was not bored. → ______
나는 심심하지 않았어.

11. We are not interested in mobile games. → ______
우리는 모바일 게임에 관심이 없어.

12. This bench was not made of wood. → ______
이 벤치는 나무로 만들어지지 않았어.

13. They were not fired. → ______
그들은 해고되지 않았어.

14. My allowance was not spent on buying snacks. → ______
내 용돈은 군것질거리를 사는 데 쓰이지 않았어.



정답과 해설 p.5

# Let's Practice More!

SET 06



학습목표 3 | **다양한 수동태 문제를 풀어 보아요.**  공부한 날 :  맞은 개수 : /14개

다음 밑줄 친 부분이 옳으면 ○, 틀리면 고쳐 써 보세요.

01. Hayul was not invited by Yura. → ○
하율이는 유라에게 초대받지 않았어.

02. Is this seat take? → ______
이 자리는 주인이 있니?

03. Were those books borrowed by Jane? → ______
그 책들은 Jane에 의해 빌려졌니?

04. Was this bread baked by Paul? → ______
이 빵은 Paul에 의해서 구워졌니?

05. My file was not saving! → ______
내 파일이 저장되지 않았어!

06. The letter was write by David. → ______
그 편지는 David에 의해서 쓰여졌어.

07. Was the soccer game cancelled? → ______
축구 경기가 취소됐어?

08. It was delayed. → ______
그건 미뤄졌어.

09. Is it filling with butter cream? → ______
그것은 버터크림으로 채워져 있니?

10. The piano is play by my father. → ______
그 피아노는 나의 아버지에 의해서 연주돼.

11. The airplane was invent by the Wright brothers. → ______
비행기는 라이트형제에 의해서 발명되었어.

12. We were not pleased by the news. → ______
우리는 그 소식에 기쁘지 않았어.

13. Dinner was not preparing by Dad. → ______
저녁은 아빠에 의해서 준비되지 않았어.

14. The bag was not made by Dana. → ______
그 가방은 Dana에 의해서 만들어지지 않았어.

정답과 해설 p.5

# Let's Practice More!

SET 07

**학습목표 3 | 다양한 수동태 문제를 풀어 보아요.** 공부한 날 : 맞은 개수 : /20개

주어진 우리말 뜻을 보고 밑줄 친 부분이 옳으면 ○, 틀리면 고쳐 써 보세요.

01.

Was this picture painted by him?
이 그림은 그에 의해서 그려졌니?
➔ ○

02.
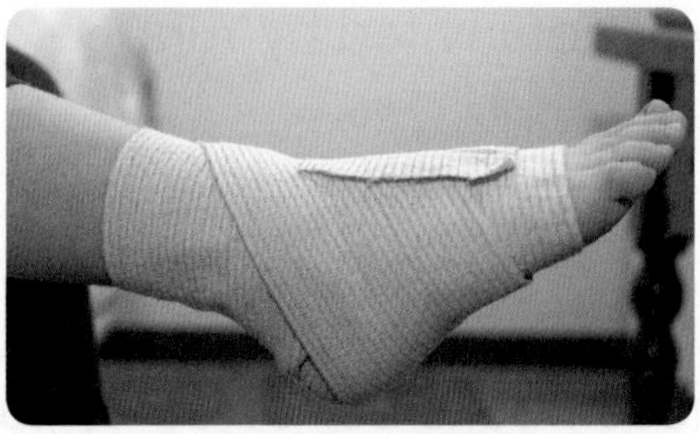

Are your leg broken?
너의 다리가 부러진 거니?
➔ ______

03. I was bitten by a dog. ➔ ______
나는 개에게 물렸어.

04. Were you attacked by Mina's dog? ➔ ______
너는 미나의 개에 의해서 공격당했니?

05. The dress was design by a young designer. ➔ ______
그 드레스는 젊은 디자이너에 의해서 디자인되었어.

06. Was the meeting cancelled by her? ➔ ______
그 회의는 그녀에 의해서 취소되었니?

07. The park is cleaned by us. ➔ ______
그 공원은 우리에 의해 청소된다.

08. Are you excited? ➔ ______
너 신나니?

09. I am not ground. ➔ ______
나는 외출금지 된 게 아니야.

10. His room was cleaned! ➔ ______
그의 방이 청소되었어!



정답과 해설 p.5

11. 

The museum is visit by many people.

그 박물관은 많은 사람들에 의해서 방문된다.

➜ ____________

12. 

Was the building built by them?

그 건물은 그들에 의해서 지어졌니?

➜ ____________

13. It is not fixed yet. ➜ ____________

그건 아직 고쳐지지 않았어.

14. The school picnic were not cancelled. ➜ ____________

학교 소풍은 취소되지 않았어.

15. They are loving by many fans. ➜ ____________

그들은 많은 팬들로부터 사랑받아.

16. Were the computer fixed by him? ➜ ____________

컴퓨터가 그에 의해서 고쳐졌나요?

17. Was the memo writing by Dana? ➜ ____________

그 메모는 다나에 의해서 쓰여졌니?

18. Were the dishes wash by dad? ➜ ____________

그릇들은 아빠에 의해서 씻어졌니? (아빠는 설거지를 하셨니?)

19. Was the bathroom cleaned by Hayul? ➜ ____________

화장실은 하율이에 의해서 청소되었니?

20. Was the ship make in Greece? ➜ ____________

그 배는 그리스에서 만들어졌니?

정답과 해설 p.5

# Let's Practice More!

SET 08

학습목표 3 | 다양한 수동태 문제를 풀어 보아요. 공부한 날 : 맞은 개수 : /20개

주어진 우리말 뜻을 보고 밑줄 친 부분을 어법에 맞게 고쳐 써 보세요.

01.

Are you grounding?

너 외출금지 된 거야?

→ grounded

02.

Was this party planning by Jane?

이 파티는 Jane에 의해 계획되었니?

→ ____________

03. This building was not build in 1989. → ____________

이 건물은 1989년에 지어지지 않았어.

04. Was your allowance raising? → ____________

너의 용돈은 올랐니?

05. Is he disappoint? → ____________

그는 실망했니?

06. My cell phone was not lose. → ____________

나의 핸드폰은 분실되지 않았어.

07. Are we sending to the haunted house? → ____________

우리는 유령의 집으로 보내지니?

08. This seat is not take. → ____________

이 자리는 주인이 없어.

09. Was your smart phone steal? → ____________

너의 스마트폰은 도난당했니?



정답과 해설 p.5

10. I am not boring. ➔ ____________
나는 지루해 하지 않아.

11. 

Her grades were not raise.
그녀의 성적은 오르지 않았어.

➔ ____________

12. 

Was this soup cook by Mom?
이 스프는 엄마가 요리하셨니?

➔ ____________

13. These cookies were not bake yesterday. ➔ ____________
이 쿠키들은 어제 구워지지 않았어.

14. Is this seat taking? ➔ ____________
이 자리는 주인이 있니?

15. I am not interesting in mobile games. ➔ ____________
나는 모바일 게임에 관심이 없어.

16. This chair was not make of wood. ➔ ____________
이 의자는 나무로 만들어지지 않았어.

17. Was she bear in Korea? ➔ ____________
그녀는 한국에서 태어났니?

18. I was not firing. ➔ ____________
나는 해고되지 않았어.

19. My allowance was not spend on buying snacks. ➔ ____________
내 용돈은 군것질거리를 사는 데 쓰이지 않았어.

20. Was the computer fixing by him? ➔ ____________
컴퓨터가 그에 의해서 고쳐졌니?

정답과 해설 p.5

# 실전테스트

CHAPTER 01

공부한 날 :

복습한 날 :

부모님 확인 :

CHAPTER 01 수동태

● 정답과 해설은 별책 5쪽에서 확인하세요!!

## 01

다음 [보기]의 단어를 과거분사로 바르게 고쳐 쓴 것을 고르세요.

[보기] eat

① eaten ② ate
③ eated ④ eating

## 02

다음 표의 빈칸에 [보기]의 단어를 알맞게 분류해서 쓰세요.

[보기] breaking, broken, running, run, closed

| 현재분사 | 과거분사 |
|---|---|
| | |

## 03

다음 문장을 수동태로 고쳐 쓰세요.

He stole my purse.

⇨ ______________________________

## 04

다음 중 과거분사와 현재분사가 바르게 짝지어지지 않은 것을 고르세요.

| | 과거분사 | 현재분사 |
|---|---|---|
| ① | gone | going |
| ② | opened | opening |
| ③ | run | running |
| ④ | walk | walking |

[05~06] 다음 중 동사원형과 과거분사의 형태가 올바르게 짝지어진 것을 고르세요.

## 05

① fall – fell ② ride – riden
③ ring – rung ④ work – worken

## 06

① become – become
② make – make
③ eat – aten
④ see – sawn

## 07

다음 문장의 밑줄 친 부분을 바르게 고친 것을 고르세요.

A lot of homework was giving by her.

① gave ② given
③ gives ④ give

## 08

다음 중 현재분사와 과거분사가 알맞게 짝지어진 것을 고르세요.

① eating – ate ② closing – closed
③ stealing – stole ④ running – ran

## 09

다음 중 문장의 형태가 나머지와 다른 것을 고르세요.

① The door is closed.
② The ball was hit.
③ I am kicking the ball.
④ My pen was lost.

## 10

다음 문장이 수동태인지 능동태인지 구분하여 쓰세요.

(1) He is running. ________
(2) The window is broken. ________
(3) I saw that movie. ________
(4) The cookie was made by her. ________

## 11

다음 밑줄 친 부분의 쓰임이 어색한 것을 고르세요.

① The book is written by her.
② Was this car bought by him?
③ The glass is broken not by him.
④ Are the dogs fed by him?

## 12

다음 글자들을 배열하여 분사를 만들고 그 뜻과 분사의 종류를 쓰세요.

s o e
l t n

단어:
뜻:
분사의 종류:

[13~17] 다음 문장이 수동태이면 '수'에, 능동태이면 '능'에 ○표 하세요.

13
The movie was directed by me. ( 수 / 능 )

14
He put on his rainboots. ( 수 / 능 )

15
My room was cleaned by me. ( 수 / 능 )

16
She cleaned my room. ( 수 / 능 )

17
I walked to the park. ( 수 / 능 )

[18~22] 다음 문장을 [보기]와 같이 바꿔 쓰세요.

[보기] She kicked the tree.
→ The tree was kicked by her.

18
We made a plan.
⇨ ______________________

19
They filled the bottle.
⇨ ______________________

20
Susan found the notebooks.
⇨ ______________________

21
He changes the light bulb.
⇨ ______________________

22
We locked the door.
⇨ ______________________

[23~24] 다음 문장에서 틀린 부분을 찾아 바르게 고쳐 문장을 다시 쓰세요.(단, 주어는 바꾸지 마세요.)

23

My glasses were breaking by him.

24

Read the book if you're interesting.

[25~26] 다음 단어들을 순서에 맞게 배열하여 문장을 완성하세요.

25

( playing / He / tennis now / is ).

⇨ ______________________

26

( is / eaten / Japan / in / Sushi ).

⇨ ______________________

[27~30] 다음 문장을 의문문으로 바꾸세요.

27

It was made by the carpenters.

⇨ ______________________

28

This table is moved by my classmates.

⇨ ______________________

29

The chairs were fixed by him.

⇨ ______________________

30

Chopsticks are used by many Asians.

⇨ ______________________

# Chapter 02 관계대명사

이 챕터에서는 공통된 단어를 가진 두 문장을 한 문장으로 만드는 '관계대명사'에 대해 배워 보아요.

☆ 학습 방향 및 배울 내용 미리보기 ☆

- [ ] **Unit 01 :** I know the girl **who** won the race.
**관계대명사**
선행사와 관계대명사에 대해 알아보아요.

▼

- [ ] **Unit 02 :** I have a Nintendo **which** has many games.
**관계대명사의 종류**
선행사로 사람을 나타내는 단어가 오는지, 사물(동물)을 나타내는 단어가 오는지에 따라 쓸 수 있는 관계대명사가 달라요.

## 단어 미리보기

이 챕터에 나올 단어들 중 이미 알고 있는 단어가 있나요?
맞는 뜻을 골라 체크해 봐요.

날짜 : 이름 : 알고 있는 단어의 수 : /24개

| No. | 아는 단어 | 단어 | 품사 | 알맞은 뜻에 체크 표시해 봐요. | | | |
|---|---|---|---|---|---|---|---|
| 1 | ☑ | brightly | 부사 | 밝게 | ☑ | 어둡게 | ☐ |
| 2 | ☐ | lose | 동사 | 잊다 | ☐ | 잃어버리다 | ☐ |
| 3 | ☐ | bark | 동사 | 타다 | ☐ | 짖다 | ☐ |
| 4 | ☐ | borrow | 동사 | 빌리다 | ☐ | 빌려주다 | ☐ |
| 5 | ☐ | next door | 부사 | 옆집에 | ☐ | 다음에 | ☐ |
| 6 | ☐ | police | 명사 | 소방관 | ☐ | 경찰 | ☐ |
| 7 | ☐ | thief | 명사 | 경찰 | ☐ | 도둑 | ☐ |
| 8 | ☐ | someday | 부사 | 언젠가 | ☐ | 어딘가 | ☐ |
| 9 | ☐ | skirt | 명사 | 바지 | ☐ | 치마 | ☐ |
| 10 | ☐ | marry | 동사 | 이혼하다 | ☐ | 결혼하다 | ☐ |
| 11 | ☐ | ending | 명사 | 시작 | ☐ | 결말 | ☐ |
| 12 | ☐ | rabbit | 명사 | 토끼 | ☐ | 거북이 | ☐ |
| 13 | ☐ | carrot | 명사 | 양파 | ☐ | 당근 | ☐ |
| 14 | ☐ | mind | 명사 | 마음 | ☐ | 몸 | ☐ |
| 15 | ☐ | raise | 동사 | 기르다 | ☐ | 떠오르다 | ☐ |
| 16 | ☐ | bake | 동사 | 굽다 | ☐ | 찌다 | ☐ |
| 17 | ☐ | hair | 명사 | 뇌 | ☐ | 머리카락 | ☐ |
| 18 | ☐ | once | 부사 | 자주 | ☐ | 한때 | ☐ |
| 19 | ☐ | race | 명사 | 경주 | ☐ | 쌀 | ☐ |
| 20 | ☐ | brave | 형용사 | 겁 많은 | ☐ | 용감한 | ☐ |
| 21 | ☐ | kind | 형용사 | 친절한 | ☐ | 못된 | ☐ |
| 22 | ☐ | watch | 명사 | 벽 | ☐ | 시계 | ☐ |
| 23 | ☐ | finger | 명사 | 손가락 | ☐ | 반지 | ☐ |
| 24 | ☐ | healthy | 형용사 | 아픈 | ☐ | 건강한 | ☐ |

관계대명사

# UNIT 01 I know the girl who won the race.

❖ POiNT ❖

관계대명사는 공통된 단어를 가지고 있는 두 문장을 하나로 연결해주는 역할을 해요.

- I know the girl.
  나는 그 소녀를 알아.
- The girl won the race.
  그 소녀는 경주에서 우승했어.

첫 번째 문장의 the girl과 두 번째 문장의 The girl은 같은 사람이에요.
이 두 문장을 하나로 만들고 싶다면 어떻게 해야 할까요?

선행사 ← → 관계대명사

I know / the girl / who won the race.
나는 알아 / 그 소녀를 / 경주에서 우승한

두 번째 문장의 The girl을 빼고 그 자리에 두 문장을 하나로 연결시켜주는 관계대명사 who를 넣어줬어요!
위 문장의 the girl처럼, 관계대명사의 앞에 위치하는 명사를 선행사라고 한답니다.
연결된 문장은 뒤의 문장(who won the race)이 선행사(the girl)를 꾸며주는 것처럼 해석하면 돼요.

## Check and Write

**다음 문장에서 관계대명사를 찾아 빈칸에 쓰세요.**

1. I have a brother who is two years old.
   나는 (나이가) 두 살인 남동생이 있다.
   who

2. She has a dog which is very loyal.
   그녀는 아주 충성스러운 강아지 한 마리를 가지고 있다.

3. I know Sihu who has many friends.
   나는 많은 친구들을 가지고 있는 시후를 안다.

4. I know the girl who smiles brightly.
   나는 밝게 웃는 그 여자아이를 안다.

5. She found the cat which was lost.
   그녀는 길을 잃은 고양이를 발견했다.

정답과 해설 p.6

# UNIT 02 I have a Nintendo which has many games.

관계대명사의 종류

**대표적인 관계대명사인 who, which, that에 대해 공부해 보아요.**
**선행사가 사람이냐 사물이냐에 따라 쓸 수 있는 관계대명사가 달라지는데, that은 사람, 동물, 사물에 상관없이 쓸 수 있어요.**

## ❖ POiNT 1 ❖

### 선행사가 사람일 때

I know the girl who[that] won the race.
(the girl: 사람 선행사 / who[that]: 관계대명사)

나는 경주에서 우승한 그 소녀를 알아.

위의 문장의 선행사는 사람이기 때문에 관계대명사 who를 써 줬어요.

## ❖ POiNT 2 ❖

### 선행사가 사물일 때

I have a Nintendo which[that] has many games.
(Nintendo: 사물 선행사 / which[that]: 관계대명사)

나는 많은 게임이 있는 닌텐도를 가지고 있어.

닌텐도는 사물이기 때문에 관계대명사 which를 썼어요.
선행사가 동물일 때도 관계대명사 which를 쓴답니다.

## ❖ POiNT 3 ❖

### 관계대명사 that

I saw Mina and her dog that were playing together.
(Mina and her dog: 사람 + 동물(사물) 선행사 / that: 관계대명사)

나는 함께 놀고 있었던 미나와 그녀의 개를 봤어.

사람과 동물(사물)이 함께 선행사로 쓰일 때는 관계대명사 that을 써요.

# Check and Write



**다음 (   ) 안에서 알맞은 단어를 골라 동그라미 하세요.**

1. There is a dog ( who / which ) is barking.
   짖고 있는 개 한 마리가 있어.

2. I love my friends ( who / which ) are over there.
   나는 저기에 있는 내 친구들을 사랑해.

3. I like the cookies ( who / that ) she made.
   나는 그녀가 만든 쿠키를 좋아해.

4. Do you know the girl ( who / which ) is taking pictures?
   너는 사진을 찍고 있는 그 소녀를 아니?

5. I read the book ( who / which ) you borrowed.
   나는 네가 빌렸던 책을 읽었어.

6. I saw a girl and a dog ( who / that ) were playing together.
   나는 함께 놀고 있었던 한 소녀와 개 한 마리를 봤어.

정답과 해설 p.6

## Practice 1 관계대명사의 알맞은 쓰임을 익혀 보아요.

다음 문장의 선행사에 주의하여 who와 which 중 알맞은 관계대명사를 빈칸에 써 보세요.

### A Peaceful Sunday morning

1. Mom was watching a movie __which__ I like.
   엄마는 내가 좋아하는 영화를 보고 계셨어.

2. Dad was using the razor ______________ mom gave him. (*razor: 면도기)
   아빠는 엄마가 그에게 주신 면도기를 사용하고 계셨어.

3. I was watching dad __________ was shaving. (*shave: 면도하다)
   나는 면도를 하고 계시는 아빠를 보고 있었어.

4. My older brother was reading a book ______________ dad gave to him. 나의 형은 아빠가 그에게 주신 책을 읽고 있었어.

5. My little sister was playing with her friend __________ lives next door. 내 여동생은 옆집에 사는 그녀의 친구와 놀고 있었어.

### B A brave dog

1. I saw Mina __________ was playing with her dog in the yard.
   나는 마당에서 그녀의 개와 놀고 있는 미나를 봤어.

2. Mina has a dog ______________ is brave. (*brave: 용감한)
   미나는 용감한 개 한 마리를 가지고 있어.

3. The thief __________ broke into Mina's house was caught by the police. (*break into: ~에 침입하다)
   미나의 집에 침입했던 도둑은 경찰에 의해서 잡혔어.

4. It was all thanks to the dog __________ Mina raises.
   그것은 모두 미나가 기르는 개 덕분이었어. (*thanks to: ~ 덕분에, raise: 기르다, 키우다)

5. This is the dog __________ helped the police catch the thief!
   이것은 경찰이 도둑을 잡는 것을 도운 개야!



정답과 해설 p.6

## C An old tree

1. I am a tree __________ has lived here for 50 years.
   나는 이곳에 50년 동안 살았던 나무야.

2. I remember everyone __________ was around me.
   나는 내 주변에 있었던 모든 사람들을 기억해.

3. I saw the old man __________ was a boy once. (*once: 한때)
   나는 한때 소년이었던 노인을 봤어.

4. The old man __________ moved to another city returned here. (*return: 돌아오다)
   다른 도시로 이사를 갔던 그 노인은 여기로 돌아왔어.

5. Someday, someone __________ remembers me will visit here again.
   언젠가, 나를 기억하는 누군가가 또 이곳에 방문할 거야.

## D Happy Melissa!

1. There is a girl __________ has long hair.
   긴 머리를 가진 여자아이가 한 명 있어.

2. Melissa is a girl __________ came from Australia. (*Australia: 호주)
   Melissa는 호주에서 온 소녀야.

3. Australia is the only country __________ is also a continent. (*continent: 대륙)
   호주는 하나의 대륙이기도 한 유일한 나라야.

4. Melissa has a dog __________ is cute.
   Melissa에게는 귀여운 개 한 마리가 있어.

5. Melissa likes her dog __________ came from France.
   Melissa는 프랑스에서 온 그녀의 개를 좋아해.

정답과 해설 p.6

## Practice 2 선행사에 따른 관계대명사의 알맞은 쓰임을 익혀 보아요.

[1 – 10] 다음 문장을 읽고 선행사에 동그라미 하세요.

1.

I am eating the cookies that my mom baked.

나는 엄마가 구우신 쿠키를 먹고 있어.

2.

The girl who is writing a letter is Jane.

편지를 쓰고 있는 그 소녀는 Jane이야.

3. I don't like movies that have sad endings.

나는 슬픈 결말을 가진 영화들을 좋아하지 않아.

4. He is the friend that makes me happy.

그는 나를 행복하게 만들어주는 친구야.

5. She likes dogs which are friendly with people.

그녀는 사람들과 친하게 지내는 개들을 좋아해.

6.

I like the skirt which Jessica is wearing.

나는 Jessica가 입고 있는 그 치마가 맘에 들어.

7.

I know a doctor who can help you.

나는 당신을 도와줄 수 있는 의사 한 명을 알아요.



정답과 해설 p.6

8. He is the student who is loved by all his teachers.
그는 그의 모든 선생님들께 사랑받는 학생이야.

9. You can't marry a man that you just met!
너는 방금 만난 남자와 결혼할 수 없어!

10. Kelly had lunch with a man who is humorous.
Kelly는 유머감각이 풍부한 한 남자와 점심을 먹었어.

**[11 – 20] 다음 문장을 읽고, ( ) 안에서 알맞은 관계대명사에 동그라미 하세요.**

11.

I bought the candy
( who / that ) I like.
나는 내가 좋아하는 사탕을 샀어.

12.

Dad gave mom the flowers
( who / that ) she likes.
아빠는 엄마에게 그녀가 좋아하는 꽃을 주셨어.

13. That girl ( who / which ) is on the playground is Mina.
운동장에 있는 저 소녀는 미나야.

14. Minwoo found the watch ( who / which ) I lost yesterday.
민우는 내가 어제 잃어버린 시계를 찾았어.

15. Mom is pleased with the present ( who / which ) dad gave to her.
엄마는 아빠가 그녀에게 주신 선물에 기뻐하셔.

정답과 해설 p.6

16. 

Those are my grandparents ( who / which ) are sitting on the bench.

벤치에 앉아 있는 저 분들은 나의 조부모님이셔.

17. 

I gave my mom a carnation ( who / which ) I made.

나는 엄마께 내가 만든 카네이션을 드렸어.

18. The boy ( who / which ) often teases Mina is Junwoo. (*tease: 놀리다)

미나를 자주 놀리는 그 남자아이는 준우야.

19. My father is an American ( who / which ) comes from Chicago.

나의 아버지는 시카고에서 오신 미국인이셔.

20. Dad fell in love with mom ( who / which ) was kind to him.

아빠는 그에게 친절했던 엄마에게 반하셨어. (*fall in love with: ~에게 반하다, ~와 사랑에 빠지다)

Cultural Tips

재미로 익히는 문화상식

## 대부분의 나라는 표준시가 달라요!

Mina in Korea

Alex in America

대부분의 나라가 그 나라 고유의 표준시를 정해서 사용하고 있기 때문에 나라마다 시간이 달라요. 그렇게 나타나는 시간의 차이를 "시차"라고 한답니다. 그렇다면, 한국과의 시차가 없는 나라는 어느 나라인지 아나요? 바로 일본이에요. 한국과 일본은 표준시의 기준이 되는 선이 동경 135°선으로 일치하기 때문에 한국과 일본은 시차가 없답니다. 기억해두면 좋겠죠?



정답과 해설 p.6

## Practice 3 관계대명사가 쓰인 문장을 완성해 보아요.

[1－10] 관계대명사 who, which, that을 이용하여 두 문장을 한 문장으로 연결하세요.

1. All his friends like Minwoo.
+ Minwoo is always smiling.

➔ All his friends like Minwoo who[that] is always smiling.

그의 모든 친구들은 항상 웃고 있는 민우를 좋아해.

2. Look at the dog.
+ The dog is biting his finger.

➔ ______________________________.

그의 손가락을 물고 있는 그 개를 봐.

3. The teacher praised the boy. + The boy helped the poor. (*praise: 칭찬하다)

➔ ______________________________.

선생님은 가난한 사람들을 도와준 그 소년을 칭찬하셨어.

4. He likes the girl. + The girl has curly hair. (*curly: 곱슬곱슬한)

➔ ______________________________.

그는 곱슬머리를 가진 그 여자아이를 좋아해.

5. It was Minwoo. + Minwoo won first place. (*win first place: 우승하다)

➔ ______________________________.

우승한 건 민우였어.

6. I found the candies. + The candies were on the table.

➔ ______________________________.

나는 테이블에 있던 사탕을 찾았어.

정답과 해설 p.6

7. I saw the man. + The man was helping an old man.

→ ______________________________
______________________________.
나는 한 노인을 도와드리고 있는 그 남자를 봤어.

8. She is the teacher. + The teacher teaches us English.

→ ______________________________
______________________________.
그녀는 우리에게 영어를 가르쳐주시는 선생님이셔.

9. She has a son. + Her son raised a turtle.

→ ____________________________________________________________.
그녀에게는 거북이를 길렀던 아들이 한 명 있어.

10. This is the book. + The book is about World War II.

→ ____________________________________________________________.
이건 2차 세계 대전에 대한 책이야.

**[11 – 20] 다음 우리말 뜻과 같도록 주어진 표현을 순서에 맞게 배열하여 문장을 완성하세요.**

11. ( a machine, This is, which ) can read people's minds.
이것은 사람들의 마음을 읽을 수 있는 기계야.
→ This is a machine which can read people's minds.

12. This is the lip balm ( she gave, to me, which ).
이것은 그녀가 나에게 준 립밤이야.
→ This is the lip balm ______________________________.


정답과 해설 p.6

13. ( who, That is, my younger brother ) is painting the wall.
벽에 페인트를 칠하고 있는 저 사람은 나의 남동생이야.

➔ ______________________________ is painting the wall.

14. I respect ( help others, who, people ).
나는 다른 사람들을 도와주는 사람들을 존경해.

➔ I respect ______________________________.

15. They saw a rabbit ( carrots, which, was eating ).
그들은 당근을 먹고 있는 토끼 한 마리를 보았어.

➔ They saw a rabbit ______________________.

16. Jade is ( enjoys playing football, who, a healthy boy ).
Jade는 축구하는 것을 즐기는 건강한 소년이야.

➔ Jade is ______________________________.

17. ( who, The kid, is over there ) is my friend. 저기에 있는 아이는 나의 친구야.

➔ ______________________________ is my friend.

18. She is ( the girl, likes David, who ). 그녀가 David를 좋아하는 소녀야.

➔ She is ______________________________.

19. ( that, This is, the puppy ) my dad bought for me.
이것은 아빠가 나에게 사주신 강아지야.

➔ ______________________________
my dad bought for me.

20. ( some photos, that, Dana has ) I took. 다나는 내가 찍은 사진 몇 장을 갖고 있어.

➔ ______________________________ I took.

정답과 해설 p.6

# Let's Practice More!

SET 01

학습목표 1 | 문장에서 관계대명사와 선행사를 찾아보아요.   공부한 날 :   맞은 개수 :   /12개

다음 문장을 읽고 관계대명사에 동그라미 하세요.

01. I know the girl who dances very well.
나는 춤을 아주 잘 추는 그 소녀를 알아.

02. Mina has a dog which is brave.
미나는 용감한 개 한 마리를 가지고 있어.

03. There is a girl who has long hair.
긴 머리를 가진 여자아이가 한 명 있어.

04. I don't like movies that have sad endings.
나는 슬픈 결말을 가진 영화들을 좋아하지 않아.

05. He is the student who is loved by all his teachers.
그는 그의 모든 선생님들께 사랑받는 학생이야.

06. You can't marry a man that you just met!
너는 방금 만난 남자와 결혼할 수 없어!

07. I bought the candies that I like.
나는 내가 좋아하는 사탕을 샀어.

08. Minwoo found the watch which I lost yesterday.
민우는 내가 어제 잃어버린 시계를 찾았어.

09. I gave my mom a carnation which I made.
나는 엄마께 내가 만든 카네이션을 드렸어.

10. All his friends like Minwoo who is always smiling.
그의 모든 친구들은 항상 웃고 있는 민우를 좋아해.

11. He likes the girl who has curly hair.
그는 곱슬머리를 가진 그 여자아이를 좋아해.

12. I found the candies which were on the table.
나는 탁자 위에 있던 사탕을 찾았어.



정답과 해설 p.6

# Let's Practice More!

SET 02

학습목표 1 | 문장에서 관계대명사와 선행사를 찾아보아요. 공부한 날 : 맞은 개수 : /14개

다음 문장에서 선행사를 찾아 동그라미 하세요.

01. I read the book which was fun.
나는 재미있던 그 책을 읽었어.

02. Dad was using the razor which mom gave him.
아빠는 엄마가 그에게 주신 면도기를 사용하고 계셨어.

03. This is the dog which helped the police catch the thief!
이것은 경찰이 도둑을 잡는 것을 도운 개야!

04. I am a tree which has lived here for 50 years.
나는 이곳에 50년 동안 살았던 나무야.

05. There is a girl who has long hair.
긴 머리를 가진 여자아이가 한 명 있어.

06. Melissa has a dog which is cute.
Melissa에게는 귀여운 개 한 마리가 있어.

07. I am eating the cookies that my mom baked.
나는 엄마가 구우신 쿠키를 먹고 있어.

08. He is the friend that makes me happy.
그는 나를 행복하게 만들어주는 친구야.

09. I like the skirt which Jessica is wearing.
나는 Jessica가 입고 있는 그 치마가 맘에 들어.

10. You can't marry a man that you just met!
너는 방금 만난 남자와 결혼할 수 없어!

11. Dad gave mom the flowers that she likes.
아빠는 엄마에게 그녀가 좋아하는 꽃을 주셨어.

12. That girl who is on the playground is Mina.
운동장에 있는 저 소녀는 미나야.

13. I gave my mom a carnation which I made.
나는 엄마께 내가 만든 카네이션을 드렸어.

14. My father is an American who comes from Chicago.
나의 아버지는 시카고에서 오신 미국인이셔.

정답과 해설 p.6

# Let's Practice More!

SET 03

**학습목표 2 | 관계대명사의 적절한 쓰임을 연습해 보아요.** 공부한 날 : 맞은 개수 : /14개

**다음 ( ) 안에서 알맞은 것을 고르세요.**

01. There is a dog ( who / which ) is barking.
짖고 있는 개가 있어.

02. Mom was watching a movie ( who / which ) I like.
엄마는 내가 좋아하는 영화를 보고 계셨어.

03. I saw Mina ( who / which ) was playing with her cat in the yard.
나는 마당에서 그녀의 고양이와 놀고 있는 미나를 봤어.

04. I remember everyone ( who / which ) was around me.
나는 내 주변에 있었던 모든 사람들을 기억해.

05. I saw the old man ( who / which ) was a boy once.
나는 한 때 소년이었던 노인을 봤어.

06. It was all thanks to the dog ( who / which ) Mina raises.
그것은 모두 미나가 기르는 개 덕분이었어.

07. The guy ( who / which ) moved to another city returned here.
다른 도시로 이사를 갔던 그 남자는 여기로 돌아왔어.

08. Australia is the only country ( who / that ) is also a continent.
호주는 하나의 대륙이기도 한 유일한 나라야.

09. Melissa likes her dog ( who / which ) came from Germany.
Melissa는 독일에서 온 그녀의 개를 좋아해.

10. The girl ( who / which ) is writing a letter is Jane.
편지를 쓰고 있는 그 소녀는 Jane이야.

11. She likes dogs ( who / which ) are friendly with people.
그녀는 사람들과 친하게 지내는 개들을 좋아해.

12. Kelly had lunch with a man ( who / which ) is humorous.
Kelly는 유머감각이 풍부한 한 남자와 점심을 먹었어.

13. Minwoo found the watch ( who / which ) I lost yesterday.
민우는 내가 어제 잃어버린 시계를 찾았어.

14. Those are my grandparents ( who / which ) are sitting on the bench.
벤치에 앉아 있는 저 분들은 나의 조부모님이셔.



정답과 해설 p.6

# Let's Practice More!

SET 04

**학습목표 2 | 관계대명사의 적절한 쓰임을 연습해 보아요.** 공부한 날 : 맞은 개수 : /12개

**다음 문장을 읽고 밑줄 친 부분이 맞으면 O표, 틀리면 고쳐 써 보세요.**



01. I like the cake <u>who</u> my mom made. → which[that]
나는 우리 엄마가 만드신 그 케이크를 좋아해.

02. I was watching dad <u>who</u> was shaving. → ______
나는 면도를 하고 계시는 아빠를 보고 있었어.

03. Mina has a dog <u>who</u> is brave. → ______
미나는 용감한 개 한 마리를 가지고 있어.

04. My little sister was playing with her friend <u>who</u> lives next door. → ______
내 여동생은 옆집에 사는 그녀의 친구와 놀고 있었어.

05. My older brother was reading a book <u>which</u> dad gave to him. → ______
내 형은 아빠가 그에게 주신 책을 읽고 있었어.

06. Someday, someone <u>that</u> remembers me will visit here again. → ______
언젠가, 나를 기억하는 누군가가 또 이곳에 방문할 거야.

07. There is a boy <u>which</u> has blue hair. → ______
파란색 머리를 가진 남자아이가 한 명 있어.

08. Catherine has a cat <u>who</u> is cute. → ______
Catherine에게는 귀여운 고양이 한 마리가 있어.

09. Marta is a girl <u>which</u> comes from Spain. → ______
Marta는 스페인에서 온 소녀야.

10. I don't like movies <u>that</u> have sad endings. → ______
나는 슬픈 결말을 가진 영화들을 좋아하지 않아.

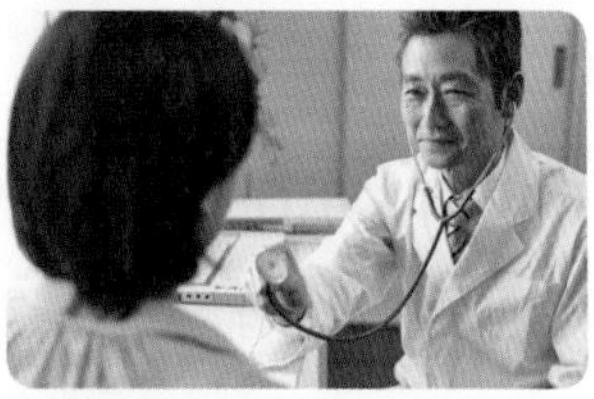

11. I know a doctor <u>which</u> can help you. → ______
나는 당신을 도와줄 수 있는 의사 한 명을 알아요.

12. He is the student <u>which</u> is loved by all his teachers. → ______
그는 그의 모든 선생님들께 사랑받는 학생이야.

정답과 해설 p.6

# Let's Practice More!

SET 05

**학습목표 2 | 관계대명사의 적절한 쓰임을 연습해 보아요.** 공부한 날 : 맞은 개수 : /14개

**다음 ( ) 안에서 알맞은 관계대명사를 모두 고르세요.**

01. I was watching dad ( who / that ) was shaving.
나는 면도를 하고 계시는 아빠를 보고 있었어.

02. I saw the girl and the dog ( who / that ) were playing.
나는 놀고 있는 소녀와 개를 봤어.

03. My little sister was playing with her friend ( who / that ) lives next door.
내 여동생은 옆집에 사는 그녀의 친구와 놀고 있었어.

04. I saw Charlie ( who / which ) was having fun with his turtle in the yard.
나는 마당에서 그의 거북이와 재미있게 놀고 있는 Charlie를 봤어.

05. Mina has the dog ( who / which ) is brave. 미나는 용감한 개 한 마리를 가지고 있어.

06. It was all thanks to the cat ( which / that ) Sunny raises.
그것은 모두 Sunny가 기르는 고양이 덕분이었어.

07. There are boys and girls ( who / that ) have long hair.
긴 머리를 가진 소년들과 소녀들이 있다.

08. I remember everyone ( who / which ) was around me.
나는 내 주변에 있었던 모든 사람들을 기억해.

09. I am a tree ( who / which ) has lived here for 50 years.
나는 이곳에 50년 동안 살았던 나무야.

10. Australia is the only country ( which / that ) is also a continent.
호주는 하나의 대륙이기도 한 유일한 나라야.

11. She likes dogs ( who / which ) are friendly with people.
그녀는 사람들과 친하게 지내는 개들을 좋아해.

12. The boy ( who / that ) is writing a letter is Jasper.
편지를 쓰고 있는 그 소년은 Jasper야.

13. Christina had lunch with a man ( who / which ) is humorous.
Christina는 유머감각이 풍부한 한 남자와 점심을 먹었어.

14. The boy ( who / that ) often teases Mina is Junwoo.
미나를 자주 놀리는 그 남자아이는 준우야.



정답과 해설 p.6

# Let's Practice More!

SET 06

**학습목표 2 | 관계대명사의 적절한 쓰임을 연습해 보아요.** 공부한 날 : 맞은 개수 : /14개

**다음 문장의 밑줄 친 부분을 어법에 맞게 고치세요.**

01. I love my parents <u>which</u> love me. 나는 나를 사랑하시는 내 부모님을 사랑해. → who[that]

02. I saw the old man <u>which</u> was a boy once. → ______
나는 한 때 소년이었던 노인을 봤어.

03. My father is an American <u>which</u> comes from LA. → ______
나의 아버지는 LA에서 오신 미국인이셔.

04. Melissa has a dog <u>who</u> is cute. Melissa에게는 귀여운 개 한 마리가 있어. → ______

05. I don't like movies <u>who</u> have sad endings. → ______
나는 슬픈 결말을 가진 영화들을 좋아하지 않아.

06. He is the friend <u>which</u> makes me happy. → ______
그는 나를 행복하게 만들어주는 친구야.

07. He is the student <u>which</u> is loved by all his teachers. → ______
그는 그의 모든 선생님들께 사랑받는 학생이야.

08. Those boys <u>which</u> are on the playground are James and Tom. 운동장에 있는 저 소년들이 James와 Tom이야. → ______

09. Those are my grandparents <u>which</u> are sitting on the bench. → ______
벤치에 앉아 있는 저 분들은 나의 조부모님이셔.

10. Dad fell in love with mom <u>which</u> was kind to him. → ______
아빠는 그에게 친절했던 엄마에게 반하셨어.

11. I know the girl <u>which</u> dances very well. → ______
나는 춤을 아주 잘 추는 그 소녀를 알아.

12. I read the book <u>who</u> was fun. 나는 재미있던 그 책을 읽었어. → ______

13. There is a dog <u>who</u> is barking. 짖고 있는 개가 있어. → ______

14. We are trees <u>who</u> have lived here for 100 years. → ______
우리는 이곳에 100년 동안 살았던 나무들이야.

정답과 해설 p.6

# Let's Practice More!

SET 07

**학습목표 3 | 관계대명사를 이용해 다양한 표현을 만들어 보아요.** 공부한 날 : 맞은 개수 : /20개

우리말 뜻을 보고 ( ) 안에 있는 단어들을 올바르게 배열하여 문장을 다시 써보세요.

**01.** Do you know ( girl, the, who ) is singing?
너는 노래를 부르고 있는 그 소녀를 아니?
➜ Do you know the girl who is singing ?

**02.** I bought ( candies, the, that ) I like. 나는 내가 좋아하는 그 사탕들을 샀어.
➜ ______________________________.

**03.** Mom is pleased with ( which, present, the ) dad gave to her.
엄마는 아빠가 그녀에게 주신 선물에 기뻐하셔.
➜ ______________________________.

**04.** My grandmother is ( comes, who, a French ) from Lyon.
나의 할머니는 Lyon에서 오신 프랑스인이셔.
➜ ______________________________.

**05.** I like ( the, that, dress ) Rebecca is wearing.
나는 Rebecca가 입고 있는 그 드레스가 마음에 들어.
➜ ______________________________.

**06.** People like ( are, which, dogs ) friendly with them. 사람들은 그들과 친하게 지내는 개들을 좋아해.
➜ ______________________________.

**07.** I know ( who, lawyer, a ) can help you. 나는 당신을 도와줄 수 있는 변호사 한 명을 알아요.
➜ ______________________________.

**08.** You can't marry ( a, that, man ) you just met! 너는 방금 만난 남자와 결혼할 수 없어!
➜ ______________________________!

**09.** Dad gave mom ( that, flowers, the ) she likes.
아빠는 엄마에게 그녀가 좋아하는 꽃을 주셨어.
➜ ______________________________.

정답과 해설 p.6

10. I gave my mom ( carnation, a, which ) I made. 나는 엄마께 내가 만든 카네이션을 드렸어.

➜ ______________________________________________.

11. This is ( which, dog, the ) helped the police catch the thief!
이것은 경찰이 도둑을 잡는 것을 도운 개야!

➜ ______________________________________________!



12. Dad was using ( razor, the, which ) mom gave him.
아빠는 엄마가 그에게 주신 면도기를 사용하고 계셨어.

➜ ______________________________________________.

13. He was watching ( that, a, movie ) I like. 그는 내가 좋아하는 영화를 보고 있었어.

➜ ______________________________________________.

14. ( thief, The, who ) broke into Mina's house was caught by the police.
미나의 집에 침입했던 도둑은 경찰에 의해서 잡혔어.

➜ ______________________________________________.

15. ( who, tall man, The ) moved to another city returned here.
다른 도시로 이사갔던 그 키가 큰 남자는 여기로 돌아왔어.

➜ ______________________________________________.

16. Minwoo found ( watch, the, which ) I lost yesterday.
민우는 내가 어제 잃어버린 시계를 찾았어.

➜ ______________________________________________.

17. Uncle Jack fell in love with ( who, Sarah ) was kind to him.
Jack 삼촌은 그에게 친절했던 Sarah에게 반하셨어.

➜ ______________________________________________.

18. The girl ( is, who ) writing a letter is Jane.
편지를 쓰고 있는 그 소녀는 Jane이야.

➜ ______________________________________________.

19. I am eating ( that, the, cookies ) my mom baked. 나는 엄마가 구우신 쿠키를 먹고 있어.

➜ ______________________________________________.

20. My younger brother was reading ( which, a, book ) dad gave to him.
내 남동생은 아빠가 그에게 주신 책을 읽고 있었어.

➜ ______________________________________________.

정답과 해설 p.7

# Let's Practice More!

SET 08

학습목표 3 | 관계대명사를 이용해 다양한 표현을 만들어 보아요. 공부한 날 : 맞은 개수 : /20개

다음 두 문장을 하나의 문장으로 완성해 보세요.

01. I know the girl. + The girl has many friends.
→ I know the girl who[that] has many friends.
나는 많은 친구들을 가진 그 소녀를 알아.

02. Mina has a dog. + The dog is brave.
→ ______________________________.
미나는 용감한 개 한 마리를 가지고 있어.

03. My little brother was playing with his friends. + His friends live next door.
→ ______________________________.
내 남동생은 옆집에 사는 그의 친구들과 놀고 있었어.

04. I saw Mina. + Mina was playing with her dog in the yard.
→ ______________________________.
나는 마당에서 그녀의 개와 놀고 있는 미나를 봤어.

05. It was all thanks to the dog. + Mina raises the dog.
→ ______________________________.
그것은 모두 미나가 기르는 개 덕분이었어.

06. I am a tree. + The tree has lived here for 50 years.
→ ______________________________.
나는 이곳에 50년 동안 살았던 나무야.

07. All his friends like Minwoo. + Minwoo is always smiling.
→ ______________________________.
그의 모든 친구들은 항상 웃고 있는 민우를 좋아해.

08. Christian is a boy. + The boy comes from Germany.
→ ______________________________.
Christian은 독일에서 온 소년이다.

09. There is a girl. + The girl has long hair.
→ ______________________________.
긴 머리를 가진 소녀가 있다.



정답과 해설 p.7

10. Sophie likes her dog. + Her dog came from Japan.

➜ ______________________________________________.

Sophie는 일본에서 온 그녀의 개를 좋아한다.

11. I don't like movies. + Movies have sad endings.

➜ ______________________________________________.

나는 슬픈 결말을 가진 영화들을 좋아하지 않아.



12. He is the friend. + The friend makes me happy.

➜ ______________________________________________.

그는 나를 행복하게 만들어주는 친구야.

13. That girl is Charlotte. + That girl is on the playground.

➜ ______________________________________.

운동장에 있는 저 소녀는 Charlotte이야.

14. Those are my parents. + My parents are sitting on the bench.

➜ ______________________________________________.

벤치에 앉아 있는 저 분들은 나의 부모님이셔.

15. I found the man. + The man stole my key.

➜ ______________________________________________.

나는 내 열쇠를 훔쳐간 남자를 찾았다.

16. I am eating the cake. + My mom baked the cake.

➜ ______________________________________.

나는 엄마가 구우신 케이크를 먹고 있어.

17. The man is Vincent. + The man is writing a letter.

➜ ______________________________________________.

편지를 쓰고 있는 그 남자는 Vincent야.

18. Kate had lunch with a man. + The man has blue hair.

➜ ______________________________________________.

Kate는 파란 머리를 가진 한 남자와 점심을 먹었어.

19. We bought the candies. + You like the candies.

➜ ______________________________________________.

우리는 네가 좋아하는 사탕을 샀어.

20. The boy is Charlie. + The boy often teases Charlotte.

➜ ______________________________________.

Charlotte를 자주 놀리는 그 남자아이는 Charlie야.

정답과 해설 p.7

Chapter

# 03 관계대명사의 종류

이 챕터에서는 선행사가 무슨 역할을 하는지에 따라
달라지는 관계대명사에 대해 자세히 배워 보아요.

☆ 학습 방향 및 배울 내용 미리보기 ☆

☐ **Unit 01 :** She is making cupcakes **that** are colorful.

**주격 관계대명사(1)**

선행사가 뒤의 문장에서 주어 역할을 하는 주격 관계대명사의 특징에 대해 배워 보아요.

▼

☐ **Unit 02 :** Look at the girl **who** is dancing.

**주격 관계대명사(2)**

사람 주어인지, 사물(동물) 주어인지에 따라 쓸 수 있는 주격 관계대명사가 달라요.

▼

☐ **Unit 03 :** This is the book **which** I want.

**목적격 관계대명사(1)**

선행사가 뒤의 문장에서 목적어 역할을 하는 목적격 관계대명사의 특징과 생략에 대해 배워 보아요.

▼

☐ **Unit 04 :** This is the girl **whom** I like.

**목적격 관계대명사(2)**

사람 목적어인지, 사물(동물) 목적어인지에 따라 쓸 수 있는 목적격 관계대명사가 달라요.

## 단어 미리보기

이 챕터에 나올 단어들 중 이미 알고 있는 단어가 있나요?
맞는 뜻을 골라 체크해 봐요.

날짜 : 이름 : 알고 있는 단어의 수 : /24개

| No. | 아는 단어 | 단어 | 품사 | 알맞은 뜻에 체크 표시해 봐요. | | | |
|---|---|---|---|---|---|---|---|
| 1 | ✔ | colorful | 형용사 | 단색의 | ☐ | 알록달록한 | ✔ |
| 2 | ☐ | help | 명사 | 도움 | ☐ | 닫기 | ☐ |
| 3 | ☐ | trouble | 명사 | 쉬움 | ☐ | 어려움 | ☐ |
| 4 | ☐ | earring | 명사 | 귀걸이 | ☐ | 목걸이 | ☐ |
| 5 | ☐ | strawberry | 명사 | 자두 | ☐ | 딸기 | ☐ |
| 6 | ☐ | popular | 형용사 | 인기 있는 | ☐ | 인기 없는 | ☐ |
| 7 | ☐ | vacation | 명사 | 개학 | ☐ | 방학 | ☐ |
| 8 | ☐ | harm | 동사 | 보호하다 | ☐ | 해치다 | ☐ |
| 9 | ☐ | like | 전치사 | ~와 같은 | ☐ | ~와 함께 | ☐ |
| 10 | ☐ | share | 동사 | 나누다 | ☐ | 가지다 | ☐ |
| 11 | ☐ | lucky | 형용사 | 운이 좋은 | ☐ | 운이 나쁜 | ☐ |
| 12 | ☐ | impossible | 형용사 | 가능한 | ☐ | 불가능한 | ☐ |
| 13 | ☐ | introduce | 동사 | 소개하다 | ☐ | 피하다 | ☐ |
| 14 | ☐ | lawyer | 명사 | 검사 | ☐ | 변호사 | ☐ |
| 15 | ☐ | pay | 동사 | 훔치다 | ☐ | 지불하다 | ☐ |
| 16 | ☐ | memory | 명사 | 추억 | ☐ | 쪽지 | ☐ |
| 17 | ☐ | zoo | 명사 | 박물관 | ☐ | 동물원 | ☐ |
| 18 | ☐ | wish | 동사 | 원하다 | ☐ | 이기다 | ☐ |
| 19 | ☐ | miracle | 명사 | 기도 | ☐ | 기적 | ☐ |
| 20 | ☐ | tofu | 명사 | 두부 | ☐ | 토마토 | ☐ |
| 21 | ☐ | often | 부사 | 자주 | ☐ | 가끔 | ☐ |
| 22 | ☐ | catch | 동사 | 잡다 | ☐ | 던지다 | ☐ |
| 23 | ☐ | decide | 동사 | 고민하다 | ☐ | 결정하다 | ☐ |
| 24 | ☐ | red | 형용사 | 빨간 | ☐ | 파란 | ☐ |

UNIT 주격 관계대명사 (1)

# 01 She is making cupcakes that are colorful.

## ❖ POiNT 1 ❖

**앞에서 선행사가 사람이냐, 사물이냐에 따라 쓸 수 있는 관계대명사가 다르다는 것 배웠죠?
뿐만 아니라 관계대명사는 선행사가 무슨 역할(주어-주격, 목적어-목적격, 소유형용사-소유격)을 하는지에 따라서도 달라져요!**

관계대명사의 종류

| 선행사 \ 격 | 주격 | 목적격 | 소유격 |
|---|---|---|---|
| 사람 | who | who[m] | whose |
| 사물, 동물 | which | which | whose[of which] |
| 사람, 사물, 동물 | that | that | – |

## ❖ POiNT 2 ❖

### 주격 관계대명사와 동사

**주격 관계대명사의 뒤에는 반드시 동사가 와요!
동사는 선행사의 수에 일치시켜줘야 해요.**

She is making cupcakes. + The cupcakes are colorful.
그녀는 컵케이크를 만들고 있어. 그 컵케이크들은 색이 알록달록해.

She is making cupcakes that are colorful. (○)
그녀는 색이 알록달록한 컵케이크들을 만들고 있어.

She is making cupcakes that is colorful. (×)

## Check and Write

**다음 빈칸에 알맞은 be동사(am, are, is)를 써 보세요.**

1. Do you know the man who [ is ] talking to her?

너는 그녀에게 말을 하고 있는 남자를 아니?

2. I'm wearing a dress which [ ] pretty.

나는 예쁜 드레스 한 벌을 입고 있어요.

3. The cat is catching the butterflies that [ ] flying in the sky.

그 고양이는 하늘을 날고 있는 나비들을 잡고 있어.

4. They are looking at the boys who [ ] playing baseball.

그들은 야구를 하고 있는 남자 아이들을 보고 있어.

5. There is a traditional house which [ ] old. (*traditional: 전통의)

오래된 전통 가옥이 있어.

정답과 해설 p.7

UNIT

# 02 Look at the girl who is dancing.

주격 관계대명사 (2)

❖ POiNT ❖

## 주격 관계대명사

이어지는 문장에서 선행사가 주어 역할을 하는 주격 관계대명사에 대해 알아볼까요?

### 사람 주어를 나타내는 관계대명사 who

Look at the girl. + The girl is dancing.
(the girl: 사람 선행사 / The girl: 주어)

그 소녀를 봐. 그 소녀는 춤을 추고 있어.

⇨ Look at the girl who is dancing.
(who: 주격 관계대명사)

춤을 추고 있는 그 소녀를 봐.

선행사(the girl)가 뒤의 문장에서는 주어 역할을 하고 있죠?
또 the girl이 사람이기 때문에 사람을 나타내는 주격 관계대명사 who를 써요!

### 동물, 사물을 나타내는 주격 관계대명사 which

This is the pencil. + The pencil is long.
(the pencil: 사물 선행사 / The pencil: 주어)

이것은 연필이야. 그 연필은 길어.

⇨ This is the pencil which is long.
(which: 주격 관계대명사)

이것은 긴 연필이야.

### 사람, 사물, 동물을 모두 나타내는 주격 관계대명사 that

She has two dogs. + The dogs are cute.
(two dogs: 동물 선행사 / The dogs: 주어)

그녀는 개 두 마리를 가지고 있어. 그 개들은 귀여워.

⇨ She has two dogs that are cute.
(that: 주격 관계대명사)

그녀는 귀여운 개 두 마리를 가지고 있어.

## Check and Write

**다음 문장을 읽고 주격 관계대명사에 동그라미 하세요.**

1. You should read the book which is on my desk.

너는 내 책상 위에 있는 책을 읽어야 해.

2. I have a friend who has a hamster.

나는 햄스터 한 마리를 가지고 있는 친구가 있어.

3. It is the cat that is cute.

그것은 귀여운 고양이야.

4. He is the teacher who plays the piano well.

그는 피아노를 잘 치는 선생님이셔.

5. Look at the girl who is singing a song.

노래하고 있는 그 소녀를 봐.

정답과 해설 p.7

## Practice 1 주격 관계대명사의 알맞은 쓰임을 익혀 보아요.

**[A-D]** 다음 문장에 알맞은 주격 관계대명사를 보기에서 골라 빈칸에 써 보세요. (중복사용 가능)

보기 who which

## A Help!

1. There are many people ___who___ are in trouble.
어려움에 처한 사람들이 많아. (*be in trouble: 어려움에 처하다)

2. They are the people ________ need help.
그들은 도움을 필요로 하는 사람들이야.

3. There are people ________ help others.
다른 사람들을 돕는 사람들이 있어.

4. They are the people ________ have warm hearts.
그들은 따뜻한 마음을 가진 사람들이야.

5. I want to do something ________ is helpful.
나는 도움이 되는 무언가를 하고 싶어.

## B She likes everyone!

1. Do you know the girl ________ is sitting on the grass?
너 잔디 위에 앉아 있는 저 여자애를 아니?

2. Of course. She is my neighbor ________ lives next door.
물론이지. 그녀는 옆집에 사는 내 이웃이야.

3. She has two dogs ________ are brown.
그녀는 갈색 강아지 두 마리를 갖고 있어.

4. Is she the girl ________ likes you?
그녀가 너를 좋아하는 여자애니?

5. No, she likes everyone ________ is around her.
아니, 그녀는 자기 주위에 있는 모든 사람들을 좋아해.



정답과 해설 p.7

CH
03

## C She is special!

1. Yura is the student __________ is loved by all the teachers.
유라는 모든 선생님들한테 사랑받는 학생이야.

2. She is the person __________ is good at finding things.
그녀는 물건을 잘 찾는 사람이야.

3. She found my earrings __________ are heart-shaped.
그녀는 나의 하트 모양 귀걸이를 찾아줬어.

4. She found them in a box __________ was under the desk.
그녀는 그것들을 책상 아래에 있던 상자 안에서 찾았어.

5. They were the presents __________ were given to me by my friend.
그것들은 내가 친구에게서 받은 선물이었어.

## D Do not harm animals! (*harm: 해치다)

1. People __________ attack small animals are cruel.
작은 동물들을 공격하는 사람들은 잔인해. (*attack: 공격하다, cruel: 잔인한)

2. Don't throw stones at the cats __________ live on the street.
길에 사는 고양이들한테 돌을 던지지 마.

3. They are animals __________ need to be taken care of.
그들은 보살핌 받을 필요가 있는 동물들이야.

4. There are people __________ forget that animals are living things.
동물들이 생명체라는 것을 잊는 사람들이 있어. (*living things: 생명체)

5. People __________ harm animals should be punished. (*punish: 처벌하다)
동물들을 해치는 사람들은 처벌 받아야 해.

정답과 해설 p.7

## Practice 2 주격 관계대명사가 쓰인 문장을 완성해 보아요.

다음 우리말 뜻과 같도록 주어진 표현을 순서에 맞게 배열하여 문장을 완성하세요.

1. ( disappoints her, Something, that ) has happened again!

(*disappoint: 실망시키다)

그녀를 실망시키는 무언가가 또 일어났어!

➔ Something that disappoints her has happened again!

2. Strawberries are ( is popular in spring, the fruit, which ).

딸기는 봄에 인기 있는 과일이야.

➔ Strawberries are ______________________ ______________________.

3. Mom reduced ( which, is little even now, my allowance ).

엄마는 지금도 적은 내 용돈을 줄이셨어. (*reduce: 줄이다, allowance: 용돈)

➔ Mom reduced ______________________.

4. I have ( that, something, might save you some money ).

나는 네게 돈을 좀 아껴줄지도 모르는 무언가를 갖고 있어.

➔ I have ______________________.

5. I have ( two coupons, can be used, which ) to buy ice cream.

나는 아이스크림을 사는 데 쓸 수 있는 쿠폰이 두 장 있어.

➔ I have ______________________ to buy ice cream.

6. Tell me ( a story, might interest me, which ).

나를 흥미롭게 할 만한 이야기 하나를 해줘. (*interest: 흥미롭게 하다, 흥미를 갖게 하다)

➔ Tell me ______________________.



정답과 해설 p.7

7. We wait for Santa Claus ( us presents, gives, who ).

우리는 우리에게 선물을 주는 산타클로스를 기다려.

➔ We wait for Santa Claus

______________________

______________________.

8. Can I eat the strawberries ( on the table, which, are )?

식탁에 있는 딸기를 먹어도 돼요?

➔ Can I eat the strawberries

______________________

______________________?

9. We saw ( who, the actress, is famous).

우리는 유명한 여배우를 봤어.

➔ We saw ______________________________.

10. Winter vacation is like ( reenergizes us, which, an oasis ).

겨울 방학은 우리를 다시 힘내게 하는 오아시스와 같아. (*reenergize: 다시 힘내게 하다)

➔ Winter vacation is like ______________________________.

11. The books introduced ( who, people, lived, exciting lives ).

그 책들은 흥미로운 삶을 살았던 사람들을 소개해줬다. (*introduce: 소개하다)

➔ The books introduced ______________________________.

12. ( that, matters even more, There's something ); believing in yourself.

훨씬 더 중요한 무언가가 있는데, 바로 너 자신을 믿는 거야. (*matter: 중요하다)

➔ ______________________________; believing in yourself.

13. I need ( won't run away, a friend, who ). (*run away: 달아나다)

나는 달아나지 않을 친구가 필요해.

➔ I need ______________________________.

**14.** ( the girl, who, She is )
speaks three languages.
그녀는 3개 국어를 하는 소녀야. (*language: 언어)

➔ ____________________
speaks three languages.

**15.** ( that, fear, It is )
makes a dream impossible.
꿈을 불가능하게 만드는 것은 두려움이다.

➔ ____________________
makes a dream impossible.

**16.** You are ( who, the one, is lucky ).
너는 운이 좋은 사람이야.
➔ You are ______________________________.

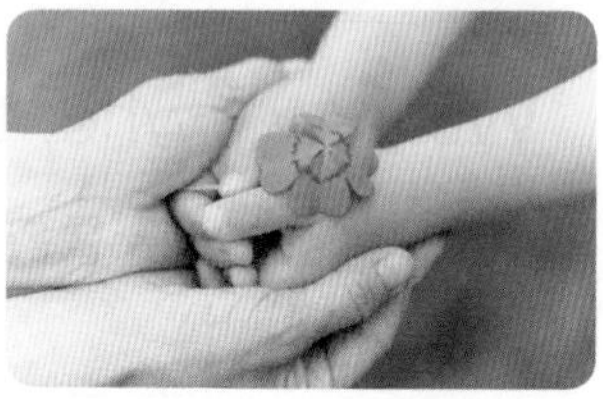

**17.** A detective is a person ( finding things, who, is good at ).
형사는 무언가를 찾는 데 능숙한 사람이야. (*detective: 형사)
➔ A detective is a person ______________________________.

**18.** ( are willing to die, Those, who ) will live.
기꺼이 죽고자 하는 이들은 살 것이다. (*be willing to: 기꺼이 ~하다)
➔ ______________________________ will live.

**19.** God helps ( help themselves, who, those ).
하늘은 스스로 돕는 자를 돕는다.
➔ God helps ______________________________.

**20.** ( two rabbits, The man, chases, who ) catches neither one.
두 마리 토끼를 쫓는 사람은 한 마리도 못 잡는다. (*chase: 쫓다, *neither: (둘 중)어느 것도 ~아닌)
➔ ______________________________ catches neither one.


정답과 해설 p.8

## Practice 3 관계대명사와 동사가 알맞게 쓰였는지 따져 보아요.

다음 문장을 읽고 밑줄 친 부분이 문법에 맞으면 ○표, 틀리면 ×표 하세요.

1. 

She is the teacher who is very fun.

그녀는 매우 재미있는 선생님이셔.

➔ ○

2. 

I like people which make me laugh.

나는 나를 웃게 만드는 사람들을 좋아해.

➔ ________

3. This boy is my little brother that bothers me.

이 남자애는 나를 귀찮게 하는 내 남동생이야. (*bother: 귀찮게 하다)

➔ ________

4. He is the teacher which is the most popular in our school.

그는 우리 학교에서 가장 인기 있는 선생님이셔. (*popular: 인기 있는) ➔ ________

5. He is one of the people who like me very much. ➔ ________

그는 나를 엄청 좋아하는 사람들 중 한 명이야.

6. He is a lawyer which helps the poor. ➔ ________

그는 가난한 사람들을 돕는 변호사야. (*lawyer: 변호사, the poor: 가난한 사람들)

7. Hayul who had a nightmare sleeps with us.

악몽을 꾼 하율이는 우리와 함께 잠을 자. (*nightmare: 악몽)

➔ ________

정답과 해설 p.8

8. 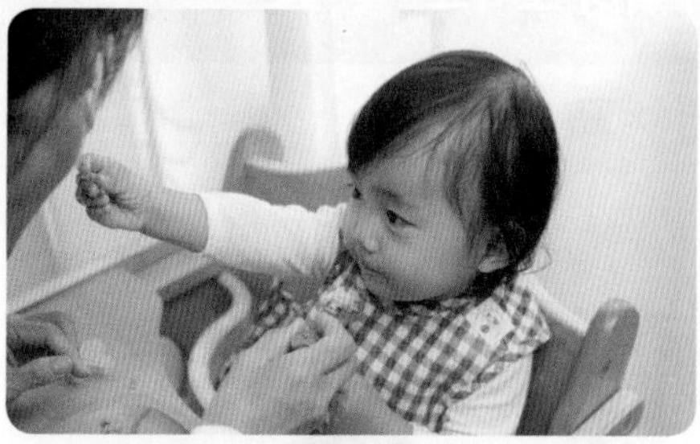

The baby who was very small has grown!

엄청 작았던 아기가 자랐어!

➔ ____________

9. 

He looked at the picture who was on the wall.

그는 벽에 걸린 그림을 봤어.

➔ ____________

10. Is there anybody which can help me? ➔ ____________

나를 도와줄 수 있는 사람 있어요?

11. There is too much homework that is difficult. ➔ ____________

어려운 숙제가 너무 많아요. (*difficult: 어려운)

12. These are the problems that requires much knowledge. ➔ ____________

이것들은 많은 지식을 요구하는 문제들이야. (*require: 요구하다, knowledge: 지식)

13. I know someone that is good at the computer. ➔ ____________

나는 컴퓨터에 능숙한 누군가를 알고 있어.

14. There are many people who makes donations to charities.

자선 단체에 기부를 하는 사람들이 많아. (*make donations: 기부하다, charity: 자선 단체) ➔ ____________

15. Melisa is a student which is good at painting.

Melisa는 그림을 잘 그리는 학생이야.

➔ ____________

정답과 해설 p.8

16. 

I have a cousin which lives in Canada.

나는 캐나다에 사는 사촌이 한 명 있어.

➔ ______________

17. 

I like people that share their talents.

나는 그들의 재능을 나누는 사람들을 좋아해.

➔ ______________

18. There are many people which will not tell us their names. ➔ ______________

우리에게 자신의 이름을 말하지 않을 사람들이 많아.

19. A person who has good thoughts is always happy. ➔ ______________

좋은 생각을 하는 사람은 항상 행복해. (*thought: 생각)

20. You have to decide what to do with the time that are given to you. 너는 너에게 주어진 시간에 무엇을 할지를 정해야 해. ➔ ______________

Cultural Tips 재미로 익히는 문화상식

## 도와주세요! – 여러 나라의 긴급 구조 전화번호

해외에 있는데 위급한 상황이 벌어졌어요.
다른 나라에서도 우리나라와 똑같이 119를 누르면 될까요?

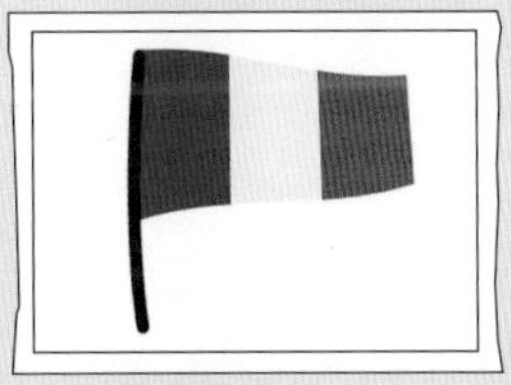

프랑스 - 112 or 15

미국 - 911

독일 - 110

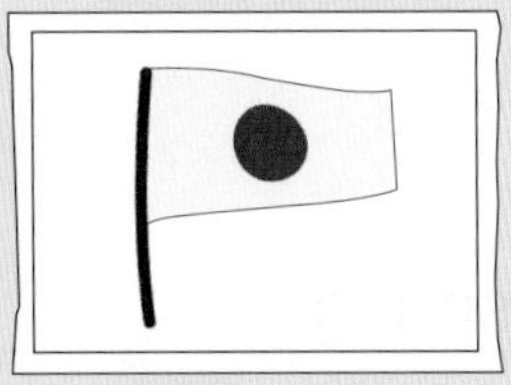

일본 - 110

영국 - 999

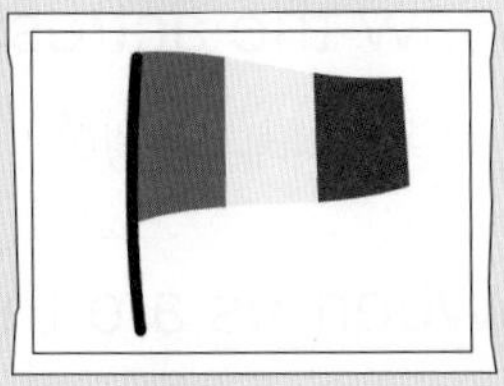

이탈리아 - 112

정답과 해설 p.8

# Let's Practice More!

SET 01

학습목표 1 | 주격 관계대명사의 개념을 익혀 보아요.　　공부한 날 :　　맞은 개수 :　　/12개

밑줄 친 부분이 선행사면 ○표, 아니면 ×표 하세요.

01. Can I eat <u>the oranges</u> which are on the table? → ○
제가 탁자 위에 있는 오렌지를 먹어도 되나요?

02. People who attack small <u>animals</u> are cruel. → ______
작은 동물들을 공격하는 사람들은 잔인해.

03. Mom reduced <u>my allowance</u> which is little even now. → ______
엄마는 지금도 적은 내 용돈을 줄이셨어.

04. <u>The books</u> introduced people who lived exciting lives. → ______
그 책들은 흥미로운 삶을 살았던 사람들을 소개해줬다.

05. <u>I</u> need a friend who won't run away. → ______
나는 달아나지 않을 친구가 필요해.

06. <u>God</u> helps those who help themselves. → ______
하늘은 스스로 돕는 자를 돕는다.

07. <u>Melissa</u> is a student who is good at painting. → ______
Melissa는 그림을 잘 그리는 학생이야.

08. <u>The baby</u> who had a nightmare sleeps with us. → ______
악몽을 꾼 그 아기는 우리와 함께 잠을 자.

09. We wait for <u>Santa Claus</u> who gives us presents. → ______
우리는 우리에게 선물을 주는 산타클로스를 기다려.

10. You are <u>the one</u> who is lucky. → ______
너는 운이 좋은 사람이야.

11. <u>We</u> saw the actress who is famous. → ______
우리는 유명한 여배우를 봤어.

12. <u>Strawberries</u> are the fruit which is popular in spring. → ______
딸기는 봄에 인기 있는 과일이야.



정답과 해설 p.8

# Let's Practice More!

SET 02

학습목표 1 | 주격 관계대명사의 개념을 익혀 보아요.  공부한 날 :  맞은 개수 : /14개

밑줄 친 관계대명사가 주어 역할을 하고 있으면 ○표, 아니면 ×표 하세요.

01. Look at the girl <u>who</u> is dancing. 춤을 추고 있는 그 소녀를 봐. → ○

02. He had a sweet voice <u>which</u> I like. → ______
그는 내가 좋아하는 달콤한 목소리를 갖고 있었어.

03. Santa brought me the bike <u>which</u> I wanted! → ______
산타가 내가 원했던 자전거를 나에게 가져다줬어!

04. Do you know that girl <u>who</u> is sitting on the grass? 너는 잔디 위에 앉아 있는 저 여자애를 아니? → ______

05. She is my neighbor <u>who</u> lives next door. → ______
그녀는 옆집에 사는 내 이웃이야.

06. Is Mary the girl <u>who</u> likes you? Mary가 너를 좋아하는 여자애니? → ______

07. She found my earrings <u>which</u> are heart-shaped. → ______
그녀는 나의 하트 모양 귀걸이를 찾아줬어.

08. There isn't a jar <u>that</u> I can't open! 내가 열 수 없는 병은 없어! → ______

09. They are people <u>who</u> forget the fact. 그들은 그 사실을 잊은 사람들이야. → ______

10. They saw the picture <u>that</u> I took. → ______
그들은 내가 찍은 사진을 봤어.

11. She is the person <u>who</u> is good at finding things. → ______
그녀는 물건을 잘 찾는 사람이야.

12. I want the bike <u>which</u> Mina has. 나는 미나가 가지고 있는 자전거를 원해요. → ______

13. I found the watch <u>which</u> she lost! 나는 그녀가 잃어버린 시계를 찾았어! → ______

14. He has two dogs <u>which</u> are brown. 그는 갈색 강아지 두 마리를 갖고 있어. → ______

정답과 해설 p.8

# Let's Practice More!

SET 03

학습목표 1 | 주격 관계대명사의 개념을 익혀 보아요.   공부한 날 :   맞은 개수 :   /14개

밑줄 친 부분이 주격 관계대명사면 ○표, 아니면 ×표 하세요.

01. I'm looking at the girl who is singing. → ○
나는 노래를 부르고 있는 소녀를 보고 있어.

02. Yura is the student who is loved by all the teachers. → ______
유라는 모든 선생님들한테 사랑받는 학생이야.

03. They were the presents which were given to me by my friend. → ______
그것들은 내가 내 친구에게서 받은 선물이었어.

04. I opened the jar that my older brother couldn't open! → ______
나는 형이 열지 못했던 병을 열었어!

05. She found them in a box which was under the desk. → ______
그녀는 그것들을 책상 아래에 있던 상자 안에서 찾았어.

06. People who harm animals should be punished. → ______
동물들을 해치는 사람들은 처벌 받아야 해.

07. The old things which you still have are not bad. → ______
네가 아직도 가지고 있는 오래된 것들은 (상태가) 나쁘지 않단다.

08. You have many memories which you share with them. → ______
너는 그들과 함께 공유하는 많은 추억들을 가지고 있어.

09. They are the people who need help. 그들은 도움이 필요한 사람들이야. → ______

10. Don't throw stones at the cats which live on the street. → ______
길에 사는 고양이들한테 돌을 던지지 마.

11. I have two coupons which can be used to buy ice cream. → ______
나는 아이스크림을 사는 데 쓸 수 있는 쿠폰이 두 장 있어.

12. Why don't you ride your bike which I bought for you? → ______
내가 너에게 사주었던 너의 자전거를 타는 게 어떠니?

13. Winter vacation is like an oasis which reenergizes us. → ______
겨울 방학은 우리를 다시 힘내게 하는 오아시스와 같아.

14. She is the girl who speaks three languages. → ______
그녀는 3개 국어를 하는 소녀야.


정답과 해설 p.8

# Let's Practice More!

SET 04

**학습목표 2 | 주격 관계대명사를 올바르게 써 보아요.**　　공부한 날 :　　맞은 개수 :　　/14개

**다음 (　) 안에 들어갈 관계대명사로 적절한 것을 모두 고르세요.**

01. She has two dogs ( that / which / who ) are very cute.
그녀는 매우 귀여운 두 마리의 개를 가지고 있다.

02. She likes everyone ( that / which ) is around her.
그녀는 자기 주위에 있는 모든 사람들을 좋아해.

03. People ( that / which / who ) attack small animals are cruel.
작은 동물들을 공격하는 사람들은 잔인해.

04. There are many people ( that / which / who ) are in trouble.
어려움에 처한 사람들이 많아.

05. There's something ( that / who ) matters even more.
훨씬 더 중요한 무언가가 있어.

06. We saw the actress ( that / which / who ) is famous. 우리는 유명한 여배우를 봤어.

07. These are the problems ( that / which / who ) require much knowledge.
이것들은 많은 지식을 요구하는 문제들이야.

08. He looked at the picture ( that / which / who ) was on the wall.
그는 벽에 걸린 그림을 봤어.

09. She is the teacher ( that / which / who ) is very fun. 그녀는 매우 재미있는 선생님이셔.

10. Tell me a story ( that / which / who ) might interest me.
나를 흥미롭게 할 만한 이야기 하나를 해줘.

11. Something ( that / who ) disappoints her has happened again!
그녀를 실망시키는 무언가가 또 일어났어!

12. Those ( which / who ) are willing to die will live.
기꺼이 죽고자 하는 이들은 살 것이다.

13. I have something ( that / who ) might save you some money.
나는 너에게 돈을 좀 아껴줄지도 모르는 무언가를 갖고 있어.

14. A detective is a person ( that / which / who ) is good at finding things.
형사는 무언가를 찾는 데 능숙한 사람이야.

정답과 해설 p.8

# Let's Practice More!

SET 05

**학습목표 2 | 주격 관계대명사를 올바르게 써 보아요.** 공부한 날 : 맞은 개수 : /14개

**다음 문장을 읽고 밑줄 친 부분이 맞으면 ○표, 틀리면 고쳐 써 보세요.**

01. There is a cat who bites a pencil. 연필을 무는 고양이 한 마리가 있다. → which[that]

02. They are the people who have warm hearts. → ______
그들은 따뜻한 마음을 가진 사람들이야.

03. I want to do something that is helpful. → ______
나는 도움이 되는 무언가를 하고 싶어.

04. She is the girl who speaks three languages. → ______
그녀는 3개 국어를 하는 소녀야.

05. The man which chases two rabbits catches neither one. → ______
두 마리 토끼를 쫓는 사람은 한 마리도 못 잡는다.

06. I like people which make me laugh. → ______
나는 나를 웃게 만드는 사람들을 좋아해.

07. He is the teacher who is the most popular in our school. → ______
그는 우리 학교에서 가장 인기 있는 선생님이셔.

08. I know someone that is good at the computer. → ______
나는 컴퓨터에 능숙한 누군가를 알고 있어.

09. There are many people who won't tell us their names. → ______
우리에게 자신의 이름을 말하지 않을 사람들이 많아.

10. It was the present who was given to me by my parents. → ______
그것은 내가 부모님께 받은 선물이었어.

11. Hayul who had a nightmare sleeps with us. → ______
악몽을 꾼 하율이는 우리와 함께 잠을 자.

12. Is there anybody that can help me? → ______
나를 도와줄 수 있는 사람 있어요?

13. He is one of the people which like me very much. → ______
그는 나를 엄청 좋아하는 사람들 중에 한 명이야.

14. I have a cousin who lives in Canada. → ______
나는 캐나다에 사는 사촌이 한 명 있어.



정답과 해설 p.8

# Let's Practice More!

SET 06

**학습목표 3 | 주격 관계대명사의 수 일치를 연습해 보아요.** 공부한 날 : 맞은 개수 : /14개

다음 문장을 읽고 ( ) 안에서 올바른 것을 고르세요.

01. There are three dogs which ( is / are ) playing in the yard.
마당에서 놀고 있는 3마리의 개가 있다.

02. Do you know that boy who ( is / are ) sitting on the grass?
넌 잔디 위에 앉아 있는 저 남자애를 아니?

03. My friend has two dogs which ( is / are ) white.
내 친구는 하얀색 강아지 두 마리를 갖고 있어.

04. Don't throw stones at the cats which ( lives / live ) on the street.
길에 사는 고양이들한테 돌을 던지지 마.

05. People who ( harms / harm ) animals should be punished.
동물들을 해치는 사람들은 처벌 받아야 해.

06. Jeremy is the person who ( is / are ) good at finding things.
Jeremy는 물건을 잘 찾는 사람이야.

07. The children wait for Santa Claus who ( gives / give ) them presents.
그 아이들은 그들에게 선물을 주는 산타클로스를 기다려.

08. There's something that ( matters / matter ) even more. 훨씬 더 중요한 무언가가 있어.

09. Charlotte is the girl who ( speaks / speak ) three languages.
Charlotte은 3개 국어를 하는 소녀야.

10. The baby who ( was / were ) very small has grown! 엄청 작았던 아기가 자랐어!

11. There are many people who ( makes / make ) donations to charities.
자선 단체에 기부를 하는 사람들이 많이 있어.

12. You have to decide what to do with the time that ( is / are ) given to you.
너는 너에게 주어진 시간에 무엇을 할지를 정해야 해.

13. They are the people who ( has / have ) warm hearts.
그들은 따뜻한 마음을 가진 사람들이야.

14. Can I eat the cookies which ( is / are ) on the table?
제가 탁자 위에 있는 쿠키들을 먹어도 되나요?

정답과 해설 p.8

# Let's Practice More!

SET 07

학습목표 3 | 주격 관계대명사의 수 일치를 연습해 보아요.  공부한 날 :  맞은 개수 : /20개

다음 문장을 읽고 밑줄 친 부분이 맞으면 ○표, 틀리면 고쳐 써 보세요.

01.

She is making cupcakes that is for her mother.

그녀는 그녀의 엄마를 위한 컵케이크를 만드는 중이다.

➔ are

02.

There is too much homework that is difficult.

어려운 숙제가 너무 많아요.

➔ ________

03. He is a lawyer who help the poor. ➔ ________

그는 가난한 사람들을 돕는 변호사야.

04. The police found my ring which was given to me by mom. ➔ ________

경찰이 엄마가 나에게 주신 내 반지를 찾아줬어.

05. There are many people who are in trouble. ➔ ________

어려움에 처한 사람들이 많아.

06. My dad likes everyone that are around him. ➔ ________

우리 아빠는 자기 주위에 있는 모든 사람들을 좋아해.

07. Those who are willing to die will live. ➔ ________

기꺼이 죽고자 하는 이들은 살 것이다.

08. My parents reduced my allowance which are little even now. ➔ ________

나의 부모님은 지금도 적은 내 용돈을 줄이셨어.

09. She is the teacher who is very humorous. ➔ ________

그녀는 매우 유머러스한 선생님이다.



정답과 해설 p.8

10. 

Watermelons are the fruit which are popular in summer.

수박은 여름에 인기 있는 과일이야.

➔ ____________

11. 

Can I drink some juice which are on the table?

탁자 위에 있는 주스를 좀 마셔도 될까요?

➔ ____________



12. A person who have good thoughts is always happy. ➔ ____________

좋은 생각을 하는 사람은 항상 행복해.

13. People who harms animals should be punished. ➔ ____________

동물들을 해치는 사람들은 처벌 받아야 해.

14. You are the one who are lucky. ➔ ____________

너는 운이 좋은 사람이야.

15. I know someone that is good at the computer. 나는 컴퓨터에 능숙한 누군가를 알고 있어. ➔ ____________

16. This boy is my little brother that bothers me. ➔ ____________

이 남자애가 나를 귀찮게 하는 내 남동생이야.

17. Uncle Jack found my earrings in a box which was under the desk. Jack 삼촌은 내 귀걸이를 책상 아래에 있던 상자 안에서 찾았어. ➔ ____________

18. They are the people who needs help. ➔ ____________

그들은 도움을 필요로 하는 사람들이야.

19. My friend has nephews who lives in India. ➔ ____________

내 친구는 인도에 사는 조카들이 있어. (*nephew: 조카)

20. Stray cats are animals which need to be taken care of. ➔ ____________

길고양이들은 보살핌 받을 필요가 있는 동물이야. (*stray cat: 길고양이)

정답과 해설 p.8

# Let's Practice More!

SET 08

학습목표 4 | 주격 관계대명사의 알맞은 쓰임과 수 일치를 더 연습해 보아요. 공부한 날 : 맞은 개수 : /20개

다음 문장의 밑줄 친 부분을 바르게 고쳐 쓰세요.

01. 

She was a singer which was famous.

그녀는 유명했던 가수였다.

→ who[that]

02. 

We saw the picture which were on the wall.

우리는 벽에 걸린 그림을 봤어.

→ ______

03. This kid is my neighbor who live next door. → ______

이 아이는 옆집에 사는 내 이웃이야.

04. Something who surprises her has happened again! → ______

그녀를 놀라게 하는 무언가가 또 일어났어!

05. I have something who might save you some time. → ______

나는 네게 시간을 좀 아껴줄지도 모르는 무언가를 갖고 있어.

06. She likes people who makes her laugh. → ______

그녀는 그녀를 웃게 만드는 사람들을 좋아해.

07. She is one of the people who likes me very much. → ______

그녀는 나를 엄청 좋아하는 사람들 중 한 명이야.

08. I have a coupon who can be used to buy a cake. → ______

나는 케이크를 사는 데 쓸 수 있는 쿠폰이 한 장 있어.

09. Spring break is like an oasis who reenergizes us. → ______

봄 방학은 우리를 다시 힘내게 하는 오아시스와 같아. (*spring break: 봄 방학)



정답과 해설 p.8

10. A detective is a person who are good at finding things. → ____________
형사는 무언가를 찾는 데 능숙한 사람이야.

11. People which attack small animals are cruel. → ____________
작은 동물들을 공격하는 사람들은 잔인해.

12. I have problems who require much knowledge. → ____________
나는 많은 지식을 요구하는 문제들을 가지고 있어.



13.

There are people who helps others.
다른 사람들을 돕는 사람들이 있어.
→ ____________

14.

Is he the boy which likes you?
그가 너를 좋아하는 남자애니?
→ ____________

15. They were the candies which was given to me by my cousin.
그것들은 내가 내 사촌에게 받은 사탕들이었어. → ____________

16. Charlie and Eric are twins which are good at painting. → ____________
Charlie와 Eric은 그림을 잘 그리는 쌍둥이다.

17. Mina is the student who are loved by all the teachers. → ____________
미나는 모든 선생님들한테 사랑받는 학생이야.

18. Tell me a story who might impress me. (*impress: 감명을 주다) → ____________
나에게 감명을 줄 만한 이야기 하나를 해줘.

19. The man who chase two rabbits catches neither one. → ____________
두 마리 토끼를 쫓는 사람은 한 마리도 못 잡는다.

20. My parents like people who shares their talents. → ____________
우리 부모님은 그들의 재능을 나누는 사람들을 좋아해.

정답과 해설 p.8

# UNIT 03 This is the book which I want.

목적격 관계대명사 (1)

### ❖ POiNT 1 ❖

| 관계대명사의 종류 | | | |
|---|---|---|---|
| 선행사 \ 격 | 주격 | 소유격 | 목적격 |
| 사람 | who | whose | who[m] |
| 사물, 동물 | which | whose[of which] | which |
| 사람, 사물, 동물 | that | – | that |

### ❖ POiNT 2 ❖

**목적격 관계대명사**

이어지는 문장에서 선행사가 목적어 역할을 하는 목적격 관계대명사의 뒤에는 반드시 주어+동사가 와요.
또한 목적격 관계대명사가 목적어 역할을 하기 때문에 뒤에 이어지는 문장 안에 목적어는 없어요!

This is the book which[that] I want. (○)
주어 동사

이것은 내가 원하는 책이야.

This is the book which[that] I want the book. (×)
목적어

### ❖ POiNT 3 ❖

**목적격 관계대명사의 생략**

This is the book I want.

이것은 내가 원하는 책이야.

위의 문장에서는 관계대명사가 쓰이지 않았어요!
관계대명사가 목적격으로 사용될 때는 관계대명사를 생략할 수 있기 때문이에요!

## Check and Write

**다음 문장을 읽고 밑줄 친 관계대명사가 주격인지 목적격인지 빈칸에 써 보세요.**



1. I ate some bananas which my mom bought for me.

나는 엄마가 나를 위해 사 주신 바나나 몇 개를 먹었어.

[ 목적격 ]

2. She is a teacher who teaches English.

그녀는 영어를 가르치는 선생님이야.

[          ]

3. These are the shoes that I bought yesterday.

이것들은 어제 내가 샀던 신발들이야.

[          ]

4. Do you know Lily's little brother who is standing behind her?

너는 그녀의 뒤에 서 있는 Lily의 남동생을 아니?

[          ]

5. They are the students whom Ms. Lee teaches.

그들은 이 선생님이 가르치는 학생들이야.

[          ]

정답과 해설 p.8

UNIT 04 목적격 관계대명사 (2)

# This is the girl whom I like.

❖ POiNT ❖

**목적어 역할을 하는 목적격 관계대명사**

**사람 목적어를 나타내는 목적격 관계대명사 who(m)**

This is the girl. + I like her.

시람 선행사 / 목적어

이 아이는 그 소녀다. 나는 그녀를 좋아한다.

This is the girl who(m) I like.

목적격 관계대명사

이 아이는 내가 좋아하는 그 소녀야.

**사물, 동물 목적어를 나타내는 목적격 관계대명사 which**

This is the book. + I was reading it yesterday.

사물 선행사 / 사물 목적어

이것은 책이다. 나는 어제 그것을 읽고 있었다.

This is the book which I was reading yesterday.

목적격 관계대명사

이것은 내가 어제 읽고 있었던 그 책이다.

**사람, 사물, 동물 목적어를 나타내는 목적격 관계대명사 that**

He has a pretty cat. + I like the cat very much.

동물 선행사 / 동물 목적어

그는 예쁜 고양이를 가지고 있어. 나는 그 고양이를 매우 좋아해.

He has a pretty cat that I like very much.

목적격 관계대명사

그는 내가 매우 좋아하는 예쁜 고양이를 가지고 있어.

## Check and Write

**다음 문장에서 목적격 관계대명사를 찾아 빈칸에 쓰세요.**

1. He has two children whom he loves very much.

그는 그가 매우 사랑하는 두 명의 자식이 있어.

whom

2. This is the story that my mother read to me.

이것은 나의 엄마가 나에게 읽어주신 이야기야.

3. I have a red bag which my mom bought for me.

나는 엄마가 나에게 사주신 빨간 가방이 있어.

4. Do you know the boy who Nayeon met yesterday?

너는 나연이가 어제 만났던 남자아이를 아니?

5. She will pay for the doll that she chooses.

그녀는 그녀가 선택한 인형의 값을 지불할거야.

정답과 해설 p.8

## Practice 1 문제를 풀면서 관계대명사의 알맞은 쓰임을 익혀 보아요.

**[A-D]** 다음 문장에 알맞은 관계대명사를 보기 에서 골라 빈칸에 알맞게 써 보세요. (중복사용 가능)

보기 which whom

### A Is Santa my dad?

1. Santa brought me the bike __which__ I wanted!
   산타가 내가 원했던 자전거를 나에게 가져다줬어!
2. He had a sweet voice ________ I like.
   그는 내가 좋아하는 달콤한 목소리를 갖고 있었어.

3. The man ________ Mina met was not Santa.
   미나가 만났던 남자는 산타가 아니었어.
4. It was her dad ________ Mina loves!
   그것은 미나가 사랑하는 그녀의 아빠였어!
5. It is a secret ________ we should take to our graves!
   이건 우리가 우리 무덤까지 가지고 가야될 비밀이야!

### B He is a superman!

1. I opened the jar ________ my older brother couldn't open!
   나는 형이 열지 못했던 병을 열었어!
2. There isn't a jar ________ I can't open! 내가 열 수 없는 병은 없어!
3. In the arm-wrestling contest, I beat the boy ________ I couldn't beat last year.
   (*arm-wrestling: 팔씨름)
   나는 팔씨름 대회에서 작년에는 이길 수 없었던 그 소년을 이겼어.

4. You are the strongest boy ________ I've ever seen!
   너는 내가 지금껏 본 가장 힘센 소년이야!
5. No, my dad is the strongest man ________ I've ever seen.
   아니야, 우리 아빠가 내가 지금껏 본 가장 힘센 사람이야.



정답과 해설 p.8

## ⓒ She is sad.

1. She fought with her friend __________ she often plays with.
   그녀는 그녀가 자주 같이 노는 그녀의 친구와 싸웠어.

2. She lost her watch __________ she likes the most.
   그녀는 그녀가 가장 좋아하는 시계를 잃어버렸어.

3. I found the watch __________ she lost!
   나는 그녀가 잃어버린 시계를 찾았어!

4. She is the girl __________ I like most in the world!
   그녀는 내가 이 세상에서 제일 좋아하는 소녀야!

## Ⓓ Memories

1. I want the bike __________ Mina has.
   나는 미나가 가지고 있는 자전거를 원해요.

2. Why don't you ride your bike __________ I bought for you?
   내가 너에게 사주었던 너의 자전거를 타는 게 어떠니?

3. It is too old. It's the one __________ you bought for me when I was young!
   그건 너무 낡았어요. 그건 내가 어렸을 때 나에게 사주신 거잖아요!

4. The old things __________ you still have are not bad.
   네가 아직도 가지고 있는 오래된 것들은 (상태가) 나쁘지 않단다.

5. You have many memories __________ you share with them.
   너는 그것들과 함께 공유하는 많은 추억들을 가지고 있어. **(*share: 공유하다)**

6. Wasn't the time __________ you spent with them happy?
   네가 그것들과 보냈던 시간이 행복하지 않았니?

정답과 해설 p.8

## Practice 2 선행사에 따른 관계대명사의 알맞은 쓰임을 익혀 보아요.

[1–10] 다음 문장을 읽고 선행사에 동그라미 하세요.

1.

My dad is wearing the sweater which my mom made.

나의 아빠는 엄마가 만든 스웨터를 입고 계셔.

2.

I met the friends whom I like the most.

나는 내가 가장 좋아하는 친구들을 만났어.

3. I have the textbook which we will be using today.

나는 우리가 오늘 사용할 교과서를 갖고 있어. (*textbook: 교과서)

4. He has a dark side which he never shows to anybody.

그는 누구에게도 절대 보여주지 않는 어두운 면이 있어.

5. There's something that I didn't tell you.

내가 너에게 말하지 않았던 게 있어.

6. A laugh is the only weapon that we have. (*weapon: 무기)

웃음은 우리가 가진 유일한 무기야.



정답과 해설 p.8

7. She drew the scene which she saw. (*scene: 장면)

그녀는 그녀가 본 장면을 그렸어.

8. That's the funniest thing that I've ever heard.

내가 지금껏 들어본 가장 웃기는 일이야.

9. Mina caught the ball which I threw to her. (*throw: 던지다)

미나는 내가 그녀에게 던진 공을 잡았어.

10. It's a secret which I didn't tell to anybody.

그것은 내가 아무에게도 말하지 않은 비밀이야.

**[11–20] 다음 문장을 읽고, (  ) 안에서 알맞은 관계대명사에 동그라미 하세요.**

11.

He has a pretty cat
( whom / which ) I like.

그는 내가 좋아하는 예쁜 고양이를 가지고 있어.

12.

I will have a Russian Blue Cat
( whom / that ) I like.

나는 내가 좋아하는 러시안 블루 고양이를 키울 거야.

13. The winter vacation ( whom / that ) I've waited for starts today!

내가 기다려왔던 겨울 방학이 오늘 시작돼!

(*wait for: ~을 기다리다)

정답과 해설 p.8

14. I will go sledding ( whom / that ) is interesting.

나는 재미있는 썰매타기를 하러 갈 거야. (*sledding: 썰매타기)

15. The TV show ( whom / which ) Mina's family watched was boring.

미나의 가족이 봤던 TV 쇼는 지루했어.

16. It was an amazing thing ( whom / that ) they experienced.

그것은 그들이 겪었던 신기한 일이었어.

17. 

Tell me everything ( whom / that ) you want for Christmas.

크리스마스에 네가 원하는 모든 것을 나에게 말해봐.

18. 

There are toys ( whom / that ) kids like under the Christmas tree.

아이들이 좋아하는 장난감들이 크리스마스 트리 아래에 있어.

19. It's a miracle that the person ( whom / which ) I like likes me.

내가 좋아하는 사람이 나를 좋아한다는 것은 기적이야.

20. He has some qualities ( who / that ) I don't have. (*quality: 자질)

그는 내가 갖고 있지 않은 몇 가지 자질들을 가지고 있어.



정답과 해설 p.8

## Practice 3 관계대명사가 쓰인 문장을 완성해 보아요.

[1–10] 관계대명사 whom, which, that을 이용하여 두 문장을 한 문장으로 연결하세요.

1. He is a lawyer. + Many people respect him. (*respect: 존경하다)

➔ He is a lawyer whom[that] many people respect.

그는 많은 사람들이 존경하는 변호사야.

2. Look at the mess! + My dog made the mess!

➔ ______________________________!

내 개가 만든 엉망진창인 상태를 봐! (*mess: 엉망진창)

3. Do you remember the boy? + We met the boy at the pool.

➔ ______________________________?

너 우리가 수영장에서 만났던 그 소년을 기억하니?

4. This is the camera.
+ My father gave me the camera.

➔ ______________________________.

이건 나의 아버지가 나에게 준 카메라야.

5. This is the story. + My father read the story to me.

➔ ______________________________.

이건 나의 아버지께서 나에게 읽어주신 이야기야.

6. These are the photos. + I like the photos.

➔ ______________________________.

이것들은 내가 좋아하는 사진들이야.

정답과 해설 p.8

7. My dog tore up the photo. + I love the photo. (*tear up:찢다)

➔ ______________________________________________.

나의 개가 내가 아주 좋아하는 사진을 찢어놨어.

8. They drew a picture of a tiger. + They saw a tiger at the zoo.

➔ ______________________________________________.

그들은 동물원에서 보았던 호랑이의 그림을 그렸어.

9. I like the candies.

+ I bought the candies at the market.

➔ ______________________________________.

나는 시장에서 구입한 그 사탕들이 좋아.

10. The boy always tells lies. + I don't like the boy.

➔ ______________________________________________.

내가 좋아하지 않는 그 소년은 항상 거짓말을 한다.

**[11–20] 다음 우리말 뜻과 같도록 주어진 표현을 순서에 맞게 배열하여 문장을 완성하세요.**

11. They saw ( the picture, I took, that ). 그들은 내가 찍은 사진을 봤어.

➔ They saw the picture that I took.

12. This is ( that, the exam, have to pass, we ).

이건 우리가 통과해야만 하는 시험이야.

➔ This is ______________________________.

13. ( that, you wish, Every dream ) will come true. 네가 원하는 모든 꿈이 이루어질 거야.

➔ ______________________________ will come true.



정답과 해설 p.8

14. There is ( no one, can talk to, I ). 내가 얘기할 수 있는 사람이 아무도 없어.

➔ There is ______________________.

15. He is ( have, the nicest teacher, we )!

그는 우리가 가진 가장 훌륭한 선생님이에요!

➔ He is ______________________!

16. (The one thing, wanted, that, I ) was a Nintendo!

내가 원했던 한 가지는 닌텐도였어요!

➔ ______________________ was a Nintendo!

17. ( whom, met yesterday, I, The girl ) was David's sister.

내가 어제 만난 소녀는 David의 여동생이었어.

➔ ______________________

was David's sister.

18. ( I talked to, The man, whom ) was very nice.

내가 이야기를 했던 그 남자는 매우 멋졌어.

➔ ______________________ was very nice.

19. ( that, the bravest thing, was, Going to the market ) he has ever done.

시장에 가는 것은 그가 지금껏 한 가장 용감한 일이었어. (*brave: 용감한)

➔ ______________________

he has ever done.

20. ( which, The tofu, he bought ) is delicious!

그가 산 두부는 맛있어! (*tofu: 두부)

➔ ______________________

is delicious!

정답과 해설 p.9

# Let's Practice More!

SET 01

학습목표 1 | 목적격 관계대명사의 개념을 익혀 보아요. 공부한 날 : 맞은 개수 : /12개

밑줄 친 부분이 뒤의 문장에서 목적어 역할을 하고 있으면 ○표, 아니면 ×표 하세요.

01. You should read the book which is on my desk. → ×
너는 내 책상 위에 있는 책을 읽어야 해.

02. The man whom Mina met was not Santa. → ____
미나가 만났던 그 남자는 산타가 아니었어.

03. She fought with her friend whom she often plays with. → ____
그녀는 그녀가 자주 같이 노는 그녀의 친구와 싸웠어.

04. He likes everyone who is around him. → ____
그는 자기 주위에 있는 모든 사람들을 좋아해.

05. Wasn't the time which you spent with them happy? → ____
네가 그들과 함께 보냈던 시간이 행복하지 않았니?

06. I met the friends whom I like the most. → ____
나는 내가 가장 좋아하는 친구들을 만났어.

07. They are animals which need to be taken care of. → ____
그들은 보살핌 받을 필요가 있는 동물들이야.

08. It's a secret which I didn't tell anybody. → ____
그것은 내가 아무에게도 말하지 않은 비밀이야.

09. He has a cute hamster which I like. → ____
그는 내가 좋아하는 귀여운 햄스터 한 마리를 가지고 있어.

10. Strawberries are the fruit which is popular in spring. → ____
딸기는 봄에 인기 있는 과일이야.

11. Tell me everything that you want for Christmas. → ____
크리스마스에 네가 원하는 모든 것을 나에게 말해봐.

12. God helps those who help themselves. → ____
하늘은 스스로 돕는 자를 돕는다.



정답과 해설 p.9

# Let's Practice More!

SET 02

학습목표 1 | 목적격 관계대명사의 개념을 익혀 보아요. 공부한 날 : 맞은 개수 : /14개

다음을 읽고 밑줄 친 부분이 목적격 관계대명사면 ○표, 아니면 ×표 하세요.

01. He is the student who plays the piano well. → ×
그는 피아노를 잘 치는 학생이다.

02. You are the strongest boy whom I've ever seen! → ______
너는 내가 지금껏 본 가장 힘센 소년이야!

03. She lost her watch which she likes the most. → ______
그녀는 그녀가 가장 좋아하는 그녀의 시계를 잃어버렸어.

04. She has two dogs which are brown. → ______
그녀는 갈색 강아지 두 마리를 갖고 있어.

05. It's the one which you bought for me when I was little! → ______
그건 내가 어렸을 때 나에게 사주신 거잖아요!

06. I want to do something that is helpful. → ______
나는 도움이 되는 무언가를 하고 싶어.

07. You have many memories which you share with them. → ______
너는 그들과 함께 공유하는 많은 추억들을 가지고 있어.

08. My dad is wearing the sweater which my mom made. → ______
우리 아빠는 엄마가 만든 스웨터를 입고 계셔.

09. We saw the actress who is famous. 우리는 유명한 여배우를 봤어. → ______

10. There is too much homework that is difficult. → ______
어려운 숙제가 너무 많아요.

11. A laugh is the only weapon that we have. → ______
웃음은 우리가 가진 유일한 무기야.

12. He likes everyone who is around him. → ______
그는 자기 주위에 있는 모든 사람들을 좋아해.

13. You have to decide what to do with the time that is given to you. → ______
너는 너에게 주어진 시간에 무엇을 할지를 정해야 해.

14. He has some qualities that I don't have. → ______
그는 내가 갖고 있지 않은 몇 가지 자질들을 가지고 있어.

정답과 해설 p.9

# Let's Practice More!

SET 03

학습목표 1 | 목적격 관계대명사의 개념을 익혀 보아요.    공부한 날 :    맞은 개수 :    /12개

다음 문장을 읽고 밑줄 친 부분이 맞으면 ○표, 아니면 ×표 하세요.

01. I ate some bananas which mom bought them for me. → ×
나는 엄마가 나를 위해 사주신 바나나 몇 개를 먹었다.

02. She is the girl whom I like her! → ________
그녀는 내가 좋아하는 소녀야!

03. Why don't you ride your bike which I bought for you? → ________
내가 너에게 사주었던 너의 자전거를 타는 게 어떠니?

04. I have the textbook which we will be using it today. → ________
나는 우리가 오늘 사용할 교과서를 갖고 있어.

05. There's something that I didn't tell you. → ________
내가 너에게 말하지 않은 게 있어.

06. She drew the scene which she saw. → ________
그녀는 그녀가 본 장면을 그렸어.

07. I will have a Russian Blue that I like it. → ________
나는 내가 좋아하는 러시안 블루 고양이를 키울 거야.

08. The winter vacation that I've waited for starts today! → ________
내가 기다려왔던 겨울 방학이 오늘 시작돼!

09. My dog tore up the photo which I love it. → ________
나의 개가 내가 아주 좋아하는 사진을 찢어 놓았어.

10. This is the exam that we have to pass. → ________
이건 우리가 통과해야만 하는 시험이야.

11. The girl whom I met her yesterday was David's sister. → ________
내가 어제 만난 소녀는 David의 여동생이었어.

12. The man whom I talked with was very nice. → ________
내가 이야기를 했던 그 남자는 매우 멋졌어.



정답과 해설 p.9

# Let's Practice More!

SET 04

**학습목표 2 | 주격 관계대명사와 목적격 관계대명사를 구분해 보아요.** 공부한 날 : 맞은 개수 : /12개

**다음 문장을 읽고 밑줄 친 관계대명사가 주격이면 '주', 목적격이면 '목'이라고 쓰세요.**

01. She drew the scene which she saw. ➜ 목

그녀는 그녀가 본 장면을 그렸어.

02. It is a secret which we should take to our graves! ➜ ______

이건 우리가 우리의 무덤까지 가지고 가야 될 비밀이야!

03. My dad is the strongest man that I've ever seen. ➜ ______

우리 아빠는 내가 지금껏 본 가장 힘센 사람이야.

04. There are toys that kids like under the Christmas tree. ➜ ______

아이들이 좋아하는 장난감들이 크리스마스 트리 아래에 있어.

05. He is a lawyer who helps the poor. ➜ ______

그는 가난한 사람들을 돕는 변호사야.

06. She is a teacher that many people respect. ➜ ______

그녀는 많은 사람들이 존경하는 선생님이야.

07. A person who has good thoughts is always happy. ➜ ______

좋은 생각을 하는 사람은 항상 행복해.

08. It was an amazing thing that they experienced. ➜ ______

그것은 그들이 겪었던 신기한 일이었어.

09. She has two turtles which are very big. ➜ ______

그녀는 매우 큰 거북이 두 마리를 갖고 있어.

10. I have two coupons which can be used to buy ice cream. ➜ ______

나는 아이스크림을 사는 데 쓸 수 있는 쿠폰이 두 장 있어.

11. Look at the mess that my dog made! ➜ ______

내 개가 만든 엉망진창인 상태를 봐!

12. This is the camera which my father gave me. ➜ ______

이건 우리 아빠가 나에게 주신 카메라야.

정답과 해설 p.9

# Let's Practice More!

SET 05

학습목표 3 | 목적격 관계대명사의 특징을 익혀 보아요.　　공부한 날 :　　맞은 개수 :　　/14개

다음 (　) 안에 들어갈 관계대명사로 적절한 것을 고르세요.

01. Do you know the boy ( that / which ) Mina met yesterday?
너는 미나가 어제 만난 소년을 아니?

02. Look at the mess ( which / whom ) my cat made! 내 고양이가 만든 엉망진창인 상태를 봐!

03. There isn't a jar ( whom / that ) I can't open! 내가 열 수 없는 병은 없어!

04. She fought with her friend ( that / which ) she likes the most.
그녀는 그녀가 가장 좋아하는 친구와 싸웠어.

05. I want the bike ( whom / which ) Melissa has.
나는 Melissa가 가지고 있는 자전거를 원해요.

06. He has a dark side ( whom / which ) he never shows to anybody.
그는 누구에게도 절대 보여주지 않는 어두운 면이 있어.

07. It is the funniest thing ( that / whom ) I've ever heard.
그건 내가 지금껏 들어본 가장 웃기는 일이야.

08. Do you remember the boy ( whom / which ) we met at the pool?
너는 우리가 수영장에서 만났던 그 소년을 기억하니?

09. This is the story ( that / whom ) my father read to me.
이건 나의 아버지께서 나에게 읽어주신 이야기야.

10. The boy ( whom / which ) I don't like always tells lies.
내가 좋아하지 않는 그 소년은 항상 거짓말을 한다.

11. Every dream ( that / whom ) you wish will come true.
네가 원하는 모든 꿈이 이루어질 거야.

12. The TV show ( whom / which ) Mina's family watched was boring.
미나의 가족이 봤던 TV쇼는 지루했어.

13. You are the tallest man ( that / which ) I've ever seen.
너는 내가 지금껏 본 가장 키 큰 사람이야.

14. Wasn't the time ( that / whom ) you spent with your friends amazing?
네가 너의 친구들과 보냈던 시간이 굉장하지 않았니?



정답과 해설 p.9

# Let's Practice More!

SET 06

학습목표 3 | 목적격 관계대명사의 특징을 익혀 보아요. 공부한 날 : 맞은 개수 : /14개

다음 문장을 읽고 밑줄 친 부분이 맞으면 ○표, 틀리면 고쳐 써 보세요.

01. He has a pretty cat whom I like. → which[that]

그는 내가 좋아하는 예쁜 고양이를 가지고 있다.

02. Santa brought me the computer whom I wanted! → ______

산타는 내가 원했던 컴퓨터를 나에게 가져다줬어!

03. The man that Charlotte met was not Santa. → ______

Charlotte이 만났던 그 남자는 산타가 아니었어.

04. In the arm-wrestling contest, I beat the boy which I couldn't beat last year. 나는 팔씨름 대회에서 작년에는 이길 수 없었던 그 소년을 이겼어. → ______

05. I found the ring whom he lost! 나는 그가 잃어버린 반지를 찾았어! → ______

06. My little brother is wearing the pants that my mom made. → ______

내 남동생은 엄마가 만든 바지를 입고 있어.

07. We met the friends whom we like the most! → ______

우리는 우리가 가장 좋아하는 친구들을 만났어!

08. Mina caught the ball whom I threw to her. → ______

미나는 내가 그녀에게 던진 공을 잡았어.

09. There isn't a jar that I can't open! 내가 열 수 없는 병은 없어! → ______

10. These are the photos whom I like. → ______

이것들은 내가 좋아하는 사진들이야.

11. There is no one that I can talk to. → ______

내가 얘기할 수 있는 사람이 아무도 없어.

12. He is the nicest teacher that we have! → ______

그는 우리가 가진 가장 훌륭한 선생님이에요!

13. Going to the market was the bravest thing that he has ever done. 시장에 가는 것은 그가 지금껏 한 가장 용감한 일이었어. → ______

14. The tofu whom he bought was delicious. → ______

그가 산 두부는 맛있었어.

정답과 해설 p.9

# Let's Practice More!

SET 07

학습목표 3 | 목적격 관계대명사의 특징을 익혀 보아요.　　공부한 날 :　　맞은 개수 :　　/20개

다음 문장을 읽고 (　) 안에서 올바른 것을 고르세요.

01. This is the girl who I ( like / likes ).

이 사람이 내가 좋아하는 여자애야.

02. She has a lovely voice that I ( like / likes ).

그녀는 내가 좋아하는 사랑스러운 목소리를 갖고 있어.

03. Sarah fought with her friends whom she often ( play / plays ) with.

Sarah는 그녀가 자주 같이 노는 그녀의 친구들과 싸웠어.

04. I lost my bag which I ( like / likes ) the most.

나는 내가 가장 좋아하는 가방을 잃어버렸어.

05. She is drawing the scene which she ( see / sees ).

그녀는 그녀가 보는 풍경을 그리고 있는 중이야.

06. The old things that you still have ( is / are ) not bad.

네가 아직도 가지고 있는 오래된 것들은 (상태가) 나쁘지 않단다.

07. I have a dark side which I never ( show / shows ) to anybody.

나는 누구에게도 절대 보여주지 않는 어두운 면을 가지고 있어.

08. A laugh is the only weapon that we ( has / have ).

웃음은 우리가 가진 유일한 무기야.

09. We have a cute turtle which we ( love / loves ).

우리는 우리가 사랑하는 귀여운 거북이 한 마리를 가지고 있어.



정답과 해설 p.9

10. The movie which my friend and I saw ( was / were ) fantastic.
내 친구와 내가 본 영화는 환상적이었어.

11. Tell your parents everything that you ( want / wants ) for Christmas.
크리스마스에 네가 원하는 모든 것을 너의 부모님께 말씀드려.

12. He is the nicest teacher that we ( has / have )!
그는 우리가 가진 가장 훌륭한 선생님이에요!

13. They are lawyers whom many people ( respect / respects ).
그들은 많은 사람들이 존경하는 변호사들이야.

14. The girl that I don't like always ( tell / tells ) lies.
내가 좋아하지 않는 그 소녀는 항상 거짓말을 한다.

15. The exam we have to pass ( is / are ) not easy.
우리가 통과해야만 하는 시험은 쉽지 않다.

16. The cake he bought for us ( was / were ) delicious!
그가 우리를 위해 사온 케이크는 맛있었어!

17. We have many memories that we ( share / shares ) together.
우리는 우리가 함께 공유하는 많은 추억들을 가지고 있어.

18. I want the bike that Mina ( has / have ).
나는 미나가 가지고 있는 자전거를 원해요.

19. The guy whom Emily met ( was / were ) not Tom.
Emily가 만났던 남자는 Tom이 아니었다.

20. I will buy a blue car that I ( like / likes ).
나는 내가 좋아하는 파란색 자동차를 살 거야.

정답과 해설 p.9

# Let's Practice More!

SET 08

학습목표 4 | 목적격 관계대명사의 생략을 연습해 보아요. 공부한 날 : 맞은 개수 : /20개

밑줄 친 부분을 생략할 수 있으면 ○표, 생략할 수 없으면 ×표 하세요.

01.

This is the book which I want.

이것이 내가 원하는 책이다.

→ ○

02.

There is no one that I can talk to.

내가 얘기할 수 있는 사람이 아무도 없어.

→ ______

03. They found the laptop which I lost a week ago. → ______

그들은 내가 일주일 전에 잃어버린 노트북 컴퓨터를 찾아주었어.

04. Wasn't the time which we spent together happy? → ______

우리가 함께 보냈던 시간이 행복하지 않았니?

05. There's something that matters even more. → ______

훨씬 더 중요한 무언가가 있어.

06. Our teacher has the workbook which we will be using today. → ______

우리 선생님은 우리가 오늘 사용할 워크북을 갖고 계셔.

07. I saw the actress who is beautiful. → ______

나는 아름다운 여배우를 봤어.

08. The spring break that I've waited for starts today! → ______

내가 기다려왔던 봄 방학이 오늘 시작돼!

09. People who harm animals should be punished. → ______

동물들을 해치는 사람들은 처벌 받아야 해.



정답과 해설 p.9

10. A detective is a person who is good at finding things. ➔ ________

형사는 무언가를 찾는 데 능숙한 사람이야.

11. The one thing that I wanted was a Nintendo! ➔ ________

내가 원했던 한 가지는 닌텐도였어요!

12. The woman whom I met yesterday was David's mom. ➔ ________

내가 어제 만났던 여자는 David의 엄마였어.

13. Can we use your iPad that is in your bag? ➔ ________

우리가 당신의 가방에 있는 아이패드를 사용해도 되나요?

14.

The man whom I talked to was very kind.

내가 이야기를 했던 그 남자는 매우 친절했어.

➔ ________

15.

Is he the boy who hates you?

그가 너를 싫어하는 남자애니?

➔ ________

16. They drew a picture of a tiger that they saw at the zoo. ➔ ________

그들은 동물원에서 보았던 호랑이의 그림을 그렸어.

17. I like the candies which I bought at the market. ➔ ________

나는 시장에서 구입한 그 사탕들이 좋아.

18. Jennifer is my friend who has a dark side. ➔ ________

Jennifer는 어두운 면이 있는 내 친구야.

19. My mom is the strongest woman whom I've ever seen. ➔ ________

우리 엄마는 내가 지금껏 본 가장 힘센 여자야.

20. I like people who make donations to charities. ➔ ________

나는 자선 단체에 기부를 하는 사람들이 좋아.

CH 03

정답과 해설 p.9

# Chapter 04 관계대명사 what / 관계부사

이 챕터에서는 선행사를 포함하는
관계대명사 what과 관계부사에 대해 알아보아요.

☆ 학습 방향 및 배울 내용 미리보기 ☆

☐ **Unit 01 :** This is **what** I like.

**관계대명사 what**

앞에 선행사가 오지 않는 특수한 관계대명사 what의 특징을 배워 보아요.

▼

☐ **Unit 02 :** That's **how** we learned English.

**관계부사**

선행사로 시간, 장소, 이유, 방법 중 무엇이 오는지에 따라 어떤 관계부사를 쓰는지 익혀 보아요.

## 단어 미리보기

이 챕터에 나올 단어들 중 이미 알고 있는 단어가 있나요?
맞는 뜻을 골라 체크해 봐요.

날짜 :　　　이름 :　　　알고 있는 단어의 수 :　　　/24개

| No. | 아는 단어 | 단어 | 품사 | 알맞은 뜻에 체크 표시해 봐요. | | | |
|---|---|---|---|---|---|---|---|
| 1 | ✔ | cook | 동사 | 요리하다 | ✔ | 주문하다 | ☐ |
| 2 | ☐ | hear | 동사 | 말하다 | ☐ | 듣다 | ☐ |
| 3 | ☐ | surprising | 형용사 | 놀라운 | ☐ | 걱정되는 | ☐ |
| 4 | ☐ | way | 명사 | 방귀 | ☐ | 방법 | ☐ |
| 5 | ☐ | enter | 동사 | 들어가다 | ☐ | 나오다 | ☐ |
| 6 | ☐ | easy | 형용사 | 쉬운 | ☐ | 어려운 | ☐ |
| 7 | ☐ | believe | 동사 | 거짓말하다 | ☐ | 믿다 | ☐ |
| 8 | ☐ | act | 동사 | 때리다 | ☐ | 행동하다 | ☐ |
| 9 | ☐ | place | 명사 | 시간 | ☐ | 장소 | ☐ |
| 10 | ☐ | universe | 명사 | 우주 | ☐ | 정거장 | ☐ |
| 11 | ☐ | end | 동사 | 시작하다 | ☐ | 끝내다 | ☐ |
| 12 | ☐ | chopstick | 명사 | 숟가락 | ☐ | 젓가락 | ☐ |
| 13 | ☐ | worried | 형용사 | 걱정하는 | ☐ | 즐거운 | ☐ |
| 14 | ☐ | pants | 명사 | 치마 | ☐ | 바지 | ☐ |
| 15 | ☐ | hug | 동사 | 포옹하다 | ☐ | 입맞춤하다 | ☐ |
| 16 | ☐ | moment | 명사 | 순간 | ☐ | 포착 | ☐ |
| 17 | ☐ | free | 형용사 | 바쁜 | ☐ | 한가한 | ☐ |
| 18 | ☐ | must | 조동사 | ~할 것이다 | ☐ | ~해야 한다 | ☐ |
| 19 | ☐ | late | 형용사 | 늦은 | ☐ | 이른 | ☐ |
| 20 | ☐ | cold | 명사 | 감기 | ☐ | 기운 | ☐ |
| 21 | ☐ | together | 부사 | 따로 | ☐ | 함께 | ☐ |
| 22 | ☐ | reason | 명사 | 이유 | ☐ | 기억 | ☐ |
| 23 | ☐ | living room | 명사 | 화장실 | ☐ | 거실 | ☐ |
| 24 | ☐ | large | 형용사 | 작은 | ☐ | 큰 | ☐ |

관계대명사 what

# UNIT 01 This is what I like.

## ❖ POiNT 1 ❖

**선행사를 포함하는 특수한 관계대명사 what**

**관계대명사 what은 선행사를 포함하는 관계대명사이기 때문에 앞에 선행사가 없고, '~하는 것' 이라고 해석해요.**

**1단계**

This is the cake. + I like this cake.
사물 목적어
이것은 케이크야. 나는 이 케이크를 좋아해.

**2단계**

This is the cake which[that] I like.
선행사 목적격 관계대명사(사물)
이것은 내가 좋아하는 케이크야.

**3단계**

This is what I like.
the cake which[that]
이것은 내가 좋아하는 것이야.

## ❖ POiNT 2 ❖

**기억해요!**

**관계대명사 what은 the thing which로 고쳐 쓸 수 있어요!**
**관계대명사 what 앞에는 선행사가 없고 뒤의 문장에 목적어가 오지 않아요!**

Do you know what she likes?
= Do you know the thing which she likes?
너는 그녀가 좋아하는 것을 아니?

Do you know what she likes it? (x)

## Check and Write

빈칸에 which와 what 중 적절한 관계대명사를 쓰세요.

1. I have [ what ] you gave to me.
나는 네가 나에게 준 것을 가지고 있어.

2. She ate [   ] her mother cooked for her.
그녀는 그녀의 엄마가 그녀를 위해 요리한 것을 먹었어.

3. There is a lot of food [   ] I can eat.
내가 먹을 수 있는 음식이 많이 있어.

4. [   ] I heard is surprising.
내가 들은 것은 놀라워.

5. Do you know the song [   ] she likes?
너는 그녀가 좋아하는 노래를 아니?

정답과 해설 p.9

# UNIT 02 That's how we learned English.

❖ POiNT ❖

**관계부사는 문장에서 부사를 대신하고, 선행사로 시간, 장소, 이유, 방법을 나타내는 단어들이 와요.**
**또한, 관계부사는 부사를 대신하기 때문에 뒤에 오는 문장이 완전하다는 걸 명심하세요!**

| 선행사 | 관계부사 |
|---|---|
| 시간 (the time, the day, the month 등) | when |
| 장소 (the place, the city, the country 등) | where |
| 이유 (the reason) | why |
| 방법 (the way) | how |

I know the time. + My mom will come back home at that time.
(the time: 선행사 / at that time: 부사)

나는 시간을 안다. 우리 엄마가 그때에 집에 돌아오실 것이다.

**두 문장을 연결하기 위해서 선행사 뒤에 시간을 나타내는 관계부사 when을 쓰고, 뒤의 문장 전체를 선행사를 꾸며주는 형용사처럼 해석해요.**

⇨ I know the time when my mom will come back home.
(the time: 선행사 / when: 관계부사)

나는 우리 엄마가 집에 돌아오실 시간을 알아.

This is the reason. + He did it for this reason.
(the reason: 선행사 / for this reason: 부사)

이것은 그 이유이다. 그가 이 이유 때문에 그것을 했다.

**두 문장을 연결하기 위해서 선행사 뒤에 이유를 나타내는 관계부사 why를 써요.**

⇨This is the reason why he did it. 이것은 그가 그것을 한 이유이다.
(the reason: 선행사 / why: 관계부사)

**단! 선행사 the way와 관계부사 how는 동시에 쓰지 않고 꼭 둘 중에 하나만 쓸 수 있어요.**

That's the way. + We learned English in this way.
그게 방식이야. 우리는 이런 방식으로 영어를 배웠어.

That's how we learned English. = That's the way we learned English.
그게 우리가 영어를 배웠던 방식이야.

# Check and Write

다음 보기 중 적절한 관계부사를 찾아 빈칸에 쓰세요. (중복 사용 가능)

| 보기 | when | where | why | how |
|---|---|---|---|---|

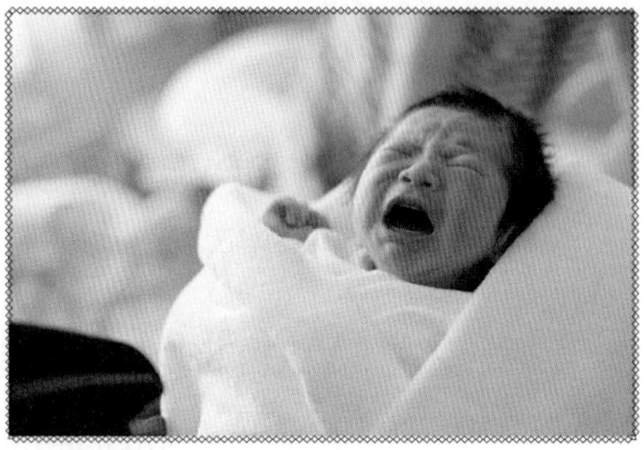

1. Do you know the place [ where ] you were born?
너는 네가 태어났던 장소를 아니?

2. This is [ ] she made the pie.
이것이 그녀가 파이를 만든 방법이야.

3. I'll never forget the day [ ] we won the game.
나는 우리가 그 경기에서 이겼던 날을 잊지 못할 거야.

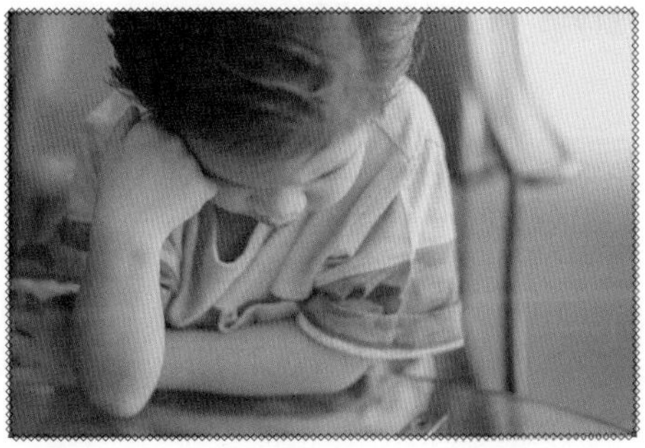

4. He didn't tell me the reason [ ] he was angry.
그는 그가 화난 이유를 내게 말하지 않았어.

5. I went to Paris [ ] Eric lives.
나는 Eric이 살고 있는 파리에 갔어.

정답과 해설 p.9

## Practice 1 관계대명사 what과 관계부사의 알맞은 쓰임을 익혀 보아요.

다음 문장에 알맞은 표현을 보기 에서 골라 빈칸에 알맞게 써 보세요. (중복 사용 가능)

### A We are together!

보기 when why What how where

1. I'll never forget the day ___when___ we first won the game.
   나는 우리가 그 경기에서 처음으로 이겼던 날을 절대 잊지 않을 거야.

2. We played soccer on the field ________ it was slippery. (*slippery: 미끄러운)
   우리는 미끄러웠던 경기장에서 축구를 했어.
3. That's the reason ________ I caught a cold that day. 그게 내가 그날 감기에 걸린 이유야.
4. But that's ________ we play the game.
   하지만 그게 우리가 경기를 하는 방식이야.
5. ________ is important to us is the time when we are together. 우리에게 중요한 것은 우리가 같이 있는 시간이야.

### B Mom was angry!

보기 when the way where why what

1. Mom told me the reason ________ she was so angry.
   엄마는 나에게 그녀가 왜 그렇게 화가 났는지 말해주셨어.
2. Dad didn't remember the day ________ they first met.
   아빠는 그들이 처음 만났던 날을 기억하지 못하셨어.
3. Dad went to the flower shop ________ he first bought the flowers for her. 아빠는 그가 그녀를 위해 처음으로 꽃을 샀던 꽃집에 가셨어.
4. He gave her ________ she likes.
   그는 그녀에게 그녀가 좋아하는 것을 주셨어.



정답과 해설 p.9

5. That's ________________ he says sorry.
그것이 그가 미안하다고 말하는 방식이야.

## C Do not fight!

보기 what where the way why

1. I don't like ________________ she reads my thoughts.
나는 그녀가 내 생각들을 읽는 방식이 맘에 안 들어.

2. That is the reason ________________ we fought.
그게 우리가 싸운 이유야.

3. I felt really bad about ________________ I did.
나는 내가 했던 것에 대해 정말로 기분이 좋지 않았어.

4. So, I went to the house ________________ she lived.
그래서 나는 그녀가 사는 집에 갔어.

5. I'm sorry about ________________ I acted. 내가 행동한 방식에 대해 미안해.

6. She also felt sorry about ________________ she did.
그녀도 그녀가 했던 것에 대해 미안하게 생각했어.

## D Come to my house!

보기 where why what

1. My house has many rooms ________________ we can study.
나의 집은 우리가 공부할 수 있는 방이 많아.

2. We have a large living room ________________
there is a big table. 우리는 큰 테이블 하나가 있는 큰 거실이 있어.

3. Mom cooks us ________________ we want.
엄마는 우리에게 우리가 원하는 것을 요리해주셔.

4. That's ________________ my friends like to come to my house.
그게 내 친구들이 우리 집에 오기를 좋아하는 이유야.

정답과 해설 p.9

## Practice 2 관계대명사 what과 관계부사를 상황에 맞게 쓸 수 있어요.

[1 – 10] 다음 문장을 읽고, 우리말 뜻을 참고하여 ( ) 안에서 알맞은 것을 골라 동그라미 하세요.

1.

( Which / What ) she wants to be is a cook.

그녀가 되고 싶은 것은 요리사야.

2.

Last year was the year ( what / when ) I entered school.

작년은 내가 학교에 입학한 해야.

3. That's ( what / the way ) we start the day.

그것은 우리가 하루를 시작하는 방식이야.

4. This is the school ( where / what ) my older brother goes.

이곳은 나의 형이 다니는 학교야.

5. Do you remember the day ( which / when ) you were late for school?

너 학교에 지각했던 날 기억해?

6. She told me the reason ( where / why ) she liked him.

그녀는 내게 그녀가 그를 좋아했던 이유를 말해줬어.



정답과 해설 p.9

7. This is ( that / what ) we were looking for!
이게 우리가 찾고 있던 거야!

8. We must choose between ( which / what ) is right and ( which / what ) is easy.
우리는 옳은 것과 쉬운 것 사이에서 선택해야 한다.



9. You become ( what / that ) you believe.
당신은 당신이 믿는 것이(믿는대로) 된다.

10. I recall the time ( when / where ) I was happy. (*recall: 떠올리다)
나는 내가 행복했었던 시간을 떠올려.

**[11 – 20] 우리말 뜻을 참고하여 다음 문장의 빈칸에 when, where, why, how 중에서 알맞은 관계부사를 써 보세요.**

11.

Taking a nap is ___how___ I refresh myself.
낮잠 자는 건 내가 기운을 되찾는 방법이야.
(*refresh oneself: 기운을 되찾다)

12.

He likes the times ________ he plays computer games.
그는 컴퓨터 게임을 하는 시간을 좋아해.

13. This is ________ we use chopsticks.
이게 우리가 젓가락을 사용하는 방식이야.

정답과 해설 p.9

14. I know the city ___________ I was born.
나는 내가 태어난 도시를 알아.

15. That's the reason ___________ we are worried.
그것이 우리가 걱정하는 이유야.

16. Tell me ___________ I can make up with him. (*make up with: ~와 화해하다)
나에게 그와 화해할 수 있는 방법을 말해줘.

17.

This is the reason ___________ they fought.
이게 그들이 싸운 이유야.

18.

This is the place ___________ they first met.
이곳은 그들이 처음 만났던 장소야.

19. That's the reason ___________ the baby is crying.
그게 그 아기가 울고 있는 이유야.

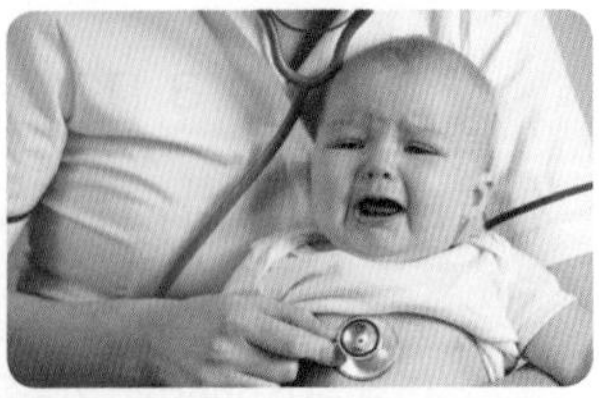

20. I want to know ___________ the universe began.
나는 우주가 어떻게 시작되었는지 알고 싶어. (*universe: 우주)

정답과 해설 p.9

## Practice 3 관계대명사 what과 관계부사가 쓰인 문장을 완성해 보아요.

다음 우리말 뜻과 같도록 주어진 표현을 순서에 맞게 배열하여 문장을 완성하세요.

1. ( what, Collecting stamps, he does, is ) in his free time.
우표 수집은 그가 여가시간에 하는 일이야.

➔ Collecting stamps is what he does ________ in his free time.

2. Could you tell me ( how, can get there, I )?
내가 거기에 도착하는 방법을 말해 줄 수 있나요?

➔ Could you tell me ________________ ________________?

3. ( we can do, What, with computers ) is amazing.
컴퓨터로 우리가 할 수 있는 것은 놀라워.

➔ ________________ is amazing.

4. I would like to ( what, show you, I've learned ).
나는 내가 배운 것을 너에게 보여주고 싶어.

➔ I would like to ________________.

5. Swimming is ( do now, what, want to, I ). 수영이 내가 지금 하고 싶은 거야.
➔ Swimming is ________________.

6. I'm looking for ( lost yesterday, I, what ). 나는 어제 내가 잃어버린 것을 찾고 있어.
➔ I'm looking for ________________.

정답과 해설 p.9

7. That's ( I, wanted to tell you, what ). 그게 내가 너에게 말하고 싶었던 거야.

➔ That's ______________________________________________.

8. ( bought, they, What ) was delicious.

그들이 산 것은 맛있었어.

➔ ____________________ was delicious.

9. Mina ( she likes, what, only eats ).

미나는 그녀가 좋아하는 것만 먹어.

➔ Mina ____________________ ____________________.

10. ( I, That's, do, what ) to end the day.

그게 내가 하루를 마무리하기 위해 하는 거야.

➔ ______________________________ to end the day.

11. ( I did, I felt bad about, what ). 나는 내가 한 것에 대해 기분이 좋지 않았어.

➔ ______________________________________________.

12. She pretends she didn't hear ( heard, she, what ).

그녀는 그녀가 들은 것을 못 들은 척 해.

➔ She pretends she didn't hear ______________________________.

13. I remember ( where, we, the place, first met ).

나는 우리가 처음 만났던 장소를 기억해.

➔ I remember ______________________________________.



정답과 해설 p.9

14. He walked to the school ( where, studies, she ).
그는 그녀가 공부하는 학교로 걸어갔어.

➔ He walked to the school ______________________________.

15. I won't forget ( when, she, the moment, hugged me ).
나는 그녀가 나를 안아줬던 순간을 잊지 않을 거야.

➔ I won't forget __________
______________________
______________________.

16. This is ( why, got married, the reason, they ).
이것이 그들이 결혼한 이유야.

➔ This is ______________
______________________
______________________.

17. ( said, she, What ) made me laugh.
그녀가 말한 것이 나를 웃게 했어.

➔ ______________________ made me laugh.

18. They wait for ( when, will be together, the day, they ).
그들은 그들이 함께 있게 될 날을 기다려.

➔ They wait for ______________________________.

19. What is ( why, like those pants, the reason, you )?
네가 저 바지를 좋아하는 이유가 뭐니?

➔ What is ______________________________?

20. We can't believe ( they, what, said ). 우리는 그들이 말한 것을 믿을 수 없어.

➔ We can't believe ______________________________.

# Let's Practice More!

SET 01

학습목표 1 | 관계대명사 what의 개념을 익혀 보아요. 공부한 날 : 맞은 개수 : /12개

다음 문장을 읽고 ( ) 안에서 알맞은 것을 골라 동그라미 하세요.

01. This is ( which / what ) I like.
이것이 내가 좋아하는 것이다.

02. Do you know the song ( which / what ) she likes?
너는 그녀가 좋아하는 노래를 아니?

03. My dad gave me cookies ( which / what ) I like the most.
나의 아빠는 내가 가장 좋아하는 쿠키를 주셨다.

04. I felt really bad about ( which / what ) I did.
나는 내가 했던 것에 대해 정말로 기분이 좋지 않았어.

05. Mom bakes the cake ( which / what ) we've wanted.
엄마는 우리가 원했던 그 케이크를 구우신다.

06. She also felt sorry about ( which / what ) she did.
그녀도 그녀가 했던 것에 대해 미안하게 생각했어.

07. We must choose between ( which / what ) is right and ( which / what ) is easy.
우리는 옳은 것과 쉬운 것 사이에서 선택해야 한다.

08. You become ( which / what ) you believe.
당신은 당신이 믿는 것이(믿는대로) 된다.

09. That's the thing ( which / what ) I do to end the day.
그게 내가 하루를 마무리하기 위해 하는 거야.

10. Swimming is ( which / what ) I want to do now.
수영이 내가 지금 하고 싶은 거야.

11. I'm looking for ( which / what ) I lost yesterday.
나는 어제 내가 잃어버린 것을 찾고 있어.

12. It is a very important thing ( which / what ) I wanted to tell you.
내가 너에게 말하고 싶었던 것은 매우 중요한 것이야.



정답과 해설 p.10

# Let's Practice More!

SET 02

학습목표 1 | 관계대명사 what의 개념을 익혀 보아요. 공부한 날 : 맞은 개수 : /14개

다음 중 밑줄 친 부분이 맞으면 ○표, 틀리면 ×표 하세요.

01. Do you know the thing what she likes? → ×
너는 그녀가 좋아하는 것을 아니?

02. This is what I like it. → ______
이것이 내가 좋아하는 것이다.

03. Mina only eats which she likes. → ______
미나는 그녀가 좋아하는 것만 먹어.

04. What they bought was delicious. → ______
그들이 산 것은 맛있었어.

05. I felt bad about what I did. → ______
나는 내가 한 것에 대해 기분이 좋지 않았어.

06. She pretends she didn't hear what she heard it. → ______
그녀는 그녀가 들은 것을 못 들은 척해.

07. We can't believe what they said. → ______
우리는 그들이 말한 것을 믿을 수 없어.

08. Something what she said made me laugh. → ______
그녀가 말한 것이 나를 웃게 했어.

09. He gave her what she likes. → ______
그는 그녀에게 그녀가 좋아하는 것을 주었어.

10. Mom cooks us what we want. → ______
엄마는 우리에게 우리가 원하는 것을 요리해주셔.

11. Collecting stamps is my hobby what I do in my free time. → ______
우표 수집은 내가 여가시간에 하는 일이야.

12. Shopping is what I want to do now. → ______
쇼핑이 내가 지금 하고 싶은 거야.

13. It is which I do to end the day. → ______
그것이 내가 하루를 마무리하기 위해 하는 거야.

14. I'm looking for what I want to be. → ______
나는 내가 되고 싶은 것을 찾는 중이야.



정답과 해설 p.10

# Let's Practice More!

SET 03

학습목표 1 | 관계대명사 what의 개념을 익혀 보아요. 공부한 날 : 맞은 개수 : /14개

다음 밑줄 친 부분의 우리말 해석으로 올바른 것을 고르세요.

01. This is the cake which I like. ( 내가 좋아하는 것 / 내가 좋아하는 )

02. This is what I like. ( 내가 좋아하는 것 / 내가 좋아하는 )

03. She felt good about what I did. ( 내가 했던 것 / 내가 한 )

04. Try this cake which I baked just now. ( 내가 구운 것 / 내가 구운 )

05. Nobody will believe what you said. ( 네가 말한 것 / 네가 말한 )

06. He bought what he needed. ( 그가 필요했던 것 / 그가 필요했던 )

07. You become what you believe. ( 네가 믿는 것 / 네가 믿는 )

08. She knows what she can do. ( 그녀가 할 수 있는 것 / 그녀가 할 수 있는)

09. I like the candies which I bought in the market. ( 내가 산 것 / 내가 산 )

10. What I need now is just water. ( 내가 필요한 것 / 내가 필요한 )

11. I am looking for the restaurant which he loved. ( 그가 사랑했던 것 / 그가 사랑했던 )

12. Jinsu has some photos which I took. ( 내가 찍은 것 / 내가 찍은 )

13. What he said is true. ( 그가 말한 것 / 그가 말한)

14. What I heard from you is shocking. ( 내가 들은 것 / 내가 들은 )



정답과 해설 p.10

# Let's Practice More!

SET 04

**학습목표 2 | 관계부사의 개념을 익혀 보아요.** 공부한 날 : 맞은 개수 : /12개



**다음 밑줄 친 부분을 보고 ( )에서 알맞은 관계부사를 고르세요.**

01. I know the time ( when / how ) mom will come back.
나는 엄마가 돌아오실 시간을 알아.

02. I'll never forget the day ( when / where ) we first won the game.
나는 우리가 그 경기에서 처음으로 이겼던 날을 절대 잊지 않을 거야.

03. That's the reason ( why / how ) I caught a cold that day.
그게 내가 그날 감기에 걸린 이유야.

04. I know the city ( where / when ) I was born.
나는 내가 태어난 도시를 알아.

05. What is important to us is the time ( when / why ) we are together.
우리에게 중요한 것은 우리가 같이 있는 시간이야.

06. Mom told me the reason ( why / when ) she was so angry.
엄마는 나에게 그녀가 왜 그렇게 화가 났는지 말해주셨어.

07. Dad didn't remember the day ( when / how ) they first met.
아빠는 그들이 처음 만났던 날을 기억하지 못하셨어.

08. I recall the time ( where / when ) I was happy.
나는 내가 행복했었던 시간을 떠올려.

09. My house has many rooms ( where / how ) we can study.
나의 집은 우리가 공부할 수 있는 방이 많아.

10. That's the reason ( when / why ) my friends like to come to my house.
그게 내 친구들이 우리 집에 오기를 좋아하는 이유야.

11. Last year was the year ( when / where ) I entered school.
작년은 내가 학교에 입학한 해야.

12. This is the place ( when / where ) they first met.
이곳은 그들이 처음 만났던 장소야.

정답과 해설 p.10

# Let's Practice More!

SET 05

**학습목표 2 | 관계부사의 개념을 익혀 보아요.** 공부한 날 : 맞은 개수 : /14개

**다음 중 밑줄 친 부분이 맞으면 ○표, 틀리면 ×표 하세요.**

01. This is <u>the way how</u> we learned English. → ×
이게 우리가 영어를 배웠던 방식이야.

02. We played soccer on <u>the field where</u> it was slippery. → ______
우리는 미끄러웠던 경기장에서 축구를 했어.

03. This was <u>the way why</u> we play the game. → ______
이것이 우리가 경기를 하는 방식이었어.

04. That is <u>the reason why</u> we fought. → ______
그게 우리가 싸운 이유야.

05. I'm sorry about <u>the way where</u> I acted. → ______
내가 행동한 방식에 대해 미안해.

06. We have <u>a large living room how</u> there is a big table. → ______
우리는 큰 테이블 하나가 있는 큰 거실이 있어.

07. Do you remember <u>the day when</u> you were late for school? → ______
너 학교에 지각했던 날 기억해?

08. Sarah told me <u>the reason why</u> she liked him. → ______
Sarah는 나에게 그녀가 그를 좋아했던 이유를 말해줬어.

09. Taking a nap is <u>how</u> I refresh myself. → ______
낮잠 자는 건 내가 기운을 되찾는 방법이야.

10. That's <u>the reason why</u> we are worried. → ______
그것이 우리가 걱정하는 이유야.

11. I remember <u>the place why</u> we first met. → ______
나는 우리가 처음 만났던 장소를 기억해.

12. I won't forget <u>the moment when</u> she hugged me. → ______
나는 그녀가 나를 안았던 순간을 잊지 않을 거야.

13. Tell me <u>the reason how</u> I can make up with him. → ______
나에게 그와 화해할 수 있는 방법을 말해줘.

14. I don't know <u>the reason why</u> the baby is crying. → ______
나는 그 아기가 울고 있는 이유를 모르겠어.



정답과 해설 p.10

# Let's Practice More!

SET 06

학습목표 2 | 관계부사의 개념을 익혀 보아요. 공부한 날 : 맞은 개수 : /14개

우리말 뜻을 참고하여 다음 문장의 밑줄 친 부분이 맞으면 ○표, 틀리면 고쳐 보세요.

01. Do you know the place when your mom was born? ➔ where
너는 너의 엄마가 태어났던 장소를 아니?

02. I don't like how she reads my thoughts. ➔ ________
나는 그녀가 내 생각들을 읽는 방식이 마음에 안 들어.

03. I went to the house where she lived. ➔ ________
나는 그녀가 사는 집에 갔어.

04. That's when we start the day. ➔ ________
그것은 우리가 하루를 시작하는 방식이야.

05. He likes the times when he plays computer games. ➔ ________
그는 컴퓨터 게임을 하는 시간을 좋아해.

06. This is why we use chopsticks. ➔ ________
이것이 우리가 젓가락을 사용하는 방식이야.

07. Did you find out the reason why they fought? ➔ ________
너는 그들이 싸운 이유를 알아냈니?

08. He walked to the school when she studies. ➔ ________
그는 그녀가 공부하는 학교로 걸어갔어.

09. We both know the reason why we got married. ➔ ________
우리 둘 다 우리가 결혼한 이유를 안다.

10. They wait for the day where they will be together. ➔ ________
그들은 그들이 함께 있게 될 날을 기다려.

11. What is the reason when you like those pants? ➔ ________
네가 저 바지를 좋아하는 이유가 뭐니?

12. That's the reason why he says sorry. ➔ ________
그것이 그가 미안하다고 말하는 방식이야.

13. I forgot the moment when we first met. ➔ ________
나는 우리가 처음 만났던 순간을 잊어버렸다.

14. That's when my family lives in India. ➔ ________
그것이 우리 가족이 인도에 사는 이유야.

정답과 해설 p.10

# Let's Practice More!

SET 07

학습목표 3 | **관계대명사 what과 관계부사를 이용해 다양한 표현을 만들어 보아요.** 공부한 날 : 맞은 개수 : /20개

**우리말 뜻을 참고하여 다음 문장의 빈칸에 when, where, why, how 중에서 알맞은 관계부사를 쓰세요.**

**01.** This is the reason ___why___ he did it.
이것은 그가 그것을 한 이유야.

**02.** Last year was the year ____________ I graduated from university. 작년은 내가 대학교를 졸업한 해였어. **(*graduate from: ~을 졸업하다)**

**03.** This is the school ____________ my little brother entered.
이곳은 내 남동생이 입학한 학교야.

**04.** I don't want to recall the time ____________ I was sad.
나는 내가 슬펐던 시간을 떠올리고 싶지 않아.

**05.** My parents don't remember the city ____________ I was born.
나의 부모님은 내가 태어난 도시를 기억하지 못한다.

**06.** She told me the reason ____________ she was so angry.
그녀는 그녀가 매우 화가 났던 이유를 나에게 말해주었다.

**07.** I want to know ____________ the universe began.
나는 우주가 어떻게 시작되었는지 알고 싶어.

**08.** It was a snowy day of December ____________ we won the Olympics.
우리가 올림픽을 우승했을 때는 12월의 눈 내리는 날이었다.

**09.** Could you tell me ____________ I can get there?
내가 거기에 도착하는 방법을 말해 줄 수 있나요?



정답과 해설 **p.10**

10. What is important to us is the time ________________ we are together.
우리에게 중요한 것은 우리가 같이 있는 시간이야.

11. Dad went to the flower shop ________________ he first bought the flowers for mom.
아빠는 그가 엄마를 위해 처음으로 꽃을 샀던 꽃집에 가셨어.

12. She was sorry about ________________ she acted.
그녀는 그녀가 행동한 방식에 대해 미안해했어.

13. No one tells me the reason ________________ he left for New York.
아무도 나에게 그가 뉴욕으로 떠난 이유를 말해주지 않는다.

14. I don't remember the place ________________ we first met.
나는 우리가 처음 만났던 곳을 기억하지 못한다.

15. They wait for the day ________________ they will be together.
그들은 그들이 함께 있게 될 날을 기다려.

16. Do you have any reason ________________ you hate him?
네가 그를 싫어하는 무슨 이유라도 있니?

17. Can you tell me ________________ I cook traditional Korean food?
나에게 한국 전통 음식을 요리하는 방법을 말해줄 수 있니?

18. I like the house ________________ you live.
나는 네가 사는 그 집이 좋아.

19. My mom came to the school ________________ I study.
나의 엄마는 내가 공부하는 학교로 왔다.

20. November 1st is the day ________________ we moved to Seattle.
11월 1일은 우리가 시애틀로 이사 간 날이다.

정답과 해설 p.10

# Let's Practice More!

SET 08

학습목표 3 | **관계대명사 what과 관계부사를 이용해 다양한 표현을 만들어 보아요.** 공부한 날 : 맞은 개수 : /20개

다음 두 문장을 관계대명사 what을 이용한 하나의 문장으로 만들어 보세요.

01. This is the thing. + I like this thing.

➔ This is what I like. 이것이 내가 좋아하는 것이다.

02. I would like to show you a thing. + I've learned the thing.

➔ ______________________. 나는 내가 배운 것을 너에게 보여주고 싶어.

03. Running is a thing. + I want to do the thing now.

➔ ______________________.

달리기가 내가 지금 하고 싶은 거야.

04. I'm looking for a thing. + I lost the thing yesterday.

➔ ______________________. 나는 어제 내가 잃어버린 것을 찾고 있어.

05. That's a thing. + I wanted to tell you the thing.

➔ ______________________. 그게 내가 너에게 말하고 싶었던 거야.

06. Mina only eats a thing. + She likes the thing.

➔ ______________________.

미나는 그녀가 좋아하는 것만 먹어.

07. That's a thing. + I do the thing to end the day.

➔ ______________________. 그게 내가 하루를 마무리하기 위해 하는 거야.

08. This is a thing. + We were looking for the thing.

➔ ______________________. 이게 우리가 찾고 있던 거야.

09. You become a thing. + You believe the thing.

➔ ______________________. 당신은 당신이 믿는 것이(믿는대로) 된다.

10. I felt bad about a thing. + I did the thing.

➔ ______________________. 나는 내가 한 것에 대해 기분이 좋지 않았어.



정답과 해설 p.10

11. She pretends she didn't hear a thing. + She heard the thing.

➔ ______________________________. 그녀는 그녀가 들은 것을 못 들은 척해.

12. We can't believe a thing. + They said the thing.

➔ ______________________________. 우리는 그들이 말한 것을 믿을 수 없어.

13. He gave her a thing. + She likes the thing.

➔ ______________________________.

그는 그녀에게 그녀가 좋아하는 것을 주었어.



14. Today's meeting was a thing. + I've waited for the thing.

➔ ______________________________.

오늘의 회의는 내가 기다려왔던 것이었다.

15. She also felt sorry about a thing. + She did the thing.

➔ ______________________________.

그녀도 그녀가 했던 것에 대해 미안하게 생각했어.

16. Mom cooks us a thing. + We want the thing.

➔ ______________________________.

엄마는 우리에게 우리가 원하는 것을 요리해주셔.

17. Collecting stamps is a thing. + He does the thing in his free time.

➔ ______________________________.

우표 수집은 그가 여가시간에 하는 일이야.

18. That's not a thing. + I meant the thing.

➔ ______________________________.

그것은 내가 의도한 것이 아니야.

19. Think about a thing. + You should do the thing first.

➔ ______________________________. 당신이 첫 번째로 해야 할 것을 생각해봐라.

20. The 9 o'clock news is a thing. + I usually watch the thing.

➔ ______________________________. 9시 뉴스는 내가 보통 보는 것이다.

정답과 해설 p.10

# 실전테스트

CHAPTER 02~04

공부한 날 :
복습한 날 :
부모님 확인 :

CHAPTER 02 관계대명사 CHAPTER 03 관계대명사의 종류 CHAPTER 04 관계대명사 what / 관계부사

●정답과 해설은 별책 11쪽에서 확인하세요!!

[01~03] [보기]에서 다음 빈칸에 들어갈 알맞은 관계부사를 고르세요.

[보기] when why
where how

## 01

2006 was the year ________ German World Cup was held.

## 02

This is the store ________ I bought my new computer.

## 03

There's another reason ________ I was late for the school.

## 04

다음 중 문법상 틀린 부분은?

He is the boy whom can sing very well.
① the boy ② whom ③ can ④ sing

## 05

다음 중 밑줄 친 부분 대신 쓸 수 있는 것을 고르세요.

She has a brother who is an actor.

① which ② that ③ whom ④ whose

## 06

다음 밑줄 친 부분 중 생략할 수 없는 것을 고르세요.

① We saw the building that my father built.
② I made some pie that you really like.
③ He went to the gym that is close to his home.
④ I like the jacket that he is wearing.

## 07

다음 문장의 빈칸에 공통으로 들어갈 알맞은 관계대명사를 고르세요.

• ________ I need is some water.
• She understood ________ I wrote.

① Which[which] ② What[what]
③ Who[who] ④ Whose[whose]

## 08

다음 빈칸에 공통으로 들어갈 수 있는 단어를 고르세요.

•I was born in Japan ________ my grandparents live.
•I am in my room ________ I can take a rest.

① where ② when
③ what ④ how

[09~14] 관계대명사를 이용하여 다음 두 문장을 한 문장으로 만드세요.

## 09

He likes the teacher.
The teacher teaches English in his school.

⇨ ______________________________
______________________________

## 10

She keeps a cat.
The cat jumps a lot.

⇨ ______________________________
______________________________

## 11

A man was reading a book.
He was sitting next to me.

⇨ ______________________________
______________________________

## 12

A truck stopped at a gas station.
It was carrying food.

⇨ ______________________________
______________________________

## 13

We should remember the people.
They clean the building for us.

⇨ ______________________________
______________________________

## 14

This is the movie.
We watched it three times.

⇨ ______________________________
______________________________

[15~17] 다음 문장의 빈칸에 들어갈 알맞은 말을 고르세요.

## 15

He is the man ______ I met yesterday.

① whom ② when
③ which ④ what

## 16

She didn't understand ______ I said.

① which ② who
③ whose ④ what

## 17

Look at the boy ______ is dancing.

① which ② who
③ whom ④ what

[18~20] 다음 문제들의 이야기가 자연스럽도록 [보기]에서 알맞은 말을 골라 그 번호를 쓰세요.

[보기] ① when Liz was born
② who likes cooking
③ that Liz likes so much

## 18

Cindy is a girl ______________. She will bake a chocolate cake for Liz.

## 19

Liz is her best friend. Tomorrow is the day ______________.

## 20

Cindy will give her the cake ______________.

## 21

다음 밑줄 친 관계대명사 중 문장에서의 쓰임이 다른 하나를 고르세요.

① I like the skirt that Jane is wearing.
② This is the chair that my father made.
③ Do you know someone that I can work with?
④ Tom bought a bag that has many pockets.

[22~23] 다음 문장의 빈칸에 공통으로 들어갈 알맞은 관계대명사를 쓰세요.

## 22

• Basketball is ________ I like to do.
• ________ she said was all true.

## 23

• Peter is the man ________ went to New York.
• The man ________ is standing next to me is Mike.

## 24

다음 중 밑줄 친 부분을 생략할 수 있는 것 두 개를 고르세요.

① What I need is cold water.
② Tell me how you made this cake.
③ I like the dog which you gave to me.
④ This is the toy that I bought yesterday.

[25~26] 우리말 해석과 같도록 빈칸에 알맞은 관계부사를 쓰세요.

## 25

나에게 전통 한국 음식을 요리하는 방법을 말해 줄래?
= Can you tell me ________ I cook traditional Korean food?

## 26

나는 내가 그녀를 처음 봤던 때를 기억해.
= I remember the time ________ I first saw her.

[27~28] 다음 문장의 밑줄 친 부분을 고쳐 쓰세요.

## 27

He is the doctor which I met.

⇨ ________________

## 28

I like this house when I live.

⇨ ________________

[29~30] 다음 우리말 해석과 그림에 맞게 주어진 단어들을 바르게 배열하여 쓰세요.

## 29

내게 필요한 것은 물이다.

( water / is / What / I / need ).

⇨ ________________

## 30

그가 해야 하는 것은 그의 숙제이다.

( he / What / his homework / is / has to do ).

⇨ ________________

Cultural Tips
재미로 익히는 문화상식

## 꾀돌이 여우는 사는 곳에 따라 생김새가 다르대요!

### 붉은여우

'여우'하면 우리가 흔히 떠올리는 종이에요.
붉은여우의 털 색에는 밝은 적색에서 오렌지색, 갈색이 있어요.
지구의 거의 모든 지역에서 서식하는데, 특히 북아메리카와 북부 아프리카, 유라시아 북부에 많이 산다고 해요.

### 사막여우

사막여우는 주로 사막지대에서 서식하는 종을 말해요.
여우류 중에서 가장 작고, 더운 환경에서 살기 때문에 열을 방출하기 위해 귀가 길대요.
너무 귀엽지 않나요?

### 북극여우

북극여우는 북유럽이나 러시아, 알래스카와 같이 매우 추운지역에 살아요.
주로 흰색 털을 가졌는데 눈 색과 비슷한 색으로 자신을 보호하기 위해서예요.
주변 환경이 추워서 털이 많고 살이 두꺼워요.
열을 방출하기 위해 귀가 긴 사막여우와는 달리 짧고 둥근 귀를 가지고 있어요.

Cultural Tips
재미로 익히는 문화상식

## 돼지와 코끼리의 거품, 아니 진흙 목욕!

돼지와 코끼리는 지금 뭘 하고 있는 걸까요?
믿기지는 않겠지만 지금 돼지와 코끼리는 바로 목욕중이랍니다!
돼지는 땀샘이 없어 스스로 체온조절을 하지 못해요. 그래서 진흙을 몸에 바르면서 체온을 낮추는 거예요.
이렇게 하면 진흙 속의 수분이 증발하면서 체온을 2℃ 떨어뜨릴 수 있답니다.
또 코끼리는 강한 햇빛에 몸이 타는 것을 막고, 모기 같은 벌레나 기생충의 공격을 막기 위해 온몸에 진흙을 바른대요.
코끼리 말고도 하마, 코뿔소도 이런 방식으로 목욕을 해요!
겉보기에는 더러워 보이지만 알고 보면 동물들도 각자의 방식으로 목욕을 하는 거랍니다!

초등영문법3800제 LEVEL 8

# 워크북

# WORKBOOK

1. **단어 쓰기 연습** mp3 음성 파일을 듣고 들려주는 단어를 세 번씩 써 보아요.
2. **Dictation Test** mp3 음성 파일을 듣고 빈칸을 채워 보세요.
3. **단어테스트** 단어 쓰기 연습을 하며 암기한 단어들을 제대로 외웠는지 확인해 보아요.
4. **워크북 정답** Dictation Test와 단어테스트의 정답

**초등영문법3800제 MP3 파일 이용 방법**

**1. 홈페이지에서 다운로드**

① 마더텅 홈페이지(www.toptutor.co.kr) 접속 → 상단 메뉴 중 [초등 · 유아]의 [교재 소개] 선택
→ 교재 목록에서 해당 교재명 찾아 선택 → 학습자료의 [mp3] 선택 후 다운로드

② 마더텅 홈페이지(www.toptutor.co.kr) 접속 → 상단 메뉴 중 [초등 · 유아] 의 [교재자료실] 선택
→ 자료실 상단의 [교재를 선택하세요.] 에서 해당 교재명 선택
→ 자료 목록에서 mp3 게시물 선택 후 다운로드

**2. 모바일 스트리밍 / 다운로드**

① 스마트폰으로 교재 뒷면의 QR코드 스캔 → MP3 스트리밍 or 다운로드

② 주소창에 m.toptutor.co.kr 또는 포털에서 '마더텅' 검색 → [MP3 자료실] 선택
→ 상단 메뉴 중 [초등 · 유아] 선택 → 해당 교재명 찾아 선택 후 MP3 스트리밍 or 다운로드

# 단어 쓰기 연습 1

초3800_8_w1

들려주는 단어를 잘 듣고, 세 번씩 써 보세요.

MP3 8권 단어 01

| | | | | |
|---|---|---|---|---|
| 01 | **be born** ⑧ 태어나다 | be born | | |
| 02 | **break** ⑧ 깨트리다 | break | | |
| 03 | **catch** ⑧ 잡다 | catch | | |
| 04 | **forget** ⑧ 잊다 | forget | | |
| 05 | **hide** ⑧ 숨기다 | hide | | |
| 06 | **hit** ⑧ 치다 | hit | | |
| 07 | **meet** ⑧ 만나다 | meet | | |
| 08 | **sell** ⑧ 팔다 | sell | | |
| 09 | **set** ⑧ 놓다 | set | | |
| 10 | **steal** ⑧ 훔치다 | steal | | |
| 11 | **think** ⑧ 생각하다 | think | | |
| 12 | **worry** ⑧ 걱정시키다 | worry | | |
| 13 | **understand** ⑧ 이해하다 | understand | | |

들려주는 단어를 잘 듣고, 세 번씩 써 보세요.

MP3 8권 단어 01

| | | | |
|---|---|---|---|
| 14 **visit** ⓢ 방문하다 | visit | | |
| 15 **send** ⓢ 보내다 | send | | |
| 16 **bite** ⓢ 물다 | bite | | |
| 17 **airplane** ⓜ 비행기 | airplane | | |
| 18 **subway** ⓜ 지하철 | subway | | |
| 19 **use** ⓢ 사용하다 | use | | |
| 20 **fix** ⓢ 고치다 | fix | | |
| 21 **bake** ⓢ 굽다 | bake | | |
| 22 **invite** ⓢ 초대하다 | invite | | |
| 23 **cancel** ⓢ 취소하다 | cancel | | |
| 24 **surprise** ⓢ 놀라게 하다 | surprise | | |
| 25 **present** ⓜ 선물 | present | | |
| 26 **please** ⓢ 기쁘게 하다 | please | | |

초3800_8_w2

# 단어 쓰기 연습 2

들려주는 단어를 잘 듣고, 세 번씩 써 보세요.

MP3 8권 단어 02

| | | | |
|---|---|---|---|
| 27 **write** ⓓ 쓰다 | write | | |
| 28 **interest** ⓓ 흥미롭게 하다 | interest | | |
| 29 **teach** ⓓ 가르치다 | teach | | |
| 30 **find** ⓓ 찾다 | find | | |
| 31 **classical** ⓗ 고전적인 | classical | | |
| 32 **book store** ⓜ 서점 | book store | | |
| 33 **plant** ⓓ 심다 | plant | | |
| 34 **clean** ⓓ 청소하다 | clean | | |
| 35 **scold** ⓓ 혼내다 | scold | | |
| 36 **gift** ⓜ 선물 | gift | | |
| 37 **because** ⓙ ~때문에 | because | | |
| 38 **ground** ⓓ 외출하지 못하게 하다 | ground | | |
| 39 **prince** ⓜ 왕자 | prince | | |

들려주는 단어를 잘 듣고, 세 번씩 써 보세요.

MP3 8권 단어 02

| | | | |
|---|---|---|---|
| 40 **save** ⓢ 구하다 | save | | |
| 41 **history** ⓜ 역사 | history | | |
| 42 **mystery** ⓜ 수수께끼 | mystery | | |
| 43 **introduce** ⓢ 소개하다 | introduce | | |
| 44 **happiness** ⓜ 행복 | happiness | | |
| 45 **darkness** ⓜ 어둠 | darkness | | |
| 46 **remember** ⓢ 기억하다 | remember | | |
| 47 **raise** ⓢ 키우다, 기르다 | raise | | |
| 48 **treat** ⓢ 치료하다 | treat | | |
| 49 **stamp** ⓜ 우표 | stamp | | |
| 50 **collect** ⓢ 모으다 | collect | | |
| 51 **skirt** ⓜ 치마 | skirt | | |
| 52 **thief** ⓜ 도둑 | thief | | |

# 단어 쓰기 연습 3

초3800_8_w3

들려주는 단어를 잘 듣고, 세 번씩 써 보세요.

MP3 8권 단어 03

|  |  | | |
| --- | --- | --- | --- |
| 01 **paint** ㊍ 그리다 | paint | | |
| 02 **eat** ㊍ 먹다 | eat | | |
| 03 **these** ㊎ 이것들의 | these | | |
| 04 **why** ㊊ 왜 | why | | |
| 05 **what** ㊌ 무엇 | what | | |
| 06 **invent** ㊍ 발명하다 | invent | | |
| 07 **tomato** ㊔ 토마토 | tomato | | |
| 08 **grow** ㊍ 키우다 | grow | | |
| 09 **diary** ㊔ 일기 | diary | | |
| 10 **picture** ㊔ 사진 | picture | | |
| 11 **take** ㊍ (사진을) 찍다 | take | | |
| 12 **lose** ㊍ 잃다 | lose | | |
| 13 **forest** ㊔ 숲 | forest | | |

들려주는 단어를 잘 듣고, 세 번씩 써 보세요.

MP3 8권 단어 03

| | | | |
|---|---|---|---|
| 14 **seat** ㉿ 자리 | seat | | |
| 15 **call** ⓢ 부르다 | call | | |
| 16 **dinner** ㉿ 저녁식사 | dinner | | |
| 17 **news** ㉿ 소식 | news | | |
| 18 **prepare** ⓢ 준비하다 | prepare | | |
| 19 **dish** ㉿ 그릇 | dish | | |
| 20 **those** ⓗ 그것들의 | those | | |
| 21 **borrow** ⓢ 빌리다 | borrow | | |
| 22 **bake** ⓢ 굽다 | bake | | |
| 23 **fill** ⓢ 채우다 | fill | | |
| 24 **meeting** ㉿ 회의 | meeting | | |
| 25 **build** ⓢ 짓다 | build | | |
| 26 **memo** ㉿ 메모 | memo | | |

# 단어 쓰기 연습 4

초3800_8_w4

들려주는 단어를 잘 듣고, 세 번씩 써 보세요.

MP3 8권 단어 04

| | | | |
|---|---|---|---|
| 27 **bathroom** 명 화장실 | bathroom | | |
| 28 **file** 명 파일 | file | | |
| 29 **save** 동 저장하다 | save | | |
| 30 **heavy** 형 무거운, 많은, 심한 | heavy | | |
| 31 **delay** 동 미루다 | delay | | |
| 32 **leg** 명 다리 | leg | | |
| 33 **bite** 동 물다 | bite | | |
| 34 **attack** 동 공격하다 | attack | | |
| 35 **dress** 명 드레스 | dress | | |
| 36 **design** 동 디자인하다 | design | | |
| 37 **designer** 명 디자이너 | designer | | |
| 38 **museum** 명 박물관 | museum | | |
| 39 **visit** 동 방문하다 | visit | | |

들려주는 단어를 잘 듣고, 세 번씩 써 보세요.

MP3 8권 단어 **04**

| | | | |
|---|---|---|---|
| 40 **excited** 형 신난 | excited | | |
| 41 **stay** 동 머물다 | stay | | |
| 42 **spend** 동 (시간·돈 등을) 쓰다 | spend | | |
| 43 **yet** 부 아직 | yet | | |
| 44 **picnic** 명 소풍 | picnic | | |
| 45 **cancel** 동 취소하다 | cancel | | |
| 46 **building** 명 건물 | building | | |
| 47 **grade** 명 성적 | grade | | |
| 48 **raise** 동 올리다 | raise | | |
| 49 **bored** 형 심심한 | bored | | |
| 50 **mobile** 형 이동하는, 이동식의 | mobile | | |
| 51 **wood** 명 나무 | wood | | |
| 52 **fire** 동 해고하다 | fire | | |

초3800_8_w5

# 단어 쓰기 연습 5

들려주는 단어를 잘 듣고, 세 번씩 써 보세요.

MP3 8권 단어 05

| | | | |
|---|---|---|---|
| 01 **race** ⓜ 시합, 경주 | race | | |
| 02 **loyal** ⓗ 충성스러운 | loyal | | |
| 03 **brightly** ⓑ 밝게, 환히 | brightly | | |
| 04 **find** ⓓ 찾다 | find | | |
| 05 **lose** ⓓ 잃어버리다 | lose | | |
| 06 **bark** ⓓ 짖다 | bark | | |
| 07 **over** ⓑ 너머 | over | | |
| 08 **borrow** ⓓ 빌리다 | borrow | | |
| 09 **use** ⓓ 사용하다 | use | | |
| 10 **razor** ⓜ 면도기 | razor | | |
| 11 **shave** ⓓ 면도하다 | shave | | |
| 12 **yard** ⓜ 마당 | yard | | |
| 13 **brave** ⓗ 용감한 | brave | | |

들려주는 단어를 잘 듣고, 세 번씩 써 보세요.

MP3 8권 단어 05

| | | | |
|---|---|---|---|
| 14 **thief** ⓜ 도둑 | thief | | |
| 15 **police** ⓜ 경찰 | police | | |
| 16 **around** ⓙ ~의 주위에 | around | | |
| 17 **once** ⓑ 언젠가, 한때 | once | | |
| 18 **return** ⓓ 돌아오다 | return | | |
| 19 **remember** ⓓ 기억하다 | remember | | |
| 20 **someday** ⓑ 언젠가 | someday | | |
| 21 **visit** ⓓ 방문하다 | visit | | |
| 22 **hair** ⓜ 머리카락 | hair | | |
| 23 **Australia** ⓜ 호주 | Australia | | |
| 24 **only** ⓗ 유일한 | only | | |
| 25 **country** ⓜ 나라 | country | | |
| 26 **also** ⓑ 또한 | also | | |

# 단어 쓰기 연습 6

초3800_8_w6

들려주는 단어를 잘 듣고, 세 번씩 써 보세요.

MP3 8권 단어 06

| | | | |
|---|---|---|---|
| 27 **continent** ⓜ 대륙 | continent | | |
| 28 **bake** ⓢ 굽다 | bake | | |
| 29 **ending** ⓜ 결말 | ending | | |
| 30 **friendly** ⓗ 다정한 | friendly | | |
| 31 **skirt** ⓜ 치마 | skirt | | |
| 32 **wear** ⓢ 입다 | wear | | |
| 33 **marry** ⓢ 결혼하다 | marry | | |
| 34 **humorous** ⓗ 재미있는 | humorous | | |
| 35 **playground** ⓜ 운동장 | playground | | |
| 36 **watch** ⓜ 시계 | watch | | |
| 37 **pleased** ⓗ 기뻐하는 | pleased | | |
| 38 **carnation** ⓜ 카네이션 | carnation | | |
| 39 **tease** ⓢ 놀리다 | tease | | |

들려주는 단어를 잘 듣고, 세 번씩 써 보세요.

MP3 8권 단어 06

| | | | |
|---|---|---|---|
| 40 **American** ⓜ 미국인 | American | | |
| 41 **kind** ⓗ 친절한 | kind | | |
| 42 **finger** ⓜ 손가락 | finger | | |
| 43 **praise** ⓓ 칭찬하다 | praise | | |
| 44 **the poor** ⓜ 가난한 사람들 | the poor | | |
| 45 **curly** ⓗ 곱슬곱슬한 | curly | | |
| 46 **raise** ⓓ 기르다 | raise | | |
| 47 **turtle** ⓜ 거북이 | turtle | | |
| 48 **about** ⓙ ~에 대한 | about | | |
| 49 **machine** ⓜ 기계 | machine | | |
| 50 **mind** ⓜ 마음 | mind | | |
| 51 **lip balm** ⓜ 립밤, 입술용 크림 | lip balm | | |
| 52 **respect** ⓓ 존경하다 | respect | | |

# 단어 쓰기 연습 7

초3800_8_w7

들려주는 단어를 잘 듣고, 세 번씩 써 보세요.

MP3 8권 단어 07

| | | | |
|---|---|---|---|
| 01 **colorful** ⓗ 알록달록한 | colorful | | |
| 02 **butterfly** ⓜ 나비 | butterfly | | |
| 03 **traditional** ⓗ 전통적인 | traditional | | |
| 04 **pencil** ⓜ 연필 | pencil | | |
| 05 **hamster** ⓜ 햄스터 | hamster | | |
| 06 **trouble** ⓜ 어려움 | trouble | | |
| 07 **help** ⓜ 도움 ⓓ 돕다 | help | | |
| 08 **heart** ⓜ 마음 | heart | | |
| 09 **warm** ⓗ 따뜻한 | warm | | |
| 10 **helpful** ⓗ 도움이 되는 | helpful | | |
| 11 **neighbor** ⓜ 이웃 | neighbor | | |
| 12 **brown** ⓗ 갈색의 | brown | | |
| 13 **earring** ⓜ 귀걸이 | earring | | |

들려주는 단어를 잘 듣고, 세 번씩 써 보세요.

MP3 8권 단어 07

| | | | |
|---|---|---|---|
| 14 **under** ㊀ ~의 아래에 | under | | |
| 15 **attack** ⓓ 공격하다 | attack | | |
| 16 **animal** ⓜ 동물 | animal | | |
| 17 **throw** ⓓ 던지다 | throw | | |
| 18 **stone** ⓜ 돌 | stone | | |
| 19 **street** ⓜ 길 | street | | |
| 20 **forget** ⓓ 잊다 | forget | | |
| 21 **fact** ⓜ 사실 | fact | | |
| 22 **harm** ⓓ 해치다 | harm | | |
| 23 **punish** ⓓ 처벌하다 | punish | | |
| 24 **disappoint** ⓓ 실망시키다 | disappoint | | |
| 25 **strawberry** ⓜ 딸기 | strawberry | | |
| 26 **fruit** ⓜ 과일 | fruit | | |

초3800_8_w8

# 단어 쓰기 연습 8

들려주는 단어를 잘 듣고, 세 번씩 써 보세요.

MP3 8권 단어 08

| | | | |
|---|---|---|---|
| 27 **popular** ⓗ 인기 있는 | popular | | |
| 28 **spring** ⓜ 봄 | spring | | |
| 29 **reduce** ⓓ 줄이다 | reduce | | |
| 30 **even** ⓑ ~도, 조차 | even | | |
| 31 **coupon** ⓜ 쿠폰, 할인권 | coupon | | |
| 32 **interest** ⓓ 흥미롭게 하다 | interest | | |
| 33 **actress** ⓜ 여배우 | actress | | |
| 34 **famous** ⓗ 유명한 | famous | | |
| 35 **vacation** ⓜ 방학 | vacation | | |
| 36 **like** ⓙ ~와 같은 | like | | |
| 37 **oasis** ⓜ 오아시스 | oasis | | |
| 38 **believe** ⓓ 믿다 | believe | | |
| 39 **introduce** ⓓ 소개하다 | introduce | | |

들려주는 단어를 잘 듣고, 세 번씩 써 보세요.

MP3 8권 단어 08

| | | | |
|---|---|---|---|
| 40 **exciting** 형 흥미로운 | exciting | | |
| 41 **matter** 동 중요하다 | matter | | |
| 42 **language** 명 언어 | language | | |
| 43 **fear** 명 두려움 | fear | | |
| 44 **impossible** 형 불가능한 | impossible | | |
| 45 **lucky** 형 운이 좋은 | lucky | | |
| 46 **detective** 명 형사 | detective | | |
| 47 **themselves** 명 그들 스스로 | themselves | | |
| 48 **chase** 동 쫓다 | chase | | |
| 49 **bother** 동 귀찮게 하다 | bother | | |
| 50 **lawyer** 명 변호사 | lawyer | | |
| 51 **nightmare** 명 악몽 | nightmare | | |
| 52 **grow** 동 자라다 | grow | | |

초3800_8_w9

# 단어 쓰기 연습 9

**들려주는 단어를 잘 듣고, 세 번씩 써 보세요.** MP3 8권 단어 **09**

| | | | |
|---|---|---|---|
| 01 **these** 대 이것들 | these | | |
| 02 **little brother** 명 남동생 | little brother | | |
| 03 **red** 형 빨간 | red | | |
| 04 **pay** 동 (값을) 지불하다 | pay | | |
| 05 **choose** 동 선택하다 | choose | | |
| 06 **bring** 동 가져오다 | bring | | |
| 07 **sweet** 형 달콤한 | sweet | | |
| 08 **voice** 명 목소리 | voice | | |
| 09 **take** 동 가져가다 | take | | |
| 10 **grave** 명 무덤 | grave | | |
| 11 **open** 동 열다 | open | | |
| 12 **jar** 명 병 | jar | | |
| 13 **arm-wrestling** 명 팔씨름 | arm-wrestling | | |

들려주는 단어를 잘 듣고, 세 번씩 써 보세요.

MP3 8권 단어 09

| | | | |
|---|---|---|---|
| 14 **beat** ⓓ 이기다 | beat | | |
| 15 **strong** ⓗ 강한 | strong | | |
| 16 **fight** ⓓ 싸우다 | fight | | |
| 17 **often** ⓑ 종종, 자주 | often | | |
| 18 **watch** ⓜ 시계 | watch | | |
| 19 **bike** ⓜ 자전거 | bike | | |
| 20 **ride** ⓓ 타다 | ride | | |
| 21 **memory** ⓜ 추억 | memory | | |
| 22 **share** ⓓ 공유하다 | share | | |
| 23 **spend** ⓓ (시간을) 보내다 | spend | | |
| 24 **wear** ⓓ 입다 | wear | | |
| 25 **textbook** ⓜ 교과서 | textbook | | |
| 26 **dark** ⓗ 어두운 | dark | | |

초3800_8_w10

# 단어 쓰기 연습 10

들려주는 단어를 잘 듣고, 세 번씩 써 보세요.

MP3 8권 단어 10

| | | | |
|---|---|---|---|
| 27 **side** ㊔ 면 | side | | |
| 28 **laugh** ㊔ 웃음 | laugh | | |
| 29 **weapon** ㊔ 무기 | weapon | | |
| 30 **draw** ㊕ 그리다 | draw | | |
| 31 **scene** ㊔ 장면 | scene | | |
| 32 **funny** ㊖ 웃긴 | funny | | |
| 33 **thing** ㊔ 것, 일 | thing | | |
| 34 **catch** ㊕ 잡다 | catch | | |
| 35 **secret** ㊔ 비밀 | secret | | |
| 36 **vacation** ㊔ 방학 | vacation | | |
| 37 **wait** ㊕ 기다리다 | wait | | |
| 38 **sledding** ㊔ 썰매 타기 | sledding | | |
| 39 **interesting** ㊖ 재미있는 | interesting | | |

들려주는 단어를 잘 듣고, 세 번씩 써 보세요.

MP3 8권 단어 10

| | | | |
|---|---|---|---|
| 40 **boring** ⓗ 지루한 | boring | | |
| 41 **amazing** ⓗ 신기한 | amazing | | |
| 42 **experience** ⓢ 경험하다 | experience | | |
| 43 **miracle** ⓜ 기적 | miracle | | |
| 44 **quality** ⓜ 자질 | quality | | |
| 45 **tofu** ⓜ 두부 | tofu | | |
| 46 **respect** ⓢ 존경하다 | respect | | |
| 47 **mess** ⓜ 엉망 진창 | mess | | |
| 48 **remember** ⓢ 기억하다 | remember | | |
| 49 **pool** ⓜ 수영장 | pool | | |
| 50 **tear** ⓢ 찢다 | tear | | |
| 51 **tiger** ⓜ 호랑이 | tiger | | |
| 52 **zoo** ⓜ 동물원 | zoo | | |

초3800_8_w11

# 단어 쓰기 연습 11

들려주는 단어를 잘 듣고, 세 번씩 써 보세요.

MP3 8권 단어 11

| | | | |
|---|---|---|---|
| 01 **cook** ㊐ 요리하다 | cook | | |
| 02 **hear** ㊐ 듣다 | hear | | |
| 03 **surprising** ㊒ 놀라운 | surprising | | |
| 04 **reason** ㊔ 이유 | reason | | |
| 05 **why** ㊕ 왜 | why | | |
| 06 **way** ㊔ 방법 | way | | |
| 07 **learn** ㊐ 배우다 | learn | | |
| 08 **pie** ㊔ 파이 | pie | | |
| 09 **place** ㊔ 장소 | place | | |
| 10 **forget** ㊐ 잊다 | forget | | |
| 11 **win** ㊐ 이기다 | win | | |
| 12 **field** ㊔ 경기장 | field | | |
| 13 **slippery** ㊒ 미끄러운 | slippery | | |

들려주는 단어를 잘 듣고, 세 번씩 써 보세요.

MP3 8권 단어 11

| | | | |
|---|---|---|---|
| 14 **cold** ⓜ 감기 | cold | | |
| 15 **important** ⓗ 중요한 | important | | |
| 16 **together** ⓑ 함께 | together | | |
| 17 **flower shop** ⓜ 꽃가게 | flower shop | | |
| 18 **thought** ⓜ 생각 | thought | | |
| 19 **fight** ⓓ 싸우다 | fight | | |
| 20 **about** ⓙ ~에 대해 | about | | |
| 21 **act** ⓓ 행동하다 | act | | |
| 22 **sorry** ⓗ 미안한 | sorry | | |
| 23 **large** ⓗ 큰 | large | | |
| 24 **living room** ⓜ 거실 | living room | | |
| 25 **table** ⓜ 탁자 | table | | |
| 26 **enter** ⓓ 들어가다 | enter | | |

# 단어 쓰기 연습 12

초3800_8_w12

들려주는 단어를 잘 듣고, 세 번씩 써 보세요.

MP3 8권 단어 12

| | | | |
|---|---|---|---|
| 27 **late** ㊒ 늦은 | late | | |
| 28 **must** ㊉ ~해야 하다 | must | | |
| 29 **choose** ㊍ 선택하다 | choose | | |
| 30 **between** ㊎ ~사이에 | between | | |
| 31 **right** ㊒ 옳은 | right | | |
| 32 **easy** ㊒ 쉬운 | easy | | |
| 33 **become** ㊍ ~이 되다 | become | | |
| 34 **believe** ㊍ 믿다 | believe | | |
| 35 **recall** ㊍ 떠올리다 | recall | | |
| 36 **refresh** ㊍ 생기를 되찾게 하다 | refresh | | |
| 37 **worried** ㊒ 걱정하는 | worried | | |
| 38 **chopstick** ㊔ 젓가락 | chopstick | | |
| 39 **city** ㊔ 도시 | city | | |

들려주는 단어를 잘 듣고, 세 번씩 써 보세요.

MP3 8권 단어 12

| | | | |
|---|---|---|---|
| 40 **be born** ㊐ 태어나다 | be born | | |
| 41 **universe** ㊐ 우주 | universe | | |
| 42 **collect** ㊐ 모으다 | collect | | |
| 43 **stamp** ㊐ 우표 | stamp | | |
| 44 **free** ㊐ 한가한 | free | | |
| 45 **amazing** ㊐ 놀라운 | amazing | | |
| 46 **swim** ㊐ 수영하다 | swim | | |
| 47 **lose** ㊐ 잃어버리다 | lose | | |
| 48 **delicious** ㊐ 맛있는 | delicious | | |
| 49 **end** ㊐ 끝내다 | end | | |
| 50 **pretend** ㊐ ~한 척하다 | pretend | | |
| 51 **moment** ㊐ 순간 | moment | | |
| 52 **remember** ㊐ 기억하다 | remember | | |

초3800_8_d1

# Dictation Test 1

MP3 8권 받아쓰기 01

Name : Date : Score : /10

**[01~10] 들려주는 문장을 잘 듣고 빈칸에 알맞은 단어를 채워 보세요.**

01. The subway ________________ ________________ by many people.
지하철은 많은 사람들에 의해 이용된다.

02. The cookies ________________ ________________ by us.
그 쿠키들은 우리에 의해 구워진다.

03. My computer was ________________ ________________ my dad.
내 컴퓨터는 나의 아빠에 의해 고쳐졌다.

04. His toys ________________ hidden ________________ Mori.
그의 장난감들은 모리에 의해 숨겨졌다.

05. The room is ________________ ________________ me.
그 방은 나에 의해 청소된다.

06. We were ________________ ________________ Mr. Kim.
우리는 김 선생님에 의해 가르쳐졌다.

07. I ________________ invited ________________ Sihu.
나는 시후에 의해 초대되었다.

08. They ________________ ________________ by many people.
그들은 많은 사람들에 의해 사랑받는다.

09. The windows were ________________ ________________ us.
그 창문들은 우리에 의해 깨졌다.

10. Eggs ________________ ________________ out today.
계란은 오늘 다 팔렸다.



정답 p.204

초3800_8_d2

# Dictation Test 2

MP3 8권 받아쓰기 02

Name : Date : Score : /10



**[01~10] 들려주는 문장을 잘 듣고 빈칸에 알맞은 단어를 채워 보세요.**

01. My bike was ________ ________ someone.
내 자전거는 누군가에 의해 훔쳐졌다.

02. My shoes ________ chewed ________ my dog.
내 신발은 내 개에 의해 물어 뜯겼다.

03. You ________ ________ by your parents.
너는 너의 부모님에 의해 사랑받는다.

04. The wall ________ ________ by her.
그 벽은 그녀에 의해 칠해진다.

05. The skirt ________ ________ by my mother.
그 치마는 나의 엄마에 의해 만들어졌다.

06. The letter ________ ________ by Sihu.
그 편지는 시후에 의해 쓰여진다.

07. The questions ________ answered ________ her.
그 질문들은 그녀에 의해 답해진다.

08. These houses ________ ________ by my grandfather.
이 집들은 나의 할아버지에 의해 지어졌다.

09. Stamps ________ collected ________ me.
우표들은 나에 의해 수집된다.

10. A dog was ________ ________ a car.
한 마리의 개가 차에 치였다.

정답 p.204

초3800_8_d3

# Dictation Test 3

MP3 8권 받아쓰기 03

Name : Date : Score : /10

**[01~10] 들려주는 문장을 잘 듣고 빈칸에 알맞은 단어를 채워 보세요.**

01. The music is __________ __________ by Jackson.
그 음악은 Jackson에 의해 연주되지 않는다.

02. __________ Spanish __________ in many countries?
스페인어는 많은 나라에서 말해지니?

03. __________ the dishes __________ by dad?
그 그릇들은 아빠에 의해 설거지되었니?

04. The candy was __________ __________ by Cathy.
그 사탕은 Cathy에 의해 먹어지지 않았다.

05. __________ tomatoes __________ by your grandmother?
토마토들이 너의 할머니에 의해 키워지니?

06. These cookies __________ not __________ by me.
이 쿠키들은 나에 의해 만들어지지 않았다.

07. __________ the computer __________ by him?
그 컴퓨터는 그에 의해 고쳐졌니?

08. His name was not __________ __________ the teacher.
그의 이름은 선생님에 의해 불리지 않았다.

09. The park __________ not __________ by us.
그 공원은 우리에 의해 청소되지 않는다.

10. __________ you attacked __________ Mina's dog?
너는 미나의 개에 의해 공격당했니?



정답 p.204

초3800_8_d4

# Dictation Test 4

MP3 8권 받아쓰기 04

Name : Date : Score : /10



**[01~10] 들려주는 문장을 잘 듣고 빈칸에 알맞은 단어를 채워 보세요.**

01. ________ those books borrowed ________ Jane?
저 책들은 Jane에 의해 빌려졌니?

02. ________ they ________ by many fans?
그들은 많은 팬들에 의해 사랑받니?

03. These shoes ________ not ________ by me.
이 신발은 나에 의해 만들어지지 않았다.

04. ________ this party planned ________ him?
이 파티는 그에 의해 계획되었니?

05. They are ________ ________ in the forest.
그들은 숲속에서 길을 잃지 않는다.

06. Her grades ________ ________ raised.
그녀의 점수는 오르지 않았다.

07. ________ your leg ________?
너의 다리는 부러졌니?

08. This seat is ________ ________.
이 자리는 주인이 없다.

09. ________ this soup ________ by your mom?
이 수프는 너의 엄마에 의해 요리되었니?

10. My files ________ ________ saved!
내 파일들은 저장되지 않았다!

정답 p.204

초3800_8_d5

# Dictation Test 5

MP3 8권 받아쓰기 05

Name : Date : Score : /10

**[01~10] 들려주는 문장을 잘 듣고 빈칸에 알맞은 단어를 채워 보세요.**

**01.** I have a brother ________________ is two years old.

나는 두 살인 남동생 한 명이 있다.

**02.** She has a dog ________________ is brave.

그녀는 용감한 개 한 마리를 가지고 있다.

**03.** I know the girl ________________ smiles brightly.

나는 밝게 웃는 그 소녀를 안다.

**04.** I like the cookies ________________ she made.

나는 그녀가 만든 쿠키들을 좋아한다.

**05.** I don't like movies ________________ have sad endings.

나는 슬픈 결말을 가지고 있는 영화를 좋아하지 않는다.

**06.** They saw rabbits ________________ were eating carrots.

그들은 당근을 먹고 있는 토끼들을 보았다.

**07.** I respect people ________________ help others.

나는 다른 이들을 도와주는 사람들을 존경한다.

**08.** Dana has some photos ________________ I took.

다나는 내가 찍은 사진들을 좀 가지고 있다.

**09.** Minwoo found the watch ________________ I lost.

민우는 내가 잃어버린 시계를 찾았다.

**10.** There is a girl ________________ has long hair.

긴 머리를 가진 소녀가 있다.



정답 p.204

초3800_8_d6

# Dictation Test 6

MP3 8권 받아쓰기 **06**



Name : Date : Score : /10

**[01~10] 들려주는 문장을 잘 듣고 빈칸에 알맞은 단어를 채워 보세요.**

01. There is a dog ________________ is barking.
    짖고 있는 개 한 마리가 있다.

02. Mina bought the candies ________________ she likes.
    미나는 그녀가 좋아하는 사탕들을 샀다.

03. I love my friends ________________ are over there.
    나는 저기 있는 내 친구들을 사랑한다.

04. This is the puppy ________________ my dad bought for me.
    이것은 나의 아빠가 나를 위해 사주셨던 강아지이다.

05. He likes dogs ________________ are friendly with people.
    그는 사람들에게 친근한 개들을 좋아한다.

06. I like the girl ________________ has curly hair.
    나는 곱슬머리를 가진 그 소녀를 좋아한다.

07. The kid ________________ is over there is my friend.
    저기 있는 아이는 내 친구이다.

08. I saw them ________________ were playing with their dog.
    나는 그들의 개와 놀고 있는 그들을 보았다.

09. I like the skirt ________________ Jessica is wearing.
    나는 Jessica가 입고 있는 그 치마를 좋아한다.

10. I am eating the cake ________________ my mom baked.
    나는 나의 엄마가 구워주신 케이크를 먹고 있다.

정답 p.204

초3800_8_d7

# Dictation Test 7

MP3 8권 받아쓰기 07

Name : Date : Score : /10

**[01~10] 들려주는 문장을 잘 듣고 빈칸에 알맞은 단어를 채워 보세요.**

01. Do you know the man ______________ is talking to her?
너는 그녀에게 말하고 있는 그 남자를 아니?

02. She has two dogs ______________ are brown.
그녀는 갈색인 두 마리의 개를 가지고 있다.

03. He looked at the picture ______________ was on the wall.
그는 벽에 있던 사진을 보았다.

04. Can I eat the strawberries ______________ are on the table?
제가 탁자 위에 있는 딸기들을 먹어도 되나요?

05. We saw the actress ______________ was famous.
우리는 유명했던 그 여배우를 보았다.

06. Look at the girl ______________ is singing a song.
노래를 부르고 있는 그 소녀를 봐.

07. I have a cousin ______________ lives in Canada.
나는 캐나다에 살고 있는 사촌이 있다.

08. I'm wearing a dress ______________ is pretty.
나는 예쁜 드레스를 입고 있다.

09. They are the people ______________ need help.
그들은 도움이 필요한 사람들이다.

10. Don't throw stones at the cats ______________ live on the street.
길에서 사는 고양이들에게 돌을 던지지 마.



정답 p.204

초3800_8_d8

# Dictation Test 8

MP3 8권 받아쓰기 08



Name : Date : Score : /10

**[01~10] 들려주는 문장을 잘 듣고 빈칸에 알맞은 단어를 채워 보세요.**

01. Do you know the girl ________________ is sitting on the grass?
너는 잔디 위에 앉아 있는 소녀를 알고 있니?

02. There are many people ________________ are in trouble.
곤경에 빠진 많은 사람들이 있다.

03. I have a friend ________________ has a hamster.
나는 햄스터를 가지고 있는 친구가 있다.

04. Look at that dog ________________ is biting his finger!
그의 손가락을 물고 있는 저 개를 봐!

05. She found the cat ________________ was lost.
그녀는 길을 잃은 고양이를 찾았다.

06. She is my neighbor ________________ lives next door.
그녀는 옆집에 살고 있는 내 이웃이다.

07. She found them in the box ________________ was under the desk.
그녀는 그것들을 책상 아래에 있던 상자 안에서 찾았다.

08. She is the teacher ________________ teaches us English.
그녀는 우리에게 영어를 가르치는 선생님이다.

09. She is the girl ________________ speaks three languages.
그녀는 세 개의 언어를 말하는 소녀이다.

10. You have to read the book ________________ is on my desk.
너는 내 책상 위에 있는 그 책을 읽어야 한다.

정답 p.204

초3800_8_d9

# Dictation Test 9

MP3 8권 받아쓰기 09

Name : Date : Score : /10

**[01~10] 들려주는 문장을 잘 듣고 빈칸에 알맞은 단어를 채워 보세요.**

01. I have a red bag ______________ my mom bought for me.
나는 나의 엄마가 나에게 사주신 빨간 가방을 가지고 있다.

02. These are the shoes ______________ I bought yesterday.
이것들은 내가 어제 산 신발이다.

03. They are the students ______________ Ms. Lee teaches.
그들은 이 선생님이 가르치는 학생들이다.

04. She lost her watch ______________ she likes.
그녀는 그녀가 좋아하는 시계를 잃어버렸다.

05. I want the bike ______________ Mina has.
나는 미나가 가지고 있는 자전거를 원한다.

06. This is the camera ______________ my father gave me.
이것은 나의 아빠가 나에게 주신 카메라이다.

07. Do you remember the boy ______________ we met at the pool?
너는 우리가 수영장에서 만났던 그 소년을 기억하니?

08. He has two children ______________ he loves very much.
그는 그가 정말 사랑하는 두 명의 아이들이 있다.

09. This is the story ______________ my mother read to me.
이것은 나의 엄마가 나에게 읽어주신 이야기이다.

10. My dad is wearing the sweater ______________ my mom made.
나의 아빠는 나의 엄마가 만드신 스웨터를 입고 계신다.



정답 p.204

초3800_8_d10

# Dictation Test 10

MP3 8권 받아쓰기 10



Name : Date : Score : /10

**[01~10] 들려주는 문장을 잘 듣고 빈칸에 알맞은 단어를 채워 보세요.**

01. This is the exam ______________ we have to pass.
이것은 우리가 통과해야만 하는 시험이다.

02. The girl ______________ I met yesterday was David's sister.
내가 어제 만난 그 소녀는 David의 여동생이다.

03. Tell me everything ______________ you want for Christmas.
네가 크리스마스에 원하는 모든 것을 나에게 말해봐.

04. There isn't a jar ______________ I can't open!
내가 열 수 없는 병은 없어!

05. The boy ______________ I don't like always tells lies.
내가 좋아하지 않는 그 소년은 항상 거짓말을 한다.

06. I ate some bananas ______________ my mom bought for me.
나는 나의 엄마가 나에게 사주신 바나나 조금을 먹었다.

07. He has a sweet voice ______________ I like.
그는 내가 좋아하는 달콤한 목소리를 가지고 있다.

08. The one thing ______________ I wanted was a Nintendo!
내가 원했던 한 가지는 닌텐도였다!

09. Look at the mess ______________ my dog made!
내 개가 만든 엉망진창인 상태를 봐!

10. He is a lawyer ______________ many people respect.
그는 많은 사람들이 존경하는 변호사이다.

정답 p.204

초3800_8_d11

# Dictation Test 11

MP3 8권 받아쓰기 **11**

Name : Date : Score : /10

**[01~10] 들려주는 문장을 잘 듣고 빈칸에 알맞은 단어를 채워 보세요.**

01. ________________ I heard is surprising.
내가 들은 것은 놀라워.

02. I went to Paris ________________ Eric lives.
나는 Eric이 살고 있는 파리에 갔어.

03. I'll never forget the day ________________ we won the game.
나는 우리가 그 게임에서 이겼던 날을 잊지 못할 거야.

04. That's ________________ we play the game.
그게 우리가 게임을 하는 방식이야.

05. Mom told me the reason ________________ she was so angry.
엄마는 나에게 그녀가 왜 그렇게 화가 났는지 말해주셨어.

06. He gave her ________________ she likes.
그는 그녀에게 그녀가 좋아하는 것을 주었어.

07. That's ________________ ________________ he says sorry.
그것이 그가 미안하다고 말하는 방식이야.

08. This is ________________ ________________ why we fought.
이것이 우리가 싸운 이유야.

09. We have a large living room ________________ there is a big table.
우리는 큰 탁자 하나가 있는 큰 거실이 있어.

10. Could you tell me ________________ I can get there?
제가 거기에 도착하는 방법을 말해 줄 수 있나요?



정답 p.204

초3800_8_d12

# Dictation Test 12

MP3 8권 받아쓰기 12

Name : Date : Score : /10

**[01~10] 들려주는 문장을 잘 듣고 빈칸에 알맞은 단어를 채워 보세요.**

01. Sorry about ______ ______ I acted.
내가 행동한 방식에 대해 미안해.

02. Last year was the year ______ I entered school.
작년은 내가 학교에 들어간 해야.

03. We must choose between ______ is right and ______ is easy.
우리는 옳은 것과 쉬운 것 사이에서 선택해야 한다.

04. I recall the time ______ I was happy.
나는 내가 행복했었던 시간을 떠올려.

05. This is ______ we use chopsticks.
이게 우리가 젓가락을 사용하는 방식이야.

06. That's the reason ______ we are worried.
그것이 우리가 걱정하는 이유야.

07. That's ______ ______ why the baby is crying.
그게 그 아기가 울고 있는 이유야.

08. I remember the place ______ we first met.
나는 우리가 처음 만났던 장소를 기억해.

09. ______ she said made me laugh.
그녀가 말한 것이 나를 웃게 했어.

10. That's ______ ______ we learned English.
그게 우리가 영어를 배웠던 방식이야.

정답 p.204

# 단어테스트 1

다음 한글 뜻을 보고 영어 표현을 적으세요. Name : Date : Score : /26

| | | | | | |
|---|---|---|---|---|---|
| 01 | | 동 태어나다 | 14 | | 동 방문하다 |
| 02 | | 동 깨트리다 | 15 | | 동 보내다 |
| 03 | | 동 잡다 | 16 | | 동 물다 |
| 04 | | 동 잊다 | 17 | | 명 비행기 |
| 05 | | 동 숨기다 | 18 | | 명 지하철 |
| 06 | | 동 치다 | 19 | | 동 사용하다 |
| 07 | | 동 만나다 | 20 | | 동 고치다 |
| 08 | | 동 팔다 | 21 | | 동 굽다 |
| 09 | | 동 놓다 | 22 | | 동 초대하다 |
| 10 | | 동 훔치다 | 23 | | 동 취소하다 |
| 11 | | 동 생각하다 | 24 | | 동 놀라게 하다 |
| 12 | | 동 걱정시키다 | 25 | | 명 선물 |
| 13 | | 동 이해하다 | 26 | | 동 기쁘게 하다 |


정답 p.204

# 단어테스트 2

다음 한글 뜻을 보고 영어 표현을 적으세요. Name : Date : Score : /26

| | | | | | |
|---|---|---|---|---|---|
| 01 | | 동 쓰다 | 14 | | 동 구하다 |
| 02 | | 동 흥미롭게 하다 | 15 | | 명 역사 |
| 03 | | 동 가르치다 | 16 | | 명 수수께끼 |
| 04 | | 동 찾다 | 17 | | 동 소개하다 |
| 05 | | 형 고전적인 | 18 | | 명 행복 |
| 06 | | 명 서점 | 19 | | 명 어둠 |
| 07 | | 동 심다 | 20 | | 동 기억하다 |
| 08 | | 동 청소하다 | 21 | | 동 키우다, 기르다 |
| 09 | | 동 혼내다 | 22 | | 동 치료하다 |
| 10 | | 명 선물 | 23 | | 명 우표 |
| 11 | | 접 ~때문에 | 24 | | 동 모으다 |
| 12 | | 동 외출하지 못하게 하다 | 25 | | 명 치마 |
| 13 | | 명 왕자 | 26 | | 명 도둑 |

정답 p.204

# 단어테스트 3

다음 한글 뜻을 보고 영어 표현을 적으세요. Name : Date : Score : /26

| | | | | | |
|---|---|---|---|---|---|
| 01 | | 동 그리다 | 14 | | 명 자리 |
| 02 | | 동 먹다 | 15 | | 동 부르다 |
| 03 | | 형 이것들의 | 16 | | 명 저녁식사 |
| 04 | | 부 왜 | 17 | | 명 소식 |
| 05 | | 대 무엇 | 18 | | 동 준비하다 |
| 06 | | 동 발명하다 | 19 | | 명 그릇 |
| 07 | | 명 토마토 | 20 | | 형 그것들의 |
| 08 | | 동 키우다 | 21 | | 동 빌리다 |
| 09 | | 명 일기 | 22 | | 동 굽다 |
| 10 | | 명 사진 | 23 | | 동 채우다 |
| 11 | | 동 (사진을) 찍다 | 24 | | 명 회의 |
| 12 | | 동 잃다 | 25 | | 동 짓다 |
| 13 | | 명 숲 | 26 | | 명 메모 |



정답 p.204

# 단어테스트 4

다음 한글 뜻을 보고 영어 표현을 적으세요. Name : Date : Score : /26

| | | | |
|---|---|---|---|
| 01 | | | 명 화장실 |
| 02 | | | 명 파일 |
| 03 | | | 동 저장하다 |
| 04 | | | 형 무거운, 많은, 심한 |
| 05 | | | 동 미루다 |
| 06 | | | 명 다리 |
| 07 | | | 동 물다 |
| 08 | | | 동 공격하다 |
| 09 | | | 명 드레스 |
| 10 | | | 동 디자인하다 |
| 11 | | | 명 디자이너 |
| 12 | | | 명 박물관 |
| 13 | | | 동 방문하다 |
| 14 | | | 형 신난 |
| 15 | | | 동 머물다 |
| 16 | | | 동 (시간·돈 등을) 쓰다 |
| 17 | | | 부 아직 |
| 18 | | | 명 소풍 |
| 19 | | | 동 취소하다 |
| 20 | | | 명 건물 |
| 21 | | | 명 성적 |
| 22 | | | 동 올리다 |
| 23 | | | 형 심심한 |
| 24 | | | 형 이동하는, 이동식의 |
| 25 | | | 명 나무 |
| 26 | | | 동 해고하다 |

정답 p.204

# 단어테스트 5

다음 한글 뜻을 보고 영어 표현을 적으세요. Name : Date : Score : /26

| | | | | | |
|---|---|---|---|---|---|
| 01 | | 명 시합, 경주 | 14 | | 명 도둑 |
| 02 | | 형 충성스러운 | 15 | | 명 경찰 |
| 03 | | 부 밝게, 환히 | 16 | | 전 ~의 주위에 |
| 04 | | 동 찾다 | 17 | | 부 언젠가, 한때 |
| 05 | | 동 잃어버리다 | 18 | | 동 돌아오다 |
| 06 | | 동 짖다 | 19 | | 동 기억하다 |
| 07 | | 부 너머 | 20 | | 부 언젠가 |
| 08 | | 동 빌리다 | 21 | | 동 방문하다 |
| 09 | | 동 사용하다 | 22 | | 명 머리카락 |
| 10 | | 명 면도기 | 23 | | 명 호주 |
| 11 | | 동 면도하다 | 24 | | 형 유일한 |
| 12 | | 명 마당 | 25 | | 명 나라 |
| 13 | | 형 용감한 | 26 | | 부 또한 |


정답 p.204

# 단어테스트 6

다음 한글 뜻을 보고 영어 표현을 적으세요. Name : Date : Score : /26

| | | | | | |
|---|---|---|---|---|---|
| 01 | | 명 대륙 | 14 | | 명 미국인 |
| 02 | | 동 굽다 | 15 | | 형 친절한 |
| 03 | | 명 결말 | 16 | | 명 손가락 |
| 04 | | 형 다정한 | 17 | | 동 칭찬하다 |
| 05 | | 명 치마 | 18 | | 명 가난한 사람들 |
| 06 | | 동 입다 | 19 | | 형 곱슬곱슬한 |
| 07 | | 동 결혼하다 | 20 | | 동 기르다 |
| 08 | | 형 재미있는 | 21 | | 명 거북이 |
| 09 | | 명 운동장 | 22 | | 전 ~에 대한 |
| 10 | | 명 시계 | 23 | | 명 기계 |
| 11 | | 형 기뻐하는 | 24 | | 명 마음 |
| 12 | | 명 카네이션 | 25 | | 명 립밤, 입술용 크림 |
| 13 | | 동 놀리다 | 26 | | 동 존경하다 |

정답 p.205

# 단어테스트 7

다음 한글 뜻을 보고 영어 표현을 적으세요. Name : Date : Score : /26

| | | | | | |
|---|---|---|---|---|---|
| 01 | | 형 알록달록한 | 14 | | 전 ~의 아래에 |
| 02 | | 명 나비 | 15 | | 동 공격하다 |
| 03 | | 형 전통적인 | 16 | | 명 동물 |
| 04 | | 명 연필 | 17 | | 동 던지다 |
| 05 | | 명 햄스터 | 18 | | 명 돌 |
| 06 | | 명 어려움 | 19 | | 명 길 |
| 07 | | 명 도움 동 돕다 | 20 | | 동 잊다 |
| 08 | | 명 마음 | 21 | | 명 사실 |
| 09 | | 형 따뜻한 | 22 | | 동 해치다 |
| 10 | | 형 도움이 되는 | 23 | | 동 처벌하다 |
| 11 | | 명 이웃 | 24 | | 동 실망시키다 |
| 12 | | 형 갈색의 | 25 | | 명 딸기 |
| 13 | | 명 귀걸이 | 26 | | 명 과일 |


정답 p.205

# 단어테스트 8

다음 한글 뜻을 보고 영어 표현을 적으세요. Name : Date : Score : /26

| | | | |
|---|---|---|---|
| 01 | 형 인기 있는 | 14 | 형 흥미로운 |
| 02 | 명 봄 | 15 | 동 중요하다 |
| 03 | 동 줄이다 | 16 | 명 언어 |
| 04 | 부 ~도, 조차 | 17 | 명 두려움 |
| 05 | 명 쿠폰, 할인권 | 18 | 형 불가능한 |
| 06 | 동 흥미롭게 하다 | 19 | 형 운이 좋은 |
| 07 | 명 여배우 | 20 | 명 형사 |
| 08 | 형 유명한 | 21 | 명 그들 스스로 |
| 09 | 명 방학 | 22 | 동 쫓다 |
| 10 | 전 ~와 같은 | 23 | 동 귀찮게 하다 |
| 11 | 명 오아시스 | 24 | 명 변호사 |
| 12 | 동 믿다 | 25 | 명 악몽 |
| 13 | 동 소개하다 | 26 | 동 자라다 |

정답 p.205

# 단어테스트 9

다음 한글 뜻을 보고 영어 표현을 적으세요. Name : Date : Score : /26

| | | | | | |
|---|---|---|---|---|---|
| 01 | | 대 이것들 | 14 | | 동 이기다 |
| 02 | | 명 남동생 | 15 | | 형 강한 |
| 03 | | 형 빨간 | 16 | | 동 싸우다 |
| 04 | | 동 (값을) 지불하다 | 17 | | 부 종종, 자주 |
| 05 | | 동 선택하다 | 18 | | 명 시계 |
| 06 | | 동 가져오다 | 19 | | 명 자전거 |
| 07 | | 형 달콤한 | 20 | | 동 타다 |
| 08 | | 명 목소리 | 21 | | 명 추억 |
| 09 | | 동 가져가다 | 22 | | 동 공유하다 |
| 10 | | 명 무덤 | 23 | | 동 (시간을) 보내다 |
| 11 | | 동 열다 | 24 | | 동 입다 |
| 12 | | 명 병 | 25 | | 명 교과서 |
| 13 | | 명 팔씨름 | 26 | | 형 어두운 |



정답 p.205

# 단어테스트 10

다음 한글 뜻을 보고 영어 표현을 적으세요. Name : Date : Score : /26

| | | |
|---|---|---|
| 01 | | 명 면 |
| 02 | | 명 웃음 |
| 03 | | 명 무기 |
| 04 | | 동 그리다 |
| 05 | | 명 장면 |
| 06 | | 형 웃긴 |
| 07 | | 명 것, 일 |
| 08 | | 동 잡다 |
| 09 | | 명 비밀 |
| 10 | | 명 방학 |
| 11 | | 동 기다리다 |
| 12 | | 명 썰매 타기 |
| 13 | | 형 재미있는 |
| 14 | | 형 지루한 |
| 15 | | 형 신기한 |
| 16 | | 동 경험하다 |
| 17 | | 명 기적 |
| 18 | | 명 자질 |
| 19 | | 명 두부 |
| 20 | | 동 존경하다 |
| 21 | | 명 엉망 진창 |
| 22 | | 동 기억하다 |
| 23 | | 명 수영장 |
| 24 | | 동 찢다 |
| 25 | | 명 호랑이 |
| 26 | | 명 동물원 |

정답 p.205

# 단어테스트 11

다음 한글 뜻을 보고 영어 표현을 적으세요. Name : Date : Score : /26

| | | |
|---|---|---|
| 01 | | 동 요리하다 |
| 02 | | 동 듣다 |
| 03 | | 형 놀라운 |
| 04 | | 명 이유 |
| 05 | | 부 왜 |
| 06 | | 명 방법 |
| 07 | | 동 배우다 |
| 08 | | 명 파이 |
| 09 | | 명 장소 |
| 10 | | 동 잊다 |
| 11 | | 동 이기다 |
| 12 | | 명 경기장 |
| 13 | | 형 미끄러운 |
| 14 | | 명 감기 |
| 15 | | 형 중요한 |
| 16 | | 부 함께 |
| 17 | | 명 꽃가게 |
| 18 | | 명 생각 |
| 19 | | 동 싸우다 |
| 20 | | 전 ~에 대해 |
| 21 | | 동 행동하다 |
| 22 | | 형 미안한 |
| 23 | | 형 큰 |
| 24 | | 명 거실 |
| 25 | | 명 탁자 |
| 26 | | 동 들어가다 |



정답 p.205

# 단어테스트 12

다음 한글 뜻을 보고 영어 표현을 적으세요. Name : Date : Score : /26

| | | | | | |
|---|---|---|---|---|---|
| 01 | | 형 늦은 | 14 | | 동 태어나다 |
| 02 | | 조 ~해야 하다 | 15 | | 명 우주 |
| 03 | | 동 선택하다 | 16 | | 동 모으다 |
| 04 | | 전 ~사이에 | 17 | | 명 우표 |
| 05 | | 형 옳은 | 18 | | 형 한가한 |
| 06 | | 형 쉬운 | 19 | | 형 놀라운 |
| 07 | | 동 ~이 되다 | 20 | | 동 수영하다 |
| 08 | | 동 믿다 | 21 | | 동 잃어버리다 |
| 09 | | 동 떠올리다 | 22 | | 형 맛있는 |
| 10 | | 동 생기를 되찾게 하다 | 23 | | 동 끝내다 |
| 11 | | 형 걱정하는 | 24 | | 동 ~한 척하다 |
| 12 | | 명 젓가락 | 25 | | 명 순간 |
| 13 | | 명 도시 | 26 | | 동 기억하다 |

정답 p.205

# 워크북 정답

**Dictation Test 1**

01. is, used
02. are, baked
03. fixed, by
04. were, by
05. cleaned, by
06. taught, by
07. was, by
08. are, loved
09. broken, by
10. are, sold

**Dictation Test 2**

01. stolen, by
02. were, by
03. are, loved
04. is, painted
05. was, made
06. is, written
07. are, by
08. were, built
09. are, by
10. hit, by

**Dictation Test 3**

01. not, played
02. Is, spoken
03. Were, washed
04. not, eaten
05. Are, grown
06. were, made
07. Was, fixed
08. called, by
09. is, cleaned
10. Were, by

**Dictation Test 4**

01. Were, by
02. Are, loved
03. were, made
04. Was, by
05. not, lost
06. were, not
07. Is, broken
08. not, taken
09. Was, cooked
10. were, not

**Dictation Test 5**

01. who
02. which
03. who
04. that
05. that
06. which
07. who
08. that
09. which
10. who

**Dictation Test 6**

01. which
02. that
03. who
04. that
05. which
06. that
07. who
08. who
09. which
10. which

**Dictation Test 7**

01. who
02. which
03. which
04. that
05. that
06. who
07. that
08. which
09. who
10. which

**Dictation Test 8**

01. that
02. who
03. that
04. that
05. which
06. who
07. which
08. that
09. who
10. which

**Dictation Test 9**

01. which
02. that
03. whom
04. which
05. which
06. that
07. whom
08. whom
09. that
10. which

**Dictation Test 10**

01. that
02. whom
03. that
04. that
05. whom
06. which
07. which
08. that
09. which
10. whom

**Dictation Test 11**

01. What
02. where
03. when
04. how
05. why
06. what
07. the, way
08. the, reason
09. where
10. how

**Dictation Test 12**

01. the, way
02. when
03. what, what
04. when
05. how
06. why
07. the, reason
08. where
09. What
10. the, way

**단어테스트 1**

01. be born
02. break
03. catch
04. forget
05. hide
06. hit
07. meet
08. sell
09. set
10. steal
11. think
12. worry
13. understand
14. visit
15. send
16. bite
17. airplane
18. subway
19. use
20. fix
21. bake
22. invite
23. cancel
24. surprise
25. present
26. please

**단어테스트 2**

01. write
02. interest
03. teach
04. find
05. classical
06. book store
07. plant
08. clean
09. scold
10. gift
11. because
12. ground
13. prince
14. save
15. history
16. mystery
17. introduce
18. happiness
19. darkness
20. remember
21. raise
22. treat
23. stamp
24. collect
25. skirt
26. thief

**단어테스트 3**

01. paint
02. eat
03. these
04. why
05. what
06. invent
07. tomato
08. grow
09. diary
10. picture
11. take
12. lose
13. forest
14. seat
15. call
16. dinner
17. news
18. prepare
19. dish
20. those
21. borrow
22. bake
23. fill
24. meeting
25. build
26. memo

**단어테스트 4**

01. bathroom
02. file
03. save
04. heavy
05. delay
06. leg
07. bite
08. attack
09. dress
10. design
11. designer
12. museum
13. visit
14. excited
15. stay
16. spend
17. yet
18. picnic
19. cancel
20. building
21. grade
22. raise
23. bored
24. mobile
25. wood
26. fire

**단어테스트 5**

01. race
02. loyal
03. brightly

04. find
05. lose
06. bark
07. over
08. borrow
09. use
10. razor
11. shave
12. yard
13. brave
14. thief
15. police
16. around
17. once
18. return
19. remember
20. someday
21. visit
22. hair
23. Australia
24. only
25. country
26. also

단어테스트 6

01. continent
02. bake
03. ending
04. friendly
05. skirt
06. wear
07. marry
08. humorous
09. playground
10. watch
11. pleased
12. carnation
13. tease
14. American
15. kind
16. finger
17. praise
18. the poor
19. curly
20. raise
21. turtle
22. about
23. machine
24. mind
25. lip balm
26. respect

단어테스트 7

01. colorful
02. butterfly
03. traditional
04. pencil
05. hamster
06. trouble
07. help
08. heart
09. warm
10. helpful
11. neighbor
12. brown
13. earring
14. under
15. attack
16. animal
17. throw
18. stone
19. street
20. forget
21. fact
22. harm
23. punish
24. disappoint
25. strawberry
26. fruit

단어테스트 8

01. popular
02. spring
03. reduce
04. even
05. coupon
06. interest
07. actress
08. famous
09. vacation
10. like
11. oasis
12. believe
13. introduce
14. exciting
15. matter
16. language
17. fear
18. impossible
19. lucky
20. detective
21. themselves
22. chase
23. bother
24. lawyer
25. nightmare
26. grow

단어테스트 9

01. these
02. little brother
03. red
04. pay
05. choose
06. bring
07. sweet
08. voice
09. take
10. grave
11. open
12. jar
13. arm-wrestling
14. beat
15. strong
16. fight
17. often
18. watch
19. bike
20. ride
21. memory
22. share
23. spend
24. wear
25. textbook
26. dark

단어테스트 10

01. side
02. laugh
03. weapon
04. draw
05. scene
06. funny
07. thing
08. catch
09. secret
10. vacation
11. wait
12. sledding
13. interesting
14. boring
15. amazing
16. experience
17. miracle
18. quality
19. tofu
20. respect
21. mess
22. remember
23. pool
24. tear
25. tiger
26. zoo

단어테스트 11

01. cook
02. hear
03. surprising
04. reason
05. why
06. way
07. learn
08. pie
09. place
10. forget
11. win
12. field
13. slippery
14. cold
15. important
16. together
17. flower shop
18. thought
19. fight
20. about
21. act
22. sorry
23. large
24. living room
25. table
26. enter

단어테스트 12

01. late
02. must
03. choose
04. between
05. right
06. easy
07. become
08. believe
09. recall
10. refresh
11. worried
12. chopstick
13. city
14. be born
15. universe
16. collect
17. stamp
18. free
19. amazing
20. swim
21. lose
22. delicious
23. end
24. pretend
25. moment
26. remember

# Grammar Review

초등영문법 3800제 8권에서 배운 문법 내용을 한 번 더 정리해 보아요!

※ 정답은 뒷면(p.208)에 있습니다.

## 수동태 / 과거분사

**다음 괄호 안에 들어갈 알맞은 말을 고르세요.**

1 The window was ( breaked / broken ) by Junwoo.

그 창문은 준우에 의해서 깨졌어.

2 This house was ( built / builded ) by my grandfather.

이 집은 나의 할아버지에 의해 지어졌다.

3 Dance music is ( hearded / heard ) in this fast food restaurant.

댄스 음악이 이 패스트푸드 음식점에서 들린다.

4 A chocolate cake was ( baked / bakeed ) by mom.

초콜릿 케이크는 엄마에 의해서 구워졌어.

5 A dog was ( hit / hited ) by a car.

개 한 마리가 차에 치였어.

6 The story was ( telled / told ) by me.

그 이야기는 나에 의해서 말해졌어.

7 You are ( grounded / ground ) for a week!

너는 일주일 동안 외출금지야!

8 That seat was not ( took / taken ).

저 자리는 주인이 없었어.

9 The music is not ( played / plaied ) by Janet.

그 음악은 Janet에 의해서 연주되는 게 아니야.

10 My bike was ( stolen / stole ) by someone.

내 자전거가 누군가에 의해 훔쳐졌어. (누군가 내 자전거를 훔쳤어.)

## 관계대명사

✎ 다음 괄호 안에 들어갈 알맞은 말을 고르세요.

1 I like movies ( who / that ) have happy endings.

나는 행복한 결말을 가진 영화들을 좋아해.

2 Minwoo found the watch ( who / which ) I lost yesterday.

민우는 내가 어제 잃어버린 시계를 찾았어.

3 My teacher is an American ( who / which ) comes from Chicago.

나의 선생님은 시카고에서 오신 미국인이셔.

4 I gave my mom a carnation ( what / which ) I made.

나는 엄마께 내가 만든 카네이션 한 송이를 드렸어.

5 The girl ( who / which ) is writing a letter is Sally.

편지를 쓰고 있는 그 소녀는 Sally야.

6 Catherine has a cat ( who / that ) is cute.

Catherine에게는 귀여운 고양이 한 마리가 있어.

7 I know a doctor ( who / which ) can help you.

나는 당신을 도와줄 수 있는 의사 한 명을 알아요.

8 He looked at the picture ( who / that ) was on the wall.

그는 벽에 걸린 그림을 봤어.

9 I have a friend ( who / which ) has a hamster.

나는 햄스터 한 마리를 가지고 있는 친구가 있어.

10 Junho is a student ( who / which ) is good at painting.

준호는 그림을 잘 그리는 학생이야.

# Grammar Review Answer 정답

## 수동태 / 과거분사

| | |
|---|---|
| 1 | The window was ( breaked / broken ) by Junwoo. |
| 2 | This house was ( built / builded ) by my grandfather. |
| 3 | Dance music is ( hearded / heard ) in this fast food restaurant. |
| 4 | A chocolate cake was ( baked / bakeed ) by mom. |
| 5 | A dog was ( hit / hited ) by a car. |
| 6 | The story was ( telled / told ) by me. |
| 7 | You are ( grounded / ground ) for a week! |
| 8 | That seat was not ( took / taken ). |
| 9 | The music is not ( played / plaied ) by Janet. |
| 10 | My bike was ( stolen / stole ) by someone. |

## 관계대명사

| | |
|---|---|
| 1 | I like movies ( who / that ) have happy endings. |
| 2 | Minwoo found the watch ( who / which ) I lost yesterday. |
| 3 | My teacher is an American ( who / which ) comes from Chicago. |
| 4 | I gave my mom a carnation ( what / which ) I made. |
| 5 | The girl ( who / which ) is writing a letter is Sally. |
| 6 | Catherine has a cat ( who / that ) is cute. |
| 7 | I know a doctor ( who / which ) can help you. |
| 8 | He looked at the picture ( who / that ) was on the wall. |
| 9 | I have a friend ( who / which ) has a hamster. |
| 10 | Junho is a student ( who / which ) is good at painting. |

정답은 뒷면에서 확인하세요.

# Say and write.

그림에 알맞은 단어를 큰 소리로 말하고 빈칸에 써 보세요.

1.

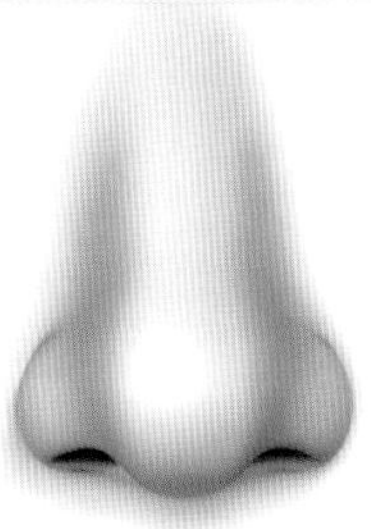

n o s e

2.

h _ _ _

3.

s _ _ _

4.

c _ _ _

5.

cl _ _ _

6.

ph _ _ _

## Say and write.

그림에 알맞은 단어를 큰 소리로 말하고 빈칸에 써 보세요.

1.

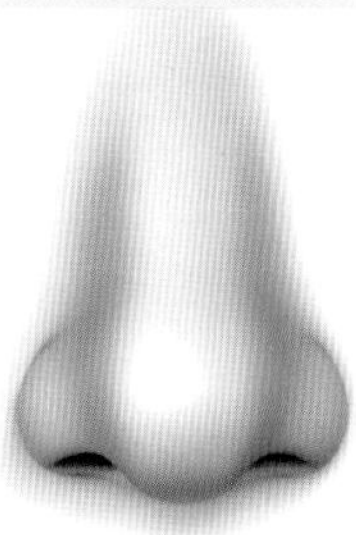

nose

2.

home

3.

soap

4.

cake

5.

cloud

6.

phone

MOTHERTONGUE
마더텅출판사
since1999.4.1.

# 초등영문법 3800제

# 정답과 해설

LEVEL 8

실력 2단계 수동태 / 관계대명사 / 관계부사

# 영문법 판매 1위,
# 초등 시리즈 초등영문법 3800제 동영상 강의

초등영문법에 필요한 것만 모았습니다.
영어에 대한 고민이 있으시면 저희 마더텅과 함께 하면 달라집니다.

**마더텅과 함께하는 단계별 레벨업 강의**
1단계부터 8단계까지 단계별 체계적인 영문법 학습

**친절한 Q&A 게시판**
친절하고 자세한 Q&A 게시판에서 강의를 수강하다 생긴 모든 궁금증을 해결

**오현진 선생님**
초등영문법 3800제 level 1~4

**어려운 영어를 쉬운 설명으로 쉽게 가보자!**

- (현) 마더텅 고등영어 강사
- (현) 대치동 새움학원 대표고등강사
- (현) 강남구청 인터넷 수능 방송 강사
- (현) 수박씨닷컴 중등영어 대표강사 [수강생 강의만족도 100%]

**최주영 선생님**
초등영문법 3800제 level 5~8

**영어, 고민하지 마시고 꽃길만 걷게 해드립니다!**

- (현) 마더텅 고등영어 강사
- (현) 대치동 위자듀 재수종합 독해 강사
- (현) 전국 중고등학교 입시진로 강사
- (전) 글로벌 1st 고등 영어 전임 강사

## 강의 구성

※ 강의 수, 가격 등은 당사 사정에 따라 변경될 수 있습니다.

| 교재명 | 가격 | 강의 수 | 수강 기간 |
|---|---|---|---|
| 초등영문법 3800제 LEVEL 1 | 5,900원 | 30강 | 150일(무료 수강연장 1회) |
| 초등영문법 3800제 LEVEL 2 | 5,900원 | 26강 | 150일(무료 수강연장 1회) |
| 초등영문법 3800제 LEVEL 3 | 5,900원 | 30강 | 150일(무료 수강연장 1회) |
| 초등영문법 3800제 LEVEL 4 | 5,900원 | 34강 | 150일(무료 수강연장 1회) |
| 초등영문법 3800제 LEVEL 5 | 5,900원 | 22강 | 150일(무료 수강연장 1회) |
| 초등영문법 3800제 LEVEL 6 | 5,900원 | 23강 | 150일(무료 수강연장 1회) |
| 초등영문법 3800제 LEVEL 7 | 5,900원 | 22강 | 150일(무료 수강연장 1회) |
| 초등영문법 3800제 LEVEL 8 | 5,900원 | 20강 | 150일(무료 수강연장 1회) |
| 초등영문법 3800제 LEVEL 1~8 | 39,900원 | 207강 | 365일(무료 수강연장 1회) |

MOTHERTONGUE 마더텅출판사 since1999.4.1. echo study (주)에코스터디

문의전화 1661-1064 (07:00~22:00) 문자 010-6640-1064 (문자수신전용) www.toptutor.co.kr 포털에서 마더텅 검색

※ 환불 요청 시 「학원의 설립 · 운영 및 과외교습에 관한 법률」에 의거하여 환불해 드립니다.

# 초등영문법 3800제

# 정답과 해설

LEVEL 8

실력 2단계

# Chapter 01 수동태

## Unit 01 격 변화와 수동태에 쓰이는 불규칙 동사

### Check and Write

▶ 본문 p.9

A 2. The cat, the cat　3. They, them

B 2. told - told　3. wrote - written

4. took - taken　5. sent - sent

6. caught - caught　7. ate - eaten

8. did - done　9. hid(ed) - hid(den)

10. won - won　11. felt - felt

12. hit - hit

## Unit 02 수동태 만드는 법

### Check and Write

▶ 본문 p.11

2. I made this airplane
나는 이 비행기를 만들었어.
3. Many people use the subway
많은 사람들이 지하철을 이용해.
4. My computer was fixed by my dad
내 컴퓨터는 우리 아빠에 의해서 고쳐졌어.

### Practice 1

▶ 본문 p.12

2. I, Sihu　3. The meeting, him
4. I, the news　5. A present, him
6. She, the news　7. It, him
8. They, many people　9. A book, you
10. He, me　12. born
13. taught　14. known
15. found　16. heard
17. read　18. sold
19. planted　20. eaten

### Practice 2

▶ 본문 p.14

2. He was scolded
3. She is sent to her room
그녀는 그녀의 방으로 보내져.
4. She was sent home from school
5. Junwoo is called a trouble maker
준우는 사고뭉치로 불려.
6. was broken by Junwoo
7. You are grounded
8. Justin was surprised at that
Justin은 그것에 깜짝 놀랐어.
9. You are loved by your parents
너는 너의 부모님에게 사랑받아.
10. I was sent by the prince
11. today is called the present
12. is introduced by her
13. Happiness is found in the darkness
행복은 어둠 속에서 발견된다.
14. They are remembered by us
그들은 우리에 의해 기억된다.
15. We were raised
16. Clara is invited by grandma
17. The letter is written by Sihu
그 편지는 시후에 의해 쓰여진다.
18. The fish was cooked by my mother
그 생선은 나의 어머니에 의해 요리되었어.
19. This picture was painted by her
이 그림은 그녀에 의해 그려졌어.
20. This box was opened by me
이 상자는 나에 의해 열렸다.

### Practice 3

▶ 본문 p.17

2. The dog was treated by the vet
그 개는 수의사에게 치료받았어.
3. A dog was hit by a car
개 한 마리가 차에 치였어.
4. His toys were hid(den) by Mori
그의 장난감들은 모리에 의해서 숨겨졌어.
5. The skirt was made by my mother
그 치마는 우리 엄마에 의해 만들어졌어.
6. A new restaurant was opened by them
새로운 식당이 그들에 의해 열렸다.
7. The thief was seen by some people
도둑은 몇몇 사람들에게 목격되었어.
8. The thief was caught by the police
도둑은 경찰에게 잡혔어.
9. The wall is painted by her
그 벽은 그녀에 의해서 페인트칠 되어져.
10. A secret was kept by them
비밀은 그들에 의해 지켜졌어.
11. The story was told by me
그 이야기는 나에 의해서 말해졌어.
12. The window was broken by Junwoo
그 창문은 준우에 의해서 깨졌어.
13. He is scolded by his mom
그는 그의 엄마에게 야단맞아.
14. The work was finished by me
그 일은 나에 의해 마무리되었어.
15. My bike was stolen by someone
내 자전거는 누군가에게 도둑맞았다.
16. My shoes are chewed by my dog
내 신발은 내 강아지에 의해서 물어뜯어져.
17. The flowerpot was broken by Kevin
화분은 Kevin에 의해서 깨졌다.
18. This house was built by my grandfather
이 집은 나의 할아버지에 의해 지어졌어.
19. The question is answered by the teacher
질문은 선생님에 의해 답변되어져.
20. A chocolate cake was baked by mom
초콜릿 케이크는 엄마에 의해서 구워졌어.

### Let's Practice More!

### Set 01

▶ 본문 p.20

02. He　03. You　04. me

05. me
06. her
07. her
08. me
09. We
10. She
11. You
12. me

**Set 02** ▶ 본문 p.21

02. introduced
03. found
04. remembered
05. raised
06. invited
07. hit
08. called
09. cooked
10. painted
11. opened
12. surprised
13. broken
14. sent

**Set 03** ▶ 본문 p.22

02. 능
03. 능
04. 수
05. 능
06. 수
07. 수
08. 능
09. 수
10. 능
11. 수
12. 능
13. 능
14. 수

**Set 04** ▶ 본문 p.23

02. 알려져 있다
03. 발견되다
04. 심어지다
05. 읽히다
06. 태어났다
07. 보내지다
08. 불리다
09. 깨졌다
10. 놀랐다
11. 길러졌다
12. 초대되다

**Set 05** ▶ 본문 p.24

02. by Sihu
03. by my mother
04. by her
05. by me
06. by them
07. by the police
08. by someone
09. by grandma
10. by her
11. by him
12. by us
13. by you
14. by me

**Set 06** ▶ 본문 p.25

02. remembered
03. heard
04. raised
05. written
06. planted
07. read
08. grounded
09. kept
10. told
11. sent
12. broken
13. called
14. chewed

**Set 07** ▶ 본문 p.26

02. surprised
03. ○
04. ○
05. ○
06. sent
07. ○
08. written
09. born
10. ○
11. eaten
12. sold
13. ○
14. called
15. broken
16. ○
17. grounded
18. ○
19. hit
20. ○

**Set 08** ▶ 본문 p.28

02. Stamps are collected by me
우표는 나에 의해서 수집된다.

03. I clean the room
나는 그 방을 청소한다.

04. His toys were hid(den) by Mori
그의 장난감들은 모리에 의해서 숨겨졌어.

05. He teaches us
그는 우리들을 가르치셔.

06. The skirt was made by my mother
그 치마는 우리 엄마에 의해 만들어졌어.

07. A new restaurant was opened by them
새로운 식당이 그들에 의해 열렸다.

08. Your parents love you
너의 부모님은 너를 사랑하셔.

09. The prince sent me to save you
왕자님은 너를 구하기 위해 나를 보내셨어.

10. My mother cooked the fish
나의 어머니는 그 생선을 요리하셨어.

11. Kevin broke the flowerpot
Kevin은 꽃병을 깨뜨렸어.

12. Junwoo broke the window
준우가 그 창문을 깼어.

13. Someone stole my bike
누군가가 내 자전거를 훔쳤어.

14. The thief was caught by the police
도둑은 경찰에게 잡혔어.

15. The thief was seen by some people
도둑은 몇몇 사람들에게 목격되었어.

16. A secret was kept by them
비밀은 그들에 의해 지켜졌어.

17. The story was told by me
그 이야기는 나에 의해서 말해졌어.

18. My grandfather built this house
나의 할아버지가 이 집을 지으셨어.

19. The teacher answers the question
선생님은 질문에 대답하셔.

20. My shoes are chewed by my dog
내 신발은 내 강아지에 의해서 물어뜯어져.

## Unit 03 수동태의 부정문

**Check and Write** ▶ 본문 p.31

2. These cookies were not made by me,
These cookies weren't made by me
이 쿠키들은 나에 의해서 만들어지지 않았어.

3. The candy was not eaten by Cathy,
The candy wasn't eaten by Cathy
그 사탕은 Cathy에 의해 먹어지지 않았어.

4. These shoes were not made for me,
These shoes weren't made for me
이 신발은 나를 위해 만들어진 게 아니었어.

## Unit 04 수동태의 의문문

**Check and Write** ▶ 본문 p.33

2. Are tomatoes grown by your grandmother
토마토는 너의 할머니에 의해서 키워지니?

3. Was the diary written by Nayeon
그 일기는 나연이에 의해서 쓰였니?

4. Were these pictures taken by you
이 사진들은 너에 의해서 찍힌 거니?

**Practice 1** ▶ 본문 p.34

2. am not
3. was not
4. is not
5. was not
6. is not
7. was not
8. were not
9. was not
10. was not
12. Were those books
13. Was this bread
14. Is it
15. Was this picture
16. Was the meeting
17. Was the building
18. Was the memo
19. Were the dishes
20. Was the bathroom

## Practice 2

▶ 본문 p.36

2. written 3. cancelled 4. delayed
5. broken 6. bitten 7. attacked
8. was 9. played 10. was invented

12. Are you excited
너 신나니?
13. The museum is visited by many people
그 박물관은 많은 사람들에 의해서 방문된다.
14. Are you grounded
너 외출금지 된 거야?
15. I am not grounded
나는 외출금지 된 게 아니야.
16. His room was cleaned
그의 방이 청소되었어!
17. They are loved by many fans
그들은 많은 팬들로부터 사랑받아.
18. Was the computer fixed by him
컴퓨터가 그에 의해서 고쳐졌나요?
19. It is not fixed
20. The school picnic was not cancelled
학교 소풍은 취소되지 않았어.

## Practice 3

▶ 본문 p.39

2. This building was not[wasn't] built in 1989
이 건물은 1989년에 지어지지 않았어.
3. My cell phone was not[wasn't] lost
나의 핸드폰은 분실되지 않았어.
4. This seat is not[isn't] taken
이 자리는 주인이 없어.
5. Her grades were not[weren't] raised
그녀의 성적은 오르지 않았어.
6. I am[I'm] not bored
나는 심심하지 않아요.
7. I am[I'm] not interested in mobile games
나는 모바일 게임에 관심이 없어요.
8. This bench was not[wasn't] made of wood
이 벤치는 나무로 만들어지지 않았어.
9. I was not[wasn't] fired
나는 해고되지 않았어.
10. My allowance was not[wasn't] spent on buying snacks
내 용돈은 군것질거리를 사는 데 쓰이지 않았어.
12. Is he disappointed
그는 실망했니?
13. Are we sent to the haunted house
우리는 유령의 집으로 보내지니?
14. Was your smart phone stolen
너의 스마트폰은 도난당했니?
15. Was this soup cooked by mom
이 스프는 엄마가 요리하셨니?
16. Was this party planned by Jane
이 파티는 Jane에 의해 계획되었니?
17. Is Spanish spoken in many countries
스페인어는 많은 나라에서 말해지니(쓰이니)?
18. Was the ship made in Greece
그 배는 그리스에서 만들어졌니?
19. Is this seat taken
이 자리는 주인이 있니?
20. Was she born in Korea
그녀는 한국에서 태어났니?

## Let's Practice More!

### Set 01

▶ 본문 p.42

02. am not 03. not taken 04. not played
05. was not 06. is not
07. not invited 08. were not 09. not prepared
10. was not 11. not saved 12. were not

### Set 02

▶ 본문 p.43

02. I was not[wasn't] bitten by a dog
나는 개에게 물리지 않았어.
03. The dress was not[wasn't] designed by a young designer
그 드레스는 젊은 디자이너에 의해서 디자인되지 않았어.
04. The piano is not[isn't] played by my father
그 피아노는 나의 아버지에 의해서 연주되지 않아.
05. The airplane was not[wasn't] invented by him
그 비행기는 그에 의해 발명되지 않았어.
06. The park is not[isn't] cleaned by us
그 공원은 우리에 의해 청소되지 않아.
07. The museum is not[isn't] visited by many people
그 박물관은 많은 사람들에 의해서 방문되지 않아.
08. I am[I'm] not grounded
나는 외출금지 된 게 아니야.
09. His room was not[wasn't] cleaned
그의 방이 청소되지 않았어!
10. They are not[They're not / They aren't] loved by many fans
그들은 많은 팬들로부터 사랑받지 않아.
11. It is not[It's not / It isn't] fixed
그건 고쳐지지 않았어.
12. The school picnic was not[wasn't] cancelled
학교 소풍은 취소되지 않았어.
13. These cookies were not[weren't] baked yesterday
이 쿠키들은 어제 구워지지 않았어.
14. This building was not[wasn't] built in 1989
이 건물은 1989년에 지어지지 않았어.

### Set 03

▶ 본문 p.44

02. Was the soccer game cancelled because of heavy rain
축구 경기가 폭우 때문에 취소됐어?
03. Was it delayed
그건 미뤄졌어?
04. Is your leg broken
너의 다리가 부러진 거니?
05. Were you attacked by Mina's dog
너는 미나의 개에 의해서 공격당했니?
06. Is this seat taken
이 자리는 주인이 있니?
07. Were those books borrowed by Jane
저 책들은 Jane에 의해 빌려졌니?
08. Was this bread baked by Paul
이 빵은 Paul에 의해서 구워졌니?
09. Is it filled with butter cream
그것은 버터크림으로 채워져 있니?

10. Was this picture painted by him
이 그림은 그에 의해서 그려졌니?

11. Was the meeting cancelled by her
그 회의는 그녀에 의해서 취소되었니?

12. Was the building built by them
그 건물은 그들에 의해서 지어졌니?

13. Was the memo written by Dana
그 메모는 다나에 의해서 쓰여졌니?

14. Are you excited
너 신나니?

**Set 04** ▶ 본문 p.45

| | | | |
|---|---|---|---|
| 02. Is | 03. sent | 04. Was | 05. made |
| 06. planned | 07. spoken | 08. Was | 09. Is |
| 10. Was | 11. cleaned | 12. Are | |

**Set 05** ▶ 본문 p.46

| | | | |
|---|---|---|---|
| 02. isn't | 03. weren't | 04. aren't | 05. wasn't |
| 06. wasn't | 07. isn't | 08. wasn't | 09. isn't |
| 10. wasn't | 11. aren't | 12. wasn't | 13. weren't |
| 14. wasn't | | | |

**Set 06** ▶ 본문 p47

| | | | |
|---|---|---|---|
| 02. taken | 03. ○ | 04. ○ | 05. saved |
| 06. written | 07. ○ | 08. ○ | 09. filled |
| 10. played | 11. invented | 12. ○ | 13. prepared |
| 14. ○ | | | |

**Set 07** ▶ 본문 p.48

| | | | |
|---|---|---|---|
| 02. Is | 03. ○ | 04. ○ | 05. designed |
| 06. ○ | 07. ○ | 08. ○ | 09. grounded |
| 10. ○ | 11. visited | 12. ○ | 13. ○ |
| 14. was | 15. loved | 16. Was | 17. written |
| 18. washed | 19. ○ | 20. made | |

**Set 08** ▶ 본문 p.50

| | | |
|---|---|---|
| 02. planned | 03. built | 04. raised |
| 05. disappointed | 06. lost | 07. sent |
| 08. taken | 09. stolen | 10. bored |
| 11. raised | 12. cooked | 13. baked |
| 14. taken | 15. interested | 16. made |
| 17. born | 18. fired | 19. spent |
| 20. fixed | | |

## Chapter 01 실전테스트 ▶ 본문 p.52

01. ①

02. 현재분사: breaking, running
과거분사: broken, run, closed

03. My purse was stolen by him.
내 지갑은 그에 의해 도난당했다.

| | | |
|---|---|---|
| 04. ④ | 05. ③ | 06. ① |
| 07. ② | 08. ② | 09. ③ |

10. (1) 능동태 (2) 수동태 (3) 능동태 (4) 수동태

| | | |
|---|---|---|
| 11. ③ | 12. stolen, 훔쳐진, 과거분사 | |
| 13. 수 | 14. 능 | 15. 수 |
| 16. 능 | 17. 능 | |

18. A plan was made by us.
계획은 우리에 의해 만들어졌다.

19. The bottle was filled by them.
그 병은 그들에 의해 채워졌다.

20. The notebooks were found by Susan.
그 공책들은 Susan에 의해 발견되었다.

21. The light bulb is changed by him.
그 전구는 그에 의해 교체된다.

22. The door was locked by us.
그 문은 우리에 의해 잠겼다.

23. My glasses were broken by him.
내 안경은 그에 의해 부러졌다.

24. Read the book if you're interested.
만약에 네가 관심이 있다면 그 책을 읽어.

25. He is playing tennis now.
그는 지금 테니스를 치고 있다.

26. Sushi is eaten in Japan.
초밥은 일본에서 먹어진다.

27. Was it made by the carpenters?
그것은 그 목수들에 의해 만들어졌니?

28. Is this table moved by my classmates?
이 탁자는 내 반 친구들에 의해 옮겨지니?

29. Were the chairs fixed by him?
그 의자들은 그에 의해 수리되었니?

30. Are chopsticks used by many Asians?
젓가락은 많은 아시아인들에 의해 사용되니?

# Chapter 02 관계대명사

## Unit 01 관계대명사

### Check and Write
▶ 본문 p.59

2. which 3. who 4. who 5. which

## Unit 02 관계대명사의 종류

### Check and Write
▶ 본문 p.61

2. who 3. that 4. who
5. which 6. that

### Practice 1
▶ 본문 p.62

A 2. which 3. who 4. which 5. who
B 1. who 2. which 3. who
4. which 5. which
C 1. which 2. who 3. who
4. who 5. who
D 1. who 2. who 3. which
4. which 5. which

### Practice 2
▶ 본문 p.64

2. The girl 3. movies 4. the friend
5. dogs 6. the skirt 7. a doctor
8. the student 9. a man 10. a man
12. that 13. who 14. which
15. which 16. who 17. which
18. who 19. who 20. who

### Practice 3
▶ 본문 p.67

2. Look at the dog which[that] is biting his finger
그의 손가락을 물고 있는 그 개를 봐.
3. The teacher praised the boy who[that] helped the poor
선생님은 가난한 사람들을 도와준 그 소년을 칭찬하셨어.
4. He likes the girl who[that] has curly hair
그는 곱슬머리를 가진 그 여자아이를 좋아해.
5. It was Minwoo who[that] won first place
우승한 건 민우였어.
6. I found the candies which[that] were on the table
나는 테이블에 있던 사탕을 찾았어.
7. I saw the man who[that] was helping an old man
나는 한 노인을 도와드리고 있는 그 남자를 봤어.
8. She is the teacher who[that] teaches us English
그녀는 우리에게 영어를 가르쳐주시는 선생님이셔.
9. She has a son who[that] raised a turtle
그녀에게는 거북이를 길렀던 아들이 한 명 있어.
10. This is the book which[that] is about World War II
이건 2차 세계 대전에 대한 책이야.
12. which she gave to me
13. That is my younger brother who
14. people who help others
15. which was eating carrots
16. a healthy boy who enjoys palying football
17. The kid who is over there
18. the girl who likes David
19. This is the puppy that
20. Dana has some photos that

### Let's Practice More!

#### Set 01
▶ 본문 p.70

02. which 03. who 04. that 05. who
06. that 07. that 08. which 09. which
10. who 11. who 12. which

#### Set 02
▶ 본문 p.71

02. the razor 03. the dog 04. a tree
05. a girl 06. a dog 07. the cookies
08. the friend 09. the skirt 10. a man
11. the flowers 12. That girl 13. a carnation
14. an American

#### Set 03
▶ 본문 p.72

02. which 03. who 04. who 05. who
06. which 07. who 08. that 09. which
10. who 11. which 12. who 13. which
14. who

#### Set 04
▶ 본문 p.73

02. ○ 03. which[that] 04. ○
05. ○ 06. ○ 07. who[that]
08. which[that] 09. who[that] 10. ○
11. who[that] 12. who[that]

#### Set 05
▶ 본문 p.74

02. that 03. who, that 04. who
05. which 06. which, that 07. who, that
08. who 09. which 10. which, that
11. which 12. who, that 13. who
14. who, that

#### Set 06
▶ 본문 p.75

02. who[that] 03. who[that] 04. which[that]
05. which[that] 06. who[that] 07. who[that]
08. who[that] 09. who[that] 10. who[that]
11. who[that] 12. which[that] 13. which[that]
14. which[that]

#### Set 07
▶ 본문 p.76

02. I bought the candies that I like
나는 내가 좋아하는 그 사탕들을 샀어.
03. Mom is pleased with the present which dad gave to her
엄마는 아빠가 주신 선물에 기뻐하셔.
04. My grandmother is a French who comes from Lyon
나의 할머니는 Lyon에서 오신 프랑스인이셔.
05. I like the dress that Rebecca is wearing
나는 Rebecca가 입고 있는 그 드레스가 마음에 들어.
06. People like dogs which are friendly with them
사람들은 그들과 친하게 지내는 개들을 좋아해.
07. I know a lawyer who can help you

나는 당신을 도와줄 수 있는 변호사 한 명을 알아요.

08. You can't marry a man that you just met
너는 방금 만난 남자와 결혼할 수 없어!

09. Dad gave mom the flowers that she likes
아빠는 엄마에게 그녀가 좋아하는 꽃을 주셨어.

10. I gave my mom a carnation which I made
나는 엄마께 내가 만든 카네이션을 드렸어.

11. This is the dog which helped the police catch the thief
이것은 경찰이 도둑을 잡는 것을 도운 개야!

12. Dad was using the razor which mom gave him
아빠는 엄마가 주신 면도기를 사용하고 계셨어.

13. He was watching a movie that I like
그는 내가 좋아하는 영화를 보고 있었어.

14. The thief who broke into Mina's house was caught by the police
미나의 집에 침입했던 도둑은 경찰에 의해서 잡혔어.

15. The tall man who moved to another city returned here
다른 도시로 이사 갔던 그 키가 큰 남자는 여기로 돌아왔어.

16. Minwoo found the watch which I lost yesterday
민우는 내가 어제 잃어버린 시계를 찾았어.

17. Uncle Jack fell in love with Sarah who was kind to him
Jack 삼촌은 그에게 친절했던 Sarah에게 반하셨어.

18. The girl who is writing a letter is Jane
편지를 쓰고 있는 그 소녀는 Jane이야.

19. I am eating the cookies that my mom baked
나는 엄마가 구우신 쿠키를 먹고 있어.

20. My younger brother was reading a book which dad gave to him
내 남동생은 아빠가 그에게 주신 책을 읽고 있었어.

**Set 08** ▶ 본문 p.78

02. Mina has a dog which[that] is brave
미나는 용감한 개 한 마리를 가지고 있어.

03. My little brother was playing with his friends who[that] live next door
내 남동생은 옆집에 사는 그의 친구들과 놀고 있었어.

04. I saw Mina who[that] was playing with her dog in the yard
나는 마당에서 그녀의 개와 놀고 있는 미나를 봤어.

05. It was all thanks to the dog which[that] Mina raises
그것은 모두 미나가 기르는 개 덕분이었어.

06. I am a tree which[that] has lived here for 50 years
나는 이곳에 50년 동안 살았던 나무야.

07. All his friends like Minwoo who[that] is always smiling
그의 모든 친구들은 항상 웃고 있는 민우를 좋아해.

08. Christian is a boy who[that] comes from Germany
Christian은 독일에서 온 소년이다.

09. There is a girl who[that] has long hair
긴 머리를 가진 소녀가 있다.

10. Sophie likes her dog which[that] came from Japan
Sophie는 일본에서 온 그녀의 개를 좋아한다.

11. I don't like movies which[that] have sad endings
나는 슬픈 결말을 가진 영화들을 좋아하지 않아.

12. He is the friend who[that] makes me happy
그는 나를 행복하게 만들어주는 친구야.

13. That girl who[that] is on the playground is Charlotte
운동장에 있는 저 소녀는 Charlotte이야

14. Those are my parents who[that] are sitting on the bench
벤치에 앉아 있는 저 분들은 나의 부모님이셔.

15. I found the man who[that] stole my key
나는 내 열쇠를 훔쳐간 남자를 찾았다.

16. I am eating the cake which[that] my mom baked
나는 엄마가 구우신 케이크를 먹고 있어.

17. The man who[that] is writing a letter is Vincent
편지를 쓰고 있는 남자는 Vincent야.

18. Kate had lunch with a man who[that] has blue hair
Kate는 파란 머리를 가진 한 남자와 점심을 먹었어.

19. We bought the candies which[that] you like
우리는 네가 좋아하는 사탕을 샀어.

20. The boy who[that] often teases Charlotte is Charlie
Charlotte을 자주 놀리는 그 남자아이는 Charlie야.

# Chapter 03 관계대명사의 종류

## Unit 01 주격 관계대명사(1)

**Check and Write** ▶ 본문 p.83

2. is 3. are 4. are 5. is

## Unit 02 주격 관계대명사(2)

**Check and Write** ▶ 본문 p.85

2. who 3. that 4. who 5. who

**Practice 1** ▶ 본문 p.86

**A** 2. who 3. who 4. who
5. which

**B** 1. who 2. who 3. which
4. who 5. who

**C** 1. who 2. who 3. which
4. which 5. which

**D** 1. who 2. which 3. which
4. who 5. who

**Practice 2** ▶ 본문 p.88

2. the fruit which is popular in spring
3. my allowance which is little even now
4. something that might save you some money
5. two coupons which can be used
6. a story which might interest me
7. who gives us presents
8. which are on the table
9. the actress who is famous
10. an oasis which reenergizes us
11. people who lived exciting lives
12. There's something that matters even more
13. a friend who won't run away

14. She is the girl who
15. It is fear that
16. the one who is lucky
17. who is good at finding things
18. Those who are willing to die
19. those who help themselves
20. The man who chases two rabbits

**Practice 3** ▶ 본문 p.91

| | | | |
|---|---|---|---|
| 2. × | 3. ○ | 4. × | 5. ○ |
| 6. × | 7. ○ | 8. ○ | 9. × |
| 10. × | 11. ○ | 12. × | 13. ○ |
| 14. × | 15. × | 16. × | 17. ○ |
| 18. × | 19. ○ | 20. × | |

**Let's Practice More!**

**Set 01** ▶ 본문 p.94

| | | | |
|---|---|---|---|
| 02. × | 03. ○ | 04. × | 05. × |
| 06. × | 07. × | 08. ○ | 09. ○ |
| 10. ○ | 11. × | 12. × | |

**Set 02** ▶ 본문 p.95

| | | | |
|---|---|---|---|
| 02. × | 03. × | 04. ○ | 05. ○ |
| 06. ○ | 07. ○ | 08. × | 09. ○ |
| 10. × | 11. ○ | 12. × | 13. × |
| 14. ○ | | | |

**Set 03** ▶ 본문 p.96

| | | | |
|---|---|---|---|
| 02. ○ | 03. ○ | 04. × | 05. ○ |
| 06. ○ | 07. × | 08. × | 09. ○ |
| 10. ○ | 11. ○ | 12. × | 13. ○ |
| 14. ○ | | | |

**Set 04** ▶ 본문 p.97

| | | |
|---|---|---|
| 02. that | 03. that, who | 04. that, who |
| 05. that | 06. that, who | 07. that, which |
| 08. that, which | 09. that, who | 10. that, which |
| 11. that | 12. who | 13. that |
| 14. that, who | | |

**Set 05** ▶ 본문 p.98

| | | |
|---|---|---|
| 02. ○ | 03. ○ | 04. ○ |
| 05. who[that] | 06. who[that] | 07. ○ |
| 08. ○ | 09. ○ | 10. which[that] |
| 11. ○ | 12. ○ | 13. who[that] |
| 14. ○ | | |

**Set 06** ▶ 본문 p.99

| | | | |
|---|---|---|---|
| 02. is | 03. are | 04. live | 05. harm |
| 06. is | 07. gives | 08. matters | 09. speaks |
| 10. was | 11. make | 12. is | 13. have |
| 14. are | | | |

**Set 07** ▶ 본문 p.100

| | | | |
|---|---|---|---|
| 02. ○ | 03. helps | 04. ○ | 05. ○ |
| 06. is | 07. ○ | 08. is | 09. ○ |
| 10. is | 11. is | 12. has | 13. harm |
| 14. is | 15. ○ | 16. ○ | 17. ○ |
| 18. need | 19. live | 20. ○ | |

**Set 08** ▶ 본문 p.102

| | | |
|---|---|---|
| 02. was | 03. lives | 04. that[which] |
| 05. that[which] | 06. make | 07. like |
| 08. which[that] | 09. which[that] | 10. is |
| 11. who[that] | 12. which[that] | 13. help |
| 14. who[that] | 15. were | 16. who[that] |
| 17. is | 18. which[that] | 19. chases |
| 20. share | | |

## Unit 03 목적격 관계대명사(1)

**Check and Write** ▶ 본문 p.105

2. 주격　3. 목적격　4. 주격　5. 목적격

## Unit 04 목적격 관계대명사(2)

**Check and Write** ▶ 본문 p.107

2. that　3. which　4. who　5. that

**Practice 1** ▶ 본문 p.108

**A** 2. which　3. whom　4. whom　5. which
**B** 1. which　2. which　3. whom　4. whom　5. whom
**C** 1. whom　2. which　3. which　4. whom
**D** 1. which　2. which　3. which　4. which　5. which　6. which

**Practice 2** ▶ 본문 p.110

| | | |
|---|---|---|
| 2. the friends | 3. the textbook | 4. a dark side |
| 5. something | 6. the only weapon | |
| 7. the scene | 8. the funniest thing | |
| 9. the ball | 10. a secret | 12. that |
| 13. that | 14. that | 15. which |
| 16. that | 17. that | 18. that |
| 19. whom | 20. that | |

**Practice 3** ▶ 본문 p.113

2. Look at the mess which[that] my dog made
 내 개가 만든 엉망진창인 상태를 봐!
3. Do you remember the boy whom[that] we met at the pool
 너 우리가 수영장에서 만났던 그 소년을 기억하니?
4. This is the camera which[that] my father gave me
 이건 우리 아빠가 나에게 준 카메라야.
5. This is the story which[that] my father read to me
 이건 나의 아버지께서 나에게 읽어주신 이야기야.
6. These are the photos which[that] I like
 이것들은 내가 좋아하는 사진들이야.
7. My dog tore up the photo which[that] I love
 나의 개가 내가 아주 좋아하는 사진을 찢어놨어.
8. They drew a picture of a tiger which[that] they saw at the zoo
 그들은 그들이 동물원에서 보았던 호랑이의 그림을 그렸어.
9. I like the candies which[that] I bought at the market
 나는 시장에서 구입한 그 사탕들이 좋아.
10. The boy whom[that] I don't like always tells lies
 내가 좋아하지 않는 그 소년은 항상 거짓말을 한다.
12. the exam that we have to pass

13. Every dream that you wish
14. no one I can talk to
15. the nicest teacher we have
16. The one thing that I wanted
17. The girl whom I met yesterday
18. The man whom I talked to
19. Going to the market was the bravest thing that
20. The tofu which he bought

**Let's Practice More!**

**Set 01** ▶ 본문 p.116

02. ○  03. ○  04. ×  05. ○
06. ○  07. ×  08. ○  09. ○
10. ×  11. ○  12. ×

**Set 02** ▶ 본문 p.117

02. ○  03. ○  04. ×  05. ○
06. ×  07. ○  08. ○  09. ×
10. ×  11. ○  12. ×  13. ×
14. ○

**Set 03** ▶ 본문 p.118

02. ×  03. ○  04. ×  05. ○
06. ○  07. ×  08. ○  09. ×
10. ○  11. ×  12. ○

**Set 04** ▶ 본문 p.119

02. 목  03. 목  04. 목  05. 주
06. 목  07. 주  08. 목  09. 주
10. 주  11. 목  12. 목

**Set 05** ▶ 본문 p.120

02. which  03. that  04. that  05. which
06. which  07. that  08. whom  09. that
10. whom  11. that  12. which  13. that
14. that

**Set 06** ▶ 본문 p.121

02. which[that]  03. ○  04. whom[that]
05. which[that]  06. ○  07. ○
08. which[that]  09. ○  10. which[that]
11. ○  12. ○  13. ○
14. which[that]

**Set 07** ▶ 본문 p.122

02. like  03. plays  04. like  05. sees
06. are  07. show  08. have  09. love
10. was  11. want  12. have  13. respect
14. tells  15. is  16. was  17. share
18. has  19. was  20. like

**Set 08** ▶ 본문 p.124

02. ○  03. ○  04. ○  05. ×
06. ○  07. ×  08. ○  09. ×
10. ×  11. ○  12. ○  13. ×
14. ○  15. ×  16. ○  17. ○
18. ×  19. ○  20. ×

# Chapter 04 관계대명사 what / 관계부사

## Unit 01 관계대명사 what

**Check and Write** ▶ 본문 p.129

2. what  3. which  4. What  5. which

## Unit 02 관계부사

**Check and Write** ▶ 본문 p.131

2. how  3. when  4. why  5. where

**Practice 1** ▶ 본문 p.132

**A** 2. where  3. why  4. how  5. What
**B** 1. why  2. when  3. where  4. what
5. the way
**C** 1. the way  2. why  3. what  4. where
5. the way  6. what
**D** 1. where  2. where  3. what  4. why

**Practice 2** ▶ 본문 p.134

2. when  3. the way  4. where  5. when
6. why  7. what  8. what, what
9. what  10. when  12. when  13. how
14. where  15. why  16. how  17. why
18. where  19. why  20. how

**Practice 3** ▶ 본문 p.137

2. how I can get there
3. What we can do with computers
4. show you what I've learned
5. what I want to do now
6. what I lost yesterday
7. what I wanted to tell you
8. What they bought
9. only eats what she likes
10. That's what I do
11. I felt bad about what I did
나는 내가 한 것에 대해 기분이 좋지 않았어.
12. what she heard
13. the place where we first met
14. where she studies

15. the moment when she hugged me
16. the reason why they got married
17. What she said
18. the day when they will be together
19. the reason why you like those pants
20. what they said

**Let's Practice More!**

**Set 01** ▶ 본문 p.140

| | |
|---|---|
| 02. which | 03. which |
| 04. what | 05. which |
| 06. what | 07. what, what |
| 08. what | 09. which |
| 10. what | 11. what |
| 12. which | |

**Set 02** ▶ 본문 p.141

| | | |
|---|---|---|
| 02. × | 03. × | 04. ○ |
| 05. ○ | 06. × | 07. ○ |
| 08. × | 09. ○ | 10. ○ |
| 11. × | 12. ○ | 13. × |
| 14. ○ | | |

**Set 03** ▶ 본문 p.142

| | |
|---|---|
| 02. 내가 좋아하는 것 | 03. 내가 했던 것 |
| 04. 내가 구운 | 05. 네가 말한 것 |
| 06. 그가 필요했던 것 | 07. 네가 믿는 것 |
| 08. 그녀가 할 수 있는 것 | 09. 내가 산 |
| 10. 내가 필요한 것 | 11. 그가 사랑했던 |
| 12. 내가 찍은 | 13. 그가 말한 것 |
| 14. 내가 들은 것 | |

**Set 04** ▶ 본문 p.143

| | |
|---|---|
| 02. when | 03. why |
| 04. where | 05. when |
| 06. why | 07. when |
| 08. when | 09. where |
| 10. why | 11. when |
| 12. where | |

**Set 05** ▶ 본문 p.144

| | | |
|---|---|---|
| 02. ○ | 03. × | 04. ○ |
| 05. × | 06. × | 07. ○ |
| 08. ○ | 09. ○ | 10. ○ |
| 11. × | 12. ○ | 13. × |
| 14. ○ | | |

**Set 06** ▶ 본문 p.145

| | |
|---|---|
| 02. ○ | 03. ○ |
| 04. how[the way] | 05. ○ |
| 06. how[the way] | 07. ○ |
| 08. where | 09. ○ |
| 10. when | 11. why |
| 12. how[the way] | 13. ○ |
| 14. (the reason) why | |

**Set 07** ▶ 본문 p.146

| | |
|---|---|
| 02. when | 03. where |
| 04. when | 05. where |
| 06. why | 07. how |
| 08. when | 09. how |
| 10. when | 11. where |
| 12. how | 13. why |
| 14. where | 15. when |
| 16. why | 17. how |
| 18. where | 19. where |
| 20. when | |

**Set 08** ▶ 본문 p.148

02. I would like to show you what I've learned
나는 내가 배운 것을 너에게 보여주고 싶어.

03. Running is what I want to do now
달리기가 내가 지금 하고 싶은 거야.

04. I'm looking for what I lost yesterday
나는 어제 내가 잃어버린 것을 찾고 있어.

05. That's what I wanted to tell you
그게 내가 너에게 말하고 싶었던 거야.

06. Mina only eats what she likes
미나는 그녀가 좋아하는 것만 먹어.

07. That's what I do to end the day
그게 내가 하루를 마무리하기 위해 하는 거야.

08. This is what we were looking for
이게 우리가 찾고 있던 거야.

09. You become what you believe
당신은 당신이 믿는 것이(믿는대로) 된다.

10. I felt bad about what I did
나는 내가 한 것에 대해 기분이 좋지 않았어.

11. She pretends she didn't hear what she heard
그녀는 그녀가 들은 것을 못 들은 척해.

12. We can't believe what they said
우리는 그들이 말한 것을 믿을 수 없어.

13. He gave her what she likes
그는 그녀에게 그녀가 좋아하는 것을 주었어.

14. Today's meeting was what I've waited for
오늘의 회의는 내가 기다려왔던 것이었다.

15. She also felt sorry about what she did
그녀도 그녀가 했던 것에 대해 미안하게 생각했어.

16. Mom cooks us what we want
엄마는 우리에게 우리가 원하는 것을 요리해주셔.

17. Collecting stamps is what he does in his free time
우표 수집이 그가 여가시간에 하는 일이야.

18. That's not what I meant
그것은 내가 의도한 것이 아니야.

19. Think about what you should do first
당신이 첫 번째로 해야 할 것을 생각해봐라.

20. The 9 o'clock news is what I usually watch
9시 뉴스는 내가 보통 보는 것이다.

## Chapter 02~04 실전테스트

▶ 본문 p.150

01. when
02. where
03. why
04. ②
05. ②
06. ③
07. ②
08. ①
09. He likes the teacher who[that] teaches English in his school.
그는 그의 학교에서 영어를 가르치는 선생님을 좋아한다.
10. She keeps a cat which[that] jumps a lot.
그녀는 많이 점프하는 고양이를 기른다.
11. A man who[that] was sitting next to me was reading a book.
내 옆에 앉아 있었던 남자는 책을 읽고 있었다.
12. A truck which[that] was carrying food stopped at a gas station.
음식을 나르고 있었던 한 트럭이 주유소에 멈췄다.
13. We should remember the people who[that] clean the building for us.
우리는 우리를 위해 건물을 청소해주시는 분들을 기억해야 한다.
14. This is the movie which[that] we watched three times.
이것은 우리가 세 번 봤던 영화이다.
15. ①
16. ④
17. ②
18. ②
19. ①
20. ③
21. ④
22. what[What]
23. who[that]
24. ③, ④
25. how
26. when
27. who[whom / that]
28. where
29. What I need is water.
내게 필요한 것은 물이다.
30. What he has to do is his homework.
그가 해야 하는 것은 그의 숙제이다.

Cultural Tips
재미로 익히는 문화상식

## 다른 나라의 낮잠 풍습 - 시에스타(Siesta)

네, 맞아요. 다른 나라에는 시에스타라는 낮잠 시간이 있답니다.
이탈리아 · 그리스 등의 지중해 연안 국가와 라틴 아메리카의 낮잠 풍습을 말하는 것인데, 한낮의 무더위를 피해 활기를 회복하기 위한 전통이에요.
이탈리아에서는 오후 1시부터 3시 30분까지, 스페인에서는 오후 1시부터 4시까지, 그리스에서는 오후 2시부터 4시까지로 시간은 나라마다 차이가 있어요!
시에스타 중에는 일반 상점들뿐만 아니라 관공서도 문을 닫고 낮잠을 즐겨요.

Cultural Tips
재미로 익히는 문화상식

## 마트료시카(Matryoshka) - 러시아의 전통 인형

"인형 안에서 또 인형이 나와!"
마트료시카는 큰 인형 안에 그것보다 작은 인형, 그리고 더 작은 인형을 여러 개 넣을 수 있게 만든 인형이에요.
인형을 품고 있는 모습이 알을 감싼 모습 같다고 해서 '마트료시카'(Matryoshka)란 이름 대신, '알을 품은 인형'(nesting doll)으로 불리기도 해요.
인형이 무려 72개가 들어간 마트료시카도 만들어졌다고 하니 정말 대단하죠?

정답은 뒷면에서 확인하세요.

# Find and circle.

그림에 알맞은 단어를 찾아 동그라미 하세요.

1. 

z e s n a k e l n k a

2. 

c i l a d g r a p e s

3. 

m s h a v e f m o e o

4. 

b i d e l e s c a p e

# Find and circle.

그림에 알맞은 단어를 찾아 동그라미 하세요.

1. 

z e s n a k e l n k a

2. 

c i l a d g r a p e s

3. 

m s h a v e f m o e o

4. 

b i d e l e s c a p e